Introduction to Computer Music

Roger B. Dannenberg

Emeritus Professor of Computer Science, Art & Music
Carnegie Mellon University, Pittsburgh, PA, USA

CRC Press
Taylor & Francis Group
Boca Raton London New York

CRC Press is an imprint of the
Taylor & Francis Group, an **informa** business
A SCIENCE PUBLISHERS BOOK

First edition published 2027
by CRC Press
2385 NW Executive Center Drive, Suite 320, Boca Raton FL 33431

and by CRC Press
4 Park Square, Milton Park, Abingdon, Oxon, OX14 4RN

CRC Press is an imprint of Taylor & Francis Group, LLC

Library of Congress Cataloging-in-Publication Data (applied for)

ISBN: 978-1-041-32250-4 (hbk)
ISBN: 978-1-041-32254-2 (pbk)
ISBN: 978-1-003-78271-1 (ebk)

DOI: 10.1201/9781003782711

Typeset in Times New Roman
by Prime Publishing Services

Preface

Computers have become part of nearly every aspect of our daily lives. We find computers almost everywhere: communication, design and construction, health, business, automobiles, science and entertainment. Computers became part of music exploration and creation even before many other computer applications we see today. As computing experienced an exponential growth, the integration of computing into music composition, performance, production and distribution grew in proportion. Now, it is unusual to encounter any music that is untouched by computing.

With all the digital tools and possibilities that exist today, it is important for anyone interested in music creation or analysis to have some basic knowledge of computer music, which I consider to be *anything* that involves both computation and music, including music synthesis, music signal processing, music composition by computer, all forms of music analysis using computational techniques, digital musical instruments and interactive music performance systems, music recommendation systems, machine learning applied to music recognition, creation, classification, processing, digital music typography and notation, music performance over digital networks, and much more.

In fact, progress has been so rapid that there are now many specialized areas, academic conferences and publications under the broad umbrella of computer music. As students and others are attracted to one specialization or another, often with a strong background in music or engineering, they often miss out on fundamental knowledge that is not today's "hot topic." Underlying cutting-edge research in music and computation, there is a wealth of basic knowledge that may not be apparent or taught in introductory music or engineering classes, leaving researchers new to the area at a disadvantage and even unaware of the rich body of knowledge that developed across disciplines of music, electrical engineering and computer science.

This book was created for computer science students, intending to contain "what every computer scientist should know" about the subject of computer music. However, the book does *not* assume even an undergraduate degree in computer science, and much of the material can be understood with only general knowledge of computing and music. I have been inspired by my former teacher, Arthur Benade, whose class and text on Fundamentals of Musical Acoustics was a brilliant combination of intuitive explanations backed by some rigorous statements, all without requiring a mastery of music, physics, differential equations, or even calculus. He taught a mix of physics and music undergraduates, and yes, even this computer science graduate student. I cannot claim to have achieved the success of Prof. Benade's teaching across multiple disciplines, but I have tried.

This book uses the Nyquist programming language to illustrate many concepts and to provide a vehicle for further exploration of music synthesis and composition by computer. Nyquist is designed for novice programmers, but some prior programming experience will be very helpful. Nyquist has an extensive reference manual, including a language introduction, which is included when you download Nyquist.

Along with this publication, a wealth of online material including slides, video lectures, and exercises has been released. These were originally part of an online instruction system, but they have been reorganized as simple documents to allow for greater access and longevity. I hope readers and educators will find them useful.

Contents

Chapter 1

Introduction

Topics Discussed: Sound, Nyquist, SAL, Lisp and Control Constructs

Computers in all forms—desktops, laptops, mobile phones—are used to store and play music. Perhaps less obvious is the fact that music is now recorded and edited almost exclusively with computers, and computers are also used to generate sounds either by manipulating short audio clips called samples or by direct computation. In the late 1940s, engineers began to turn the theory of sampling into practice, turning sound into bits and bytes and then back into sound. Analog-to-digital converters, capable of turning one second's worth of sound into thousands of numbers made it possible to transform the acoustic waves that we hear as sound into long sequences of numbers, which were then stored in computer memories. The numbers could then be turned back into the original sound. The ability to simply record a sound had been known for quite some time. The major advance of digital representations of sound was that now sound could be manipulated very easily, just as a chunk of data (56). Advantages of employing computer music and digital audio are:

1. There are no limits to the range of sounds that a computer can help explore. In principle, *any* sound can be represented digitally, and therefore any sound can be created.

2. Computers bring precision. The process to compute or change a sound can be repeated exactly, and small incremental changes can be specified in detail. Computers facilitate microscopic changes in sounds enabling us to produce desirable sounds.

3. Computation implies automation. Computers can take over repetitive tasks. Decisions about music making can be made at different levels, from the

DOI: 10.1201/9781003782711-1

highest level of composition, form, and structure, to the minutest detail of an individual sound. Unlike with conventional music, we can use automation to hear the results of these decisions quickly, and we can refine computer programs accordingly.

4. Computers can blur the lines between the traditional roles of the composer and the performer and even the audience. We can build interactive systems where, thanks to automation, composition is taking place in real time.

The creative potential for musical composition and sound generation empowered a revolution in the world of music. That revolution in the world of electroacoustic music engendered a wonderful synthesis of music, mathematics, and computing.

1.1 Theory and Practice

This book is intended for a course that has two main components: the technology of computer music and making music with computers. The technology of computer music includes *theory*, which covers topics such as digital audio and digital signal processing, software design and languages, data structures and representation. All of these form a conceptual framework that you need to understand the field. The second aspect of the technology of computer music is putting these concepts into *practice* to make them more concrete and practical. We also make music. Making music also has a theoretical side, mainly listening to music and discussing what we find in the music. Of course, there is also a practical side of making music, consisting in this book mostly of writing programs in Nyquist, a powerful composition and sound synthesis language (19).

A composer is expected to have an understanding of acoustics and psychoacoustics. The physics of sound (acoustics) is often confused with the way in which we perceive it (psychoacoustics). We will get to these topics later. In the next section, we discuss sound's physical characteristics and common measurements. Following that, we change topics and give a brief introduction to the Nyquist language.

1.1.1 Warning! Programming!

This is not an introduction to programming! If you do not already know how to program in some language such as Python or Java, you will not understand much of the content in this book. If you already have some programming experience, you should be able to pick up Nyquist quickly with the introduction in this and the next chapter. If you find the pace is too quick, I recommend *Algorithmic Composition: A Guide to Composing Music with Nyquist* (87), which was written for non-programmers and introduces Nyquist at a slower pace. As the title implies, that book also covers more algorithmic composition techniques than this one.

You should also install Nyquist, the programming language, from SourceForge (`https:sourceforge.net/projects/nyquist`). Once installed, find the *Nyquist Reference Manual.* Whenever you have questions about Nyquist, look in the reference manual for details and more examples.

1.2 Fundamentals of Computer Sound

All musicians work with sound in some way, but many have little understanding of its properties. Computer musicians can benefit in myriad ways from an understanding of the mechanisms of sound, its objective measurements and the more subjective area of its perception. This understanding is crucial to the proper use of common studio equipment and music software, and novel compositional strategies can be derived from exploiting much of the information contained in this section.

1.2.1 What is Sound?

Sound is a complex phenomenon involving physics and perception (80). Perhaps the simplest way to explain it is to say that sound involves at least three things:

1. Something moves,
2. Something transmits the results of that movement,
3. Something (or someone) hears the results of that movement (though this is philosophically debatable).

All things that make sound move, and in some very metaphysical sense, all things that move (if they do not move too slowly or too quickly) make sound. As things move, they push and pull at the surrounding air (or water or whatever medium they occupy), causing pressure variations (compressions and rarefactions). Those pressure variations, or sound waves, are what we hear as sound. (See Figure 1.1.)

Sound is produced by a rapid variation in the average density or pressure of air molecules above and below the current atmospheric pressure. We perceive sound as these pressure fluctuations cause our eardrums to vibrate. When discussing sound, these usually minute changes in atmospheric pressure are referred to as sound pressure and the fluctuations in pressure as sound waves. Sound waves are produced by a vibrating body, be it an oboe reed, loudspeaker cone, or jet engine. The vibrating sound source disturbs surrounding air molecules, causing them to bounce off each other with a force proportional to the disturbance.

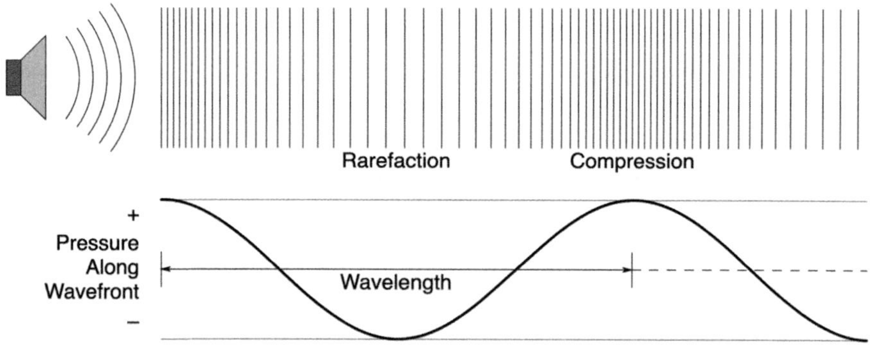

Figure 1.1: Illustration of a wave and the corresponding pressure variations in the air at an instant in time. At any given point, pressure varies with time as the wave passes through the point at the speed of sound.

The speed at which sound propagates (or travels from its source) is directly influenced by both the medium through which it travels and the factors affecting the medium, such as altitude, humidity, and temperature for gases like air. There is no sound in the vacuum of space because there are too few molecules to propagate a wave. The approximate speed of sound at 20° Celsius (68° Fahrenheit) is 1,128 feet per second (f/s).

It is important to note that the speed of sound in air is determined by the conditions of the air itself (e.g., humidity, temperature, altitude). It is not dependent upon the sound's amplitude, frequency, or wavelength.

Pressure variations travel through air as waves. Sound waves are often characterized by four basic qualities, though many more are related: frequency, amplitude, wave shape, and phase[1]. Some sound waves are periodic, in that the change from equilibrium (average atmospheric pressure) to maximum compression to maximum rarefaction back to equilibrium is repetitive. The "round trip" back to the starting point just described is called a cycle or period.

The number of cycles per unit of time is called the frequency. (See Figure 1.2.) For convenience, frequency is measured in cycles per second (cps) or the interchangeable Hertz (Hz) (60 cps = 60 Hz), named after the 19th C. physicist. 1,000 Hz is often referred to as 1 kHz (kilohertz) or simply "1k" in studio parlance.

The range of human hearing in the young is approximately 20 Hz to 20 kHz—the higher number tends to decrease with age (as do many other things). It may be quite normal for a 60-year-old to hear a maximum of 16,000 Hz. Frequencies

[1]It could be argued that phase is not a characteristic of a single wave, but only as a comparison between two or more waves.

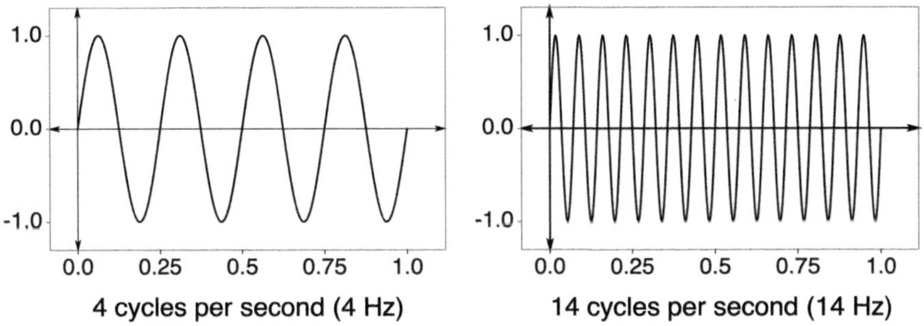

Figure 1.2: Illustration of how waveform changes with a change in frequency.

above and below the range of human hearing are also commonly used in computer music studios.

Amplitude is the objective measurement of the degree of change (positive or negative) in atmospheric pressure (the compression and rarefaction of air molecules) caused by sound waves. Sounds with greater amplitude will produce greater changes in atmospheric pressure from high pressure to low pressure to the ambient pressure present before sound was produced (equilibrium). Humans can hear atmospheric pressure fluctuations of as little as a few billionths of an atmosphere (the ambient pressure), and this amplitude is called the threshold of hearing. On the other end of the human perception spectrum, a super-loud sound near the threshold of pain may be 100,000 times the pressure amplitude of the threshold of hearing, yet only a 0.03% change at your ear drum in the actual atmospheric pressure. We hear amplitude variations over about 5 orders of magnitude from threshold to pain.

1.2.2 Analog Sound

Sound itself is a continuous wave; it is an analog signal. (See Figure 1.3.) When we record audio, we start with continuous vibrations that are analogous to the original sound waves. Capturing this continuous wave in its entirety requires an analog recording system; what the microphone receives is transformed continuously into a groove of a vinyl disk or magnetism of a tape recorder (33). Analog can be said to be the true representation of the sound at the moment it was recorded. The analog waveform is nice and smooth, while the digital version is kind of chunky. This "chunkiness" is called quantization. But does this really matter? Keep reading...

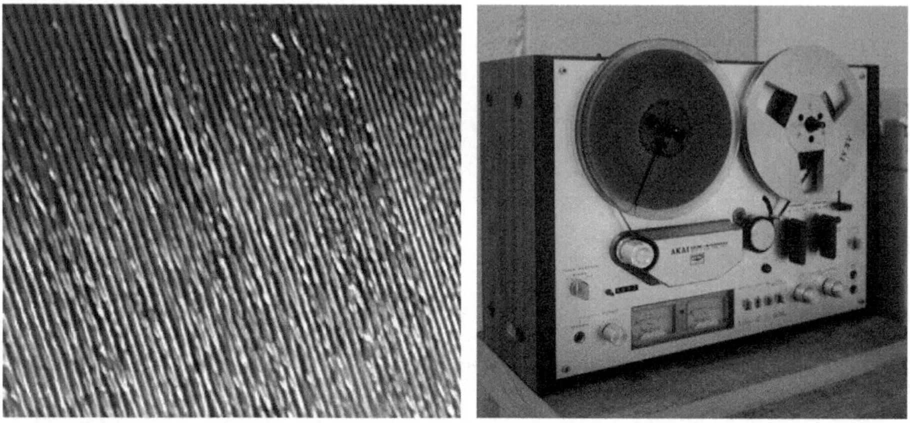

Figure 1.3: Before audio recording became digital, sounds were "carved" into vinyl records as grooves or written to tape as magnetic waveforms. Left image shows wiggles in vinyl record grooves and the right image shows a typical tape recorder used to store audio data. (Photos by the author and Fujiphilm on Unsplash.)

1.2.3 Digital Audio Representation

Sounds from the real world can be recorded and digitized using an analog-to-digital converter (ADC). As in Figure 1.4, the circuit takes a sample of the instantaneous amplitude (not frequency) of the analog waveform. Alternatively, digital synthesis software can also create samples by modeling and sampling mathematical functions or other forms of calculation. A sample in either case is defined as a measurement of the instantaneous amplitude of a real or artificial signal. Frequencies will be recreated later by playing back the sequential sample amplitudes at a specified rate. It is important to remember that frequency, phase, waveshape, etc. are not recorded in each discrete sample measurement, but will be reconstructed during the playback of the stored sequential amplitudes.

Samples are taken at a regular time interval. The rate of sample measurement is called the sampling rate (or sampling frequency). The sampling rate is responsible for the frequency response of the digitized sound.

To convert the digital audio into the analog format, we use *digital-to-analog converters*. A digital-to-analog converter, or *DAC*, is an electronic device that converts a digital code to an analog signal such as a voltage, current, or electric charge. Signals can easily be stored and transmitted in digital form; a DAC is used for the signal to be recognized by human senses or non-digital systems (69).

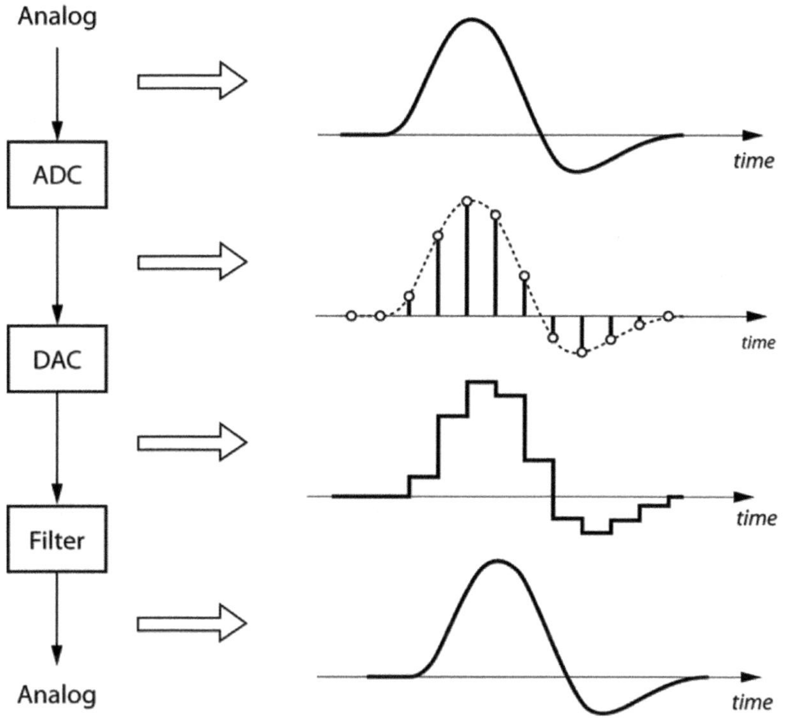

Figure 1.4: An analog waveform is converted by an ADC to digital form. Conversion back to analog is shown in two steps. First, each digital *sample* is converted to a voltage. Second, the signal is *smoothed* by a filter. (Sometimes, the filter step is assumed and the two-step process is referred to as DAC.)

1.2.4 Clipping

The input of a digital-to-analog converter is an integer, which implies there are minimum and maximum values for samples. To make calculations simpler and to avoid losing precision, we often use floating point numbers to represent and process samples[2]. For example, we might form the sum of many audio channels, exceeding the maximum sample value, but before converting to analog, we can bring the sum into range with a suitable scale factor. In this example, integer arithmetic would overflow, but floating point numbers would not.

By using floating point representations for samples, we avoid many problems of precision and numerical overflow, but we still face problems when we try to convert samples to sound because there are no floating-point converters, and

[2]A *floating point* number is a digital representation that uses the idea of scientific notation, e.g., 0.1234×10^7, by storing a sign, a fraction, and an exponent, giving a much larger range of values than an integer of the same size.

even if there were, analog circuits and amplifiers have limits. In practice, sample values are limited or "clipped" to a fixed range. This results in a particularly harsh form of distortion called *clipping*. Clipping occurs when we write too large samples to audio files or when we directly write too large samples to a DAC. (Clipping can also occur in audio recording when the input signal is too high for analog circuitry or outside the range of an analog-to-digital converter.)

There is no general remedy for clipping. Once a signal has been clipped, the original cannot be recovered. There are various ways to soften the distortion, but the only "respectable" fix is to adjust amplitudes by scaling, mixing, or even moving the microphone[3]. Figure 1.5 shows a waveform with clipping.

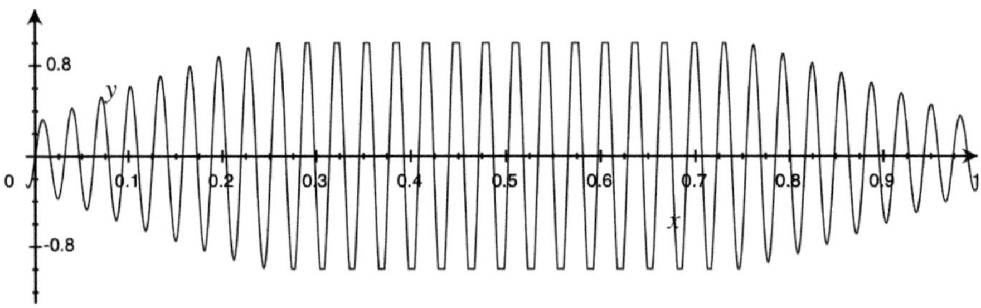

Figure 1.5: A sinusoid with increasing/decreasing volume showing audio clipping at the center of the graph.

1.2.5 The Table-Lookup Oscillator

Although we still have a lot to learn about digital audio, it is useful to look at a very concrete example of how we can use computers to *synthesize* audio in addition to simply recording and playing it back. One of the simplest synthesis algorithms is the table-lookup oscillator (70). The goal is to create a periodic, repeating signal. Ideally, we should have control over the amplitude and frequency, because scaling the amplitude makes the sound quieter or louder, and making the frequency higher makes the pitch higher.

To get started, consider Algorithm 1, which simply outputs samples sequentially and repeatedly from a table that stores one period of the repeating signal.

This will produce 120,000 samples, or about 3 seconds of audio if the sample rate is 44,100 samples per second. The frequency (rate of repetition in the signal) will be $44,100/12 = 3675$, which is near the top note of the piano. We want very fine

[3]"Louis Armstrong was famously placed 20 feet away for his solos." – Clive Thompson in `https://www.smithsonianmag.com/arts-culture/phonograph-changed-music-forever-180957677/`.

Algorithm 1 Simple table-lookup oscillator

```
// create a table with one period of the signal:
table = [0, 0.3, 0.6, 0.9, 0.6, 0.3,
         0, -0.3, -0.4, -0.9, -0.6, -0.3]
// output audio samples:
repeat 10000 times:
   for each element of table:
      write(element)
```

control over frequency, so this simple algorithm with integer-length repeating periods is not adequate. Instead, we need to use some kind of *interpolation* to allow for fractional periods. This approach is shown in Algorithm 2.

Algorithm 2 Interpolating table-lookup oscillator

```
// create a table with one period of the signal:
table = [0, 0.3, 0.6, 0.9, 0.6, 0.3,
         0, -0.3, -0.4, -0.9, -0.6, -0.3]
// make a variable to keep track of phase:
phase = 0.0
// increment phase by this to get 440 Hz:
phase_incr = 440 * len(table) / 44100.0
// output audio samples:
repeat 44100 * 10 times: // 10 seconds of audio
   i1 = floor(phase) // integer part of phase, first sample index
   frac = phase - i1 // fractional part of phase
   i2 = (i1 + 1) mod len(table) // index of next sample in table
   // linearly interpolate between two samples in the table:
   y = (1 - frac) * table[i1] + frac * table[i2]
   write(y * amplitude)
   // increment phase and wrap around when we reach the end of the table
   phase = (phase + phase_incr) mod len(table)
```

This code example is considerably longer than the first one. It uses the variable `phase` to keep track of how much of the waveform period we have output so far. After each sample is output, `phase` is incremented by `phase_incr`, which is initialized so that `phase` will reach the table length and wrap around to zero (using the `mod` operator) 440 times per second. Since `phase` is now fractional, we cannot simply write `table[phase]` to look up the value of the waveform at location `phase`. Instead, we read *two* adjacent values from the table and form a weighted sum based on the fractional part (`frac`) of `phase`. Even though the samples may not exactly repeat due to interpolation, we can control the overall frequency (or repetition rate) at which we sweep through the table very precisely.

In addition, this version of the code multiplies the computed sample (`y`) by `amplitude`. This scale factor gives us control over the overall amplitude, which is related to the loudness of the resulting sound.

In practice, we would normally use a much larger table, e.g., 2048 elements, and we would use a smoother waveform. (We will talk about why digital audio waveforms have to be smooth later.) It is common to use this technique to generate sinusoids. Of course, you *could* just call $sin(phase)$ for every sample, relying on a standard software library function, but in most cases, pre-computing values of the sin function and saving them in a table, then reading the samples from memory, is much faster than computing the sin function once per sample.

Instead of synthesizing sinusoids, we can also synthesize complex waveforms such as triangle, sawtooth, and square waves of analog synthesizers, or waveforms obtained from acoustic instruments or human voices, simply by initializing the table to the desired wave shape.

We will learn about many other synthesis algorithms and techniques, but the table-lookup oscillator is a computationally efficient method to produce sinusoids and more complex periodic signals. Besides being efficient, this method offers direct control of amplitude and frequency, which are very important control parameters for making music. The main drawback of table-lookup oscillators is that the waveform or wave shape is fixed, whereas most musical tones vary over time and with amplitude and frequency. Later, we will see alternative approaches to sound synthesis and also learn about filters, which can be used to alter wave shapes.

1.3 Nyquist, SAL, Lisp

Nyquist is a language for sound synthesis and music composition. Unlike score languages that tend to deal only with events, or signal processing languages that tend to deal only with signals and synthesis, Nyquist handles both in a single integrated system. Nyquist is also flexible and easy to use because it is based on an interactive Lisp interpreter (XLisp).

This book assumes you have programming experience in at least one language. If so, you should be able to learn SAL from this book and by consulting the *Nyquist Reference Manual* (21). If you are new to programming, I recommend *Algorithmic Composition: A Guide to Composing Music with Nyquist* (87) as a place to start.

The NyquistIDE program (Figure 1.6) combines many helpful functions and interfaces to help you get the most out of Nyquist. NyquistIDE is implemented in Java, and you will need the Java runtime system or development system installed

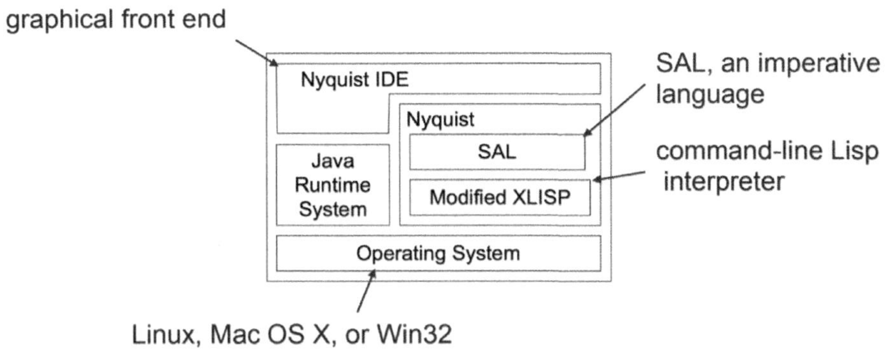

Figure 1.6: NyquistIDE System Architecture.

on your computer to use NyquistIDE. NyquistIDE helps you by providing a Lisp and SAL editor, hints for command completion and function parameters, some graphical interfaces for editing envelopes and graphical equalizers, and a panel of buttons for common operations.

1.3.1 SAL

Nyquist is based on the Lisp language. Many users found Lisp's syntax unfamiliar, and eventually Nyquist was extended with support for SAL, which is similar in semantics to Lisp, but similar in syntax to languages such as Python and Javascript. SAL comes from Heinrich Taube's music software called Common Music (93), although Nyquist's SAL is not fully compatible. Like Common Music, NyquistIDE supports two modes, Lisp and SAL. SAL mode means that Nyquist reads and evaluates SAL commands rather than Lisp. The SAL mode prompt is "`SAL> `" while the Lisp mode prompt is "`> `". When Nyquist starts, it normally enters SAL mode automatically, but certain errors may exit SAL mode. You can reenter SAL mode by typing the Lisp expression `(sal)` or finding the button labeled SAL in the IDE.

In SAL mode, you type commands in the SAL programming language. Nyquist reads the commands, compiles them into Lisp, and evaluates the commands. Some examples of SAL commands are the following:

- `print` *expression* – evaluate an expression and print the result.
- `exec` *expression* – evaluate expression but do not print the result.
- `play` *expression* – evaluate an expression and play the result, which must be a sound.
- `set` *var* = *expression* – set a variable.

1.4 Using SAL In the IDE

It is important to learn to use the NyquistIDE program, which provides an interface for editing and running Nyquist programs. The NyquistIDE is discussed in the *Nyquist Reference Manual*. You should take time to learn:

- How to switch to SAL mode. In particular, you can "pop" out to the top level of Nyquist by clicking the "Top" button; then, you can enter SAL mode by clicking the "SAL" button.
- How to run a SAL command, e.g., type `print "hello world"` in the input window at the upper left.
- How to create a new file. In particular, you should normally *save* a new empty file to a file named *something*`.sal` in order to tell the editor this is a SAL file and thereby invoke the SAL syntax coloring, indentation, support, etc.
- How to execute a file by using the *Load* menu item or keyboard shortcut.

1.5 Examples

This would be a good time to install and run the NyquistIDE. You can find Nyquist downloads on (`https://sourceforge.net/projects/nyquist`), and "read-me" files contain installation guidelines.

The program named NyquistIDE is an "integrated development environment" for Nyquist. When you run NyquistIDE, it starts the Nyquist program and displays all Nyquist output in a window. A more complete description of NyquistIDE is in Chapter "The NyquistIDE Program" in the *Nyquist Reference Manual.*

For now, all you really need to know is that you can enter Nyquist commands by typing into the upper left window. When you type return, the expression you typed is sent to Nyquist, and the results appear in the window below. You can edit files by clicking on the New File or Open File buttons. After editing some text, you can load the text into Nyquist by clicking the Load button. NyquistIDE always saves the file first; then it tells Nyquist to load the file. You will be prompted for a file name the first time you load a new file.

Try some of these examples. These are SAL commands, so be sure to enter SAL mode. Then, just type these one-by-one into the upper left window.

```
play pluck(c4)

play pluck(c4) ~ 3
```

```
play piano-note(5, fs1, 100)

play osc(c4)

play osc(c4) * osc(d4)

play pluck(c4) ~ 3

play noise() * env(0.05, 0.1, 0.5, 1, 0.5, 0.4)
```

1.6 Constants, Variables, and Functions

As in XLISP, simple constant value expressions include:

- integers (FIXNUM's), such as `1215`,
- floats (FLONUM's) such as `12.15`,
- strings (STRING's) such as `"Magna Carta"`,
- symbols (SYMBOL's) can be denoted by `quote(`*name*`)`, e.g., symbol `FOO` is denoted by `quote(foo)`. Think of symbols as unique strings. Every time you write `quote(foo)`, you get *exactly* the same identical value. Symbols in this form are not too common, but "raw" symbols, e.g., `foo`, are used to denote values of variables and to denote functions.

Additional constant expressions in SAL are:

- *lists* such as `{c 60 e 64}`. Note that there are no commas to separate list elements, and symbols in lists are not evaluated as variables but stand for themselves. Lists may contain numbers, booleans (which represent XLisp's `T` or `nil`, SAL identifiers (representing XLisp symbols), strings, SAL operators (representing XLisp symbols), and nested lists.
- *Booleans*: SAL interprets `#t` as true and `#f` as false. (But there is also the variable `t` to indicate "true," and `nil` to indicate "false." Usually we use these cleaner and prettier forms instead of `#t` and `#f`.

A curious property of Lisp and Sal is that false and the empty list are the same value. Since SAL is based on Lisp, `#f` and `{}` (the empty list) are equal.

Variables are denoted by symbols such as `count` or `duration`. Variable names may include digits and the characters `- + * $ ~ ! @ # % ^ & \ : < > . / ? _`; however, it is strongly recommended to avoid special characters when naming variables and functions. One exception is that the dash (`-`) is used to create compound names.

Recommended form: `magna-carta`, `phrase-len`; *to be avoided*: `magnaCarta`, `magna_carta`, `magnacarta`, `phraseLen`, `phrase_len`, `phraselen`.

SAL and Lisp convert all variable letters to upper case, so `foo` and `FOO` and `Foo` all denote the same variable. The preferred way to write variables and functions is in *all lower case*. (There are ways to create symbols and variables with lower case letters, but this should be avoided.)

A symbol with a leading colon (:) evaluates to itself. E.g., `:foo` has the value `:FOO`. Otherwise, a symbol denotes either a local variable, a formal parameter, or a global variable. As in Lisp, variables do not have data types or type declarations. The type of a variable is determined at runtime by its value.

Functions in SAL include both operators, e.g., `1 + 2` and standard function notation, e.g., `sqrt(2)`. The most important thing to know about operators is that *you must separate operators from operands with white space*. For example, `a + b` is an expression that denotes "a plus b", but `a+b` (no spaces) denotes the value of a variable with the unusual name of "`A+B`".

Functions are invoked using what should be familiar notation, e.g., `sin(pi)` or `max(x, 100)`. Some functions (including `max`) take a variable number of arguments. Some functions take keyword arguments, for example,

```
string-downcase("ABCD", start: 2)
```

returns `ABcd` because the keyword parameter `start: 2` says to convert to lower case starting at position 2.

1.7 Defining Functions

Before a function can be called from an expression (as described above), it must be defined. A function definition gives the function name, a list of parameters, and a statement. When a function is called, the actual parameter expressions are evaluated from left to right and the formal parameters of the function definition are set to these values. Then, the function body, a statement, is evaluated. The syntax to define functions in SAL is:

`[ define ] function` *name* `( [`*parameter* `{,` *parameter* `}*] )`
statement

This syntax *meta*-notation uses brackets [...] to denote optional elements and braces with a star {...}* to denote zero or more repetitions, but you do not literally write brackets or braces. *Italics* denote place-holders, e.g., *name* means you write the name of the function you are defining, e.g., `my-function` (remember names in SAL can have hyphens). Beginning a function definition with the keyword `define` is optional, so a minimal function definition is:

```
function three() return 3
```

Note that space and newlines are ignored, so that could be equivalently written:

```
function three()
  return 3
```

A function with two parameters is:

```
function simple-adder(a, b) return a + b
```

The formal parameters may be positional parameters that are matched with actual parameters by position from left to right. Syntactically, these are symbols and these symbols are essentially local variables that exist only until *statement* completes or a *return* statement causes the function evaluation to end. As in Lisp, parameters are passed by value, so assigning a new value to a formal parameter has no effect on the caller. However, lists and arrays are not copied, so internal changes to a list or array produce observable side effects.

Alternatively, formal parameters may be keyword parameters. Here the parameter is actually a pair: a keyword parameter, which is a symbol followed by a colon, and a default value, given by any expression. Within the body of the function, the keyword parameter is named by a symbol whose name matches the keyword parameter except there is no final colon.

```
define function foo(x: 1, y: bar(2, 3))
    display "foo", x, y

exec foo(x: 6, y: 7)
```

In this example, `x` is bound to the value 6 and `y` is bound to the value 7, so the example prints "`foo : X = 6, Y = 7`". Note that while the keyword parameters are `x:` and `y:`, the corresponding variable names in the function body are `x` and `y`, respectively.

The parameters are meaningful only within the lexical (static) scope of *statement*. They are not accessible from within other functions even if they are called by this function.

Use a `begin-end` compound statement if the body of the function should contain more than one statement or you need to define local variables. Use a `return` statement to return a value from the function. If *statement* completes without a `return`, the value false (`nil`) is returned.

See the *Nyquist Reference Manual* for complete information and details of `begin-end`, `return`, and other statements.

1.8 Simple Commands

1.8.1 exec

`exec` *expression*
Unlike most other programming languages, you cannot simply type an expression as a statement. If you want to evaluate an expression, e.g., call a function, you must use an `exec` statement. The statement simply evaluates the *expression*. For example,

```
exec set-sound-srate(22050.0)  ; change default sample rate
```

1.8.2 load

`load` *expression*
The `load` command loads a file named by *expression*, which must evaluate to a string path name for the file. To load a file, SAL interprets each statement in the file, stopping at the end of the file when an error is encountered. If the file ends in `.lsp`, the file is assumed to contain Lisp expressions, which are evaluated by the XLISP interpreter. In general, SAL files should end with the extension .sal.

1.8.3 play

`play` *expr*
The `play` statement plays the sound computed by *expr*, an expression.

1.8.4 plot

`plot` *expr*`,` *dur*`,` *n*
The `plot` statement plots the sound denoted by *expr*, an expression. If you plot a long sound, the plot statement will by default truncate the sound to 2.0 seconds and resample the signal to 1,000 points. The optional *dur* is an expression that specifies the (maximum) duration to be plotted, and the optional *n* specifies the number of points to be plotted. Executing a `plot` statement is equivalent to calling the `s-plot` function.

1.8.5 print

`print` *expr*`,` *expr* ...
The `print` statement prints the values separated by spaces and followed by a newline. There may be 0, 1, or more expressions separated by commas (,).

1.8.6 display

`display` *string*, *expression*, *expression ...*
The `display` statement is handy for debugging. When executed, `display` prints the *string* followed by a colon (:) and then, for each *expression*, the expression and its value are printed; after the last expression, a newline is printed. For example,

```
display "In function foo", bar, baz
```

prints

```
In function foo : bar = 23, baz = 5.3
```

SAL may print the expressions using Lisp syntax, e.g., if the expression is "`bar + baz`" do not be surprised if the output is:

```
    (sum bar baz) = 28.3
```

1.8.7 set

`set` *var* `op` *expression*
The `set` statement changes the value of a variable *var* according to the operator *op* and the value of *expression*. The operators are:

= The value of expression is assigned to var.

+= The value of *expression* is added to *var*.

*= The value of *var* is multiplied by the value of the *expression*.

&= The value of *expression* is inserted as the last element of the list referenced by *var*. If *var* is the empty list (denoted by `nil` or `#f`), then *var* is assigned a newly constructed list of one element, the value of *expression*.

^= The value of *expression*, a list, is appended to the list referenced by *var*. If *var* is the empty list (denoted by `nil` or `#f`), then *var* is assigned the (list) value of *expression*.

@= Pushes the value of *expression* onto the front of the list referenced by *var*. If *var* is empty (denoted by `nil` or `#f`), then *var* is assigned a newly constructed list of one element, the value of *expression*.

<= Sets the new value of *var* to the minimum of the old value of *var* and the value of *expression*.

>= Sets the new value of *var* to the maximum of the old value of *var* and the value of *expression*.

The `set` command can also perform multiple assignments separated by commas (,):

```
; example from Rick Taube's SAL description
loop
  with a, b = 0, c = 1, d = {}, e = {}, f = -1, g = 0
  for i below 5
  set a = i, b += 1, c *= 2, d &= i, e @= i, f <= i, g >= i
  finally display "results", a, b, c, d, e, f, g
end
```

1.9 Control Constructs

1.9.1 begin end

A `begin-end` statement consists of a sequence of statements surrounded by the `begin` and `end` keywords. This form is often used for function definitions and after `then` or `else` where the syntax demands a single statement but you want to perform more than one action. Variables may be declared using an optional `with` statement immediately after `begin`. For example:

```
begin
  with db = 12.0,
       linear = db-to-linear(db)
  print db, "dB represents a factor of", linear
  set scale-factor = linear
end
```

1.9.2 if then else

`if` *expression* `then` *statement* [`else` *statement*]
An `if` statement evaluates a test expression. If it is true, it evaluates the statement following `then`. If false, the statement after `else` is evaluated. Use a `begin-end` statement to evaluate more than one statement in `then` or `else` parts.

Here are some examples...

```
if x < 0 then set x = -1  ; x gets its absolute value

if x > upper-bound then
  begin
    print "x too big, setting to", upper-bound
    x = upper-bound
  end
else
  if x < lower-bound then
    begin
      print "x too small, setting to", lower-bound
      x = lower-bound
    end
```

Notice in this example that the `else` part is another `if` statement. An `if` may also be the `then` part of another `if`, so there could be two possible `if`'s with which to associate an `else`. An `else` clause always associates with the closest previous `if` that does not already have an `else` clause.

1.9.3 loop

The `loop` statement is by far the most complex statement in SAL, but it offers great flexibility for just about any kind of iteration. However, when computing sounds, *loops are generally the wrong approach*, and there are special functions such as `seqrep` and `simrep` to use iteration to create sequential and simultaneous combinations of sounds as well as special functions to iterate over *scores*, apply synthesis functions, and combine the results.

Therefore, loops are mainly for imperative programming where you want to iterate over lists, arrays, or other discrete structures. You will probably need loops at some point, so at least scan this section to see what is available, but there is no need to dwell on this section for now.

The basic function of a loop is to repeatedly evaluate a sequence of actions which are statements. The syntax for a `loop` statement is:

`loop` [*with-stmt*] { *stepping* }* { *stopping* }* { *action* }+
  [*final*] `end`

Before the loop begins, local variables may be declared in a `with` statement.

The *stepping* clauses do several things. They introduce and initialize additional local variables similar to the `with` statement. However, these local variables are updated to new values after the actions. In addition, some *stepping* clauses have associated stopping conditions, which are tested on each iteration before evaluating the actions.

There are also *stopping* clauses that provide additional tests to stop the iteration. These are also evaluated and tested on each iteration before evaluating the actions.

When some *stepping* or *stopping* condition causes the iteration to stop, the *final* clause is evaluated (if present). Local variables and their values can still be accessed in the *final* clause. After the *final* clause, the `loop` statement completes.

The *stepping* clauses are the following:

`repeat` *expression*

sets the number of iterations to the value of *expression*, which should be an integer (FIXNUM).

`for` *var* = *expression* `[ then` *expr2* `]`

introduces a new local variable named *var* and initializes it to *expression*. Before each subsequent iteration, *var* is set to the value of *expr2*. If the `then` part is omitted, *expression* is re-evaluated and assigned to *var* on each subsequent iteration. Note that this differs from a `with` statement where expressions are evaluated and variables are only assigned their values once.

`for` *var* `in` *expression*

evaluates *expression* to obtain a list and creates a new local variable initialized to the first element of the list. After each iteration, *var* is assigned the next element of the list. Iteration stops when *var* has assumed all values from the list. If the list is initially empty, the `loop` actions are not evaluated (there are zero iterations).

`for` *var* `[ from` *from-expr* `] [ [ to | below | downto | above ]`
to-expr `] [ by` *step-expr* `]`

is yet another *stepping* clause. Note that here we have introduced a new metasyntax notation: [*term1* | *term2* | *term3*] means a valid expression contains one of *term1*, *term2*, or *term3*.

This `for` clause introduces a new local variable named *var* and initialized to the value of the expression *from-expr* (with a default value of 0). After each iteration of the `loop`, *var* is incremented by the value of *step-expr* (with a default value of 1). The iteration ends when *var* is greater than the value of *to-expr* if there is a `to` clause, greater than or equal to the value of *to-expr* if there is a `below` clause, less than the value of *to-expr* if there is a `downto` clause, or less than or equal to the value of *to-expr* if there is an `above` clause. (In the cases of `downto` and `above`, the default increment value is –1. If there is no `to`, `below`, `downto`, or `above` clause, no iteration stop test is created for this *stepping* clause.)

The *stopping* clauses are the following:

`while` *expression*

The iterations are stopped when *expression* evaluates to false. Anything not false is considered to be true.

`until` *expression*

The iterations are stopped when *expression* evaluates to anything that is not false (nil).

The loop *action* consists of one or more SAL statements (indicated by the "+" in the meta-syntax).

The *final* clause is defined as follows:

`finally` *statement*

The statement is evaluated when one of the *stepping* or *stopping* clauses ends the `loop`. As always, *statement* may be a `begin-end` statement. If an *action* in the loop body evaluates a `return` statement, the `finally` statement is not executed. Loops often fall into common patterns, such as iterating a fixed number of times, performing an operation on some range of integers, collecting results in a list, and linearly searching for a solution. These forms are illustrated in the examples below.

```
; iterate 10 times
loop
  repeat 10
  print random(100)
end

; print even numbers from 10 to 20
; note that 20 is printed. On the next iteration,
;  i = 22, so i > = 22, so the loop exits.
loop
  for i from 10 below 22 by 2
  print i
end
```

```
; collect even numbers in a list
loop
  with lis
  for i from 0 to 10 by 2
  set lis @= i  ; push integers on front of list,
                ; which is much faster than append,
                ; but list is built in reverse
  finally set result = reverse(lis)
end

; now, the variable result has a list of evens
; find the first even number in a list
set result = #f  ; #f means "false"
loop
  for elem in lis
  until evenp(elem)
  finally result = elem
end
; result has first even value in lis (or it is #f)
```

1.9.4 simrep Example

We can define function `pluck-chord` as follows:

```
function pluck-chord(pitch, interval, n)
  begin
    with s = pluck(pitch)
    loop
      for i from 1 below n
      set s += pluck(pitch + interval * i)
    end
  return s
end

play pluck-chord(c3, 5, 2)
play pluck-chord(d3, 7, 4) ~ 3
play pluck-chord(c2, 10, 7) ~ 8
```

But we mentioned earlier that loops should not normally be used to compute sounds. Just to preview what is coming up ahead, here is how `pluck-chord` should be written:

```
function pluck-chord(pitch, interval, n)
  return simrep(i, n, pluck(pitch + i * interval))

play pluck-chord(c3, 5, 2)
play pluck-chord(d3, 7, 4) ~ 3
play pluck-chord(c2, 10, 7) ~ 8
```

Note that this version of the function is substantially smaller (`loop` is powerful, but sometimes a bit verbose). In addition, one could argue this `simrep` version is more correct—in the case where `n` is 0, this version returns silence, whereas the `loop` version always initializes `s` to a `pluck` sound, even if `n` is zero, so it never returns silence. The `simrep` construct and its cousin, `seqrep`, are described in the *Nyquist Reference Manual*, and we will return to them in Section 4.8.

Chapter 2

Basics of Synthesis

Topics Discussed: Unit Generators, Implementation, Functional Programming, Wavetable Synthesis, Scores in Nyquist, Score Manipulation

2.1 Unit Generators

In the 1950s, Max Mathews conceived of sound synthesis by software using networks of modules he called *unit generators* (57). Unit generators (sometimes called *ugens*) are basic building blocks for signal processing in many computer music programming languages.

Unit generators are used to construct synthesis and signal processing algorithms in software. For example, the simple unit generator `osc` generates a sinusoidal waveform at a fixed frequency. `env` generates an "envelope" to control amplitude. Multiplication of two signals can be achieved with a `mult` unit generator (created with the `*` operator), so:

```
osc(c4) * env(0.01, 0.02, 0.1, 1, 0.9, 0.8)
```

creates a sinusoid with amplitude that varies according to an envelope.

Figure 2.1 illustrates some unit generators. Lines represent audio signals, control signals, and numbers.

In many languages, unit generators can be thought of as interconnected *objects* that pass samples from object to object, performing calculations on them (20). In Nyquist, we think of unit generators as *functions* with sounds as inputs and outputs. Semantically, this is an accurate view, but since sounds can be very large (typically about 10 MB/minute), Nyquist uses a clever implementation based on *incremental lazy evaluation* so that sounds rarely exist as complete arrays of sam-

DOI: 10.1201/9781003782711-2

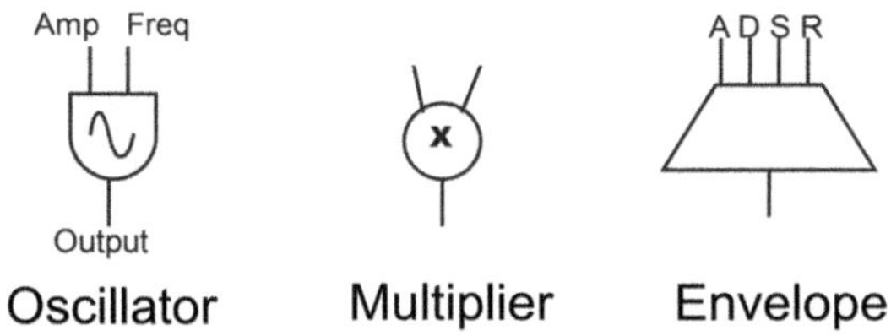

Figure 2.1: Some examples of unit generators.

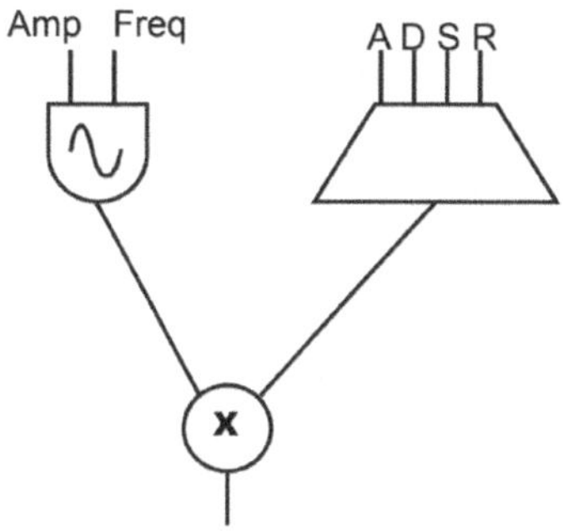

Figure 2.2: Combining unit generators.

ples. Instead, sounds are typically computed in small chunks that are "consumed" by other unit generators and quickly deleted to conserve memory (18).

Figure 2.2 shows how unit generators can be combined. Outputs from an oscillator and an envelope generator serve as inputs to the multiply unit generator in this figure.

Figure 2.3 shows how the "circuit diagram" or "signal flow diagram" notation used in Figure 2.2 relates to the functional notation of Nyquist. As you can see, wherever there is output from one unit generator to the input of another as shown on the left, we can express that as nested function calls as shown in the expression on the right.

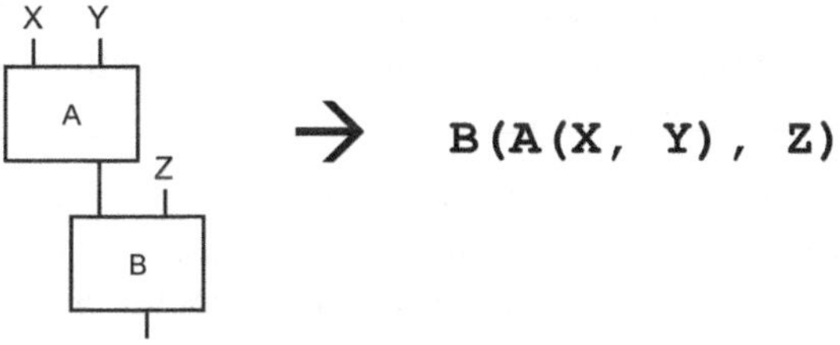

Figure 2.3: Unit generators in Nyquist.

2.1.1 Some Basic Unit Generators

The `osc` function generates a sound using a table-lookup oscillator. There are a number of optional parameters, but the default is to compute a sinusoid with an amplitude of 1.0. The parameter 60 designates a pitch of middle C. (Pitch specification will be described in greater detail later.) The result of the `osc` function is a sound. To hear a sound, you must use the play command, which plays the file through the machine's D/A converters. E.g., you can write `play osc(c4)` to play a sine tone.

It is often convenient to construct signals in Nyquist using a list of (time, value) breakpoints which are linearly interpolated to form a smooth signal. The function `pwl` is a versatile unit generator to create Piecewise Linear (PWL) signals and will be described in more detail below.

An envelope constructed by `pwl` is applied to another sound by multiplication using the multiply (*) operator. For example, you can make the simple sine tone sound smoother by giving it an envelope:

```
play osc(c4) * pwl(0.03, 1, 0.8, 1, 1)
```

While this example shows a smooth envelope multiplied by an audio signal, you can also multiply audio signals to achieve what is often called ring modulation (see also "Amplitude Modulation by Audible Frequencies" on page 69). For example:

```
play osc(c4) * osc(g4)
```

2.1.2 Evaluation

Normally, Nyquist expressions (whether written in SAL or Lisp syntax) evaluate their parameters, then apply the function. If we write `f(a, b)`, Nyquist will evaluate `a` and `b`, then pass the resulting values to function `f`.

Sounds are different. If Nyquist evaluated sounds immediately, they could be huge. Even something as simple as multiply could require memory for two huge input sounds and one equally huge output sound. Multiplying two 10-minute sounds would require 30 minutes' worth of memory, or about 300MB. This might not be a problem, but what happens if you are working with multi-channel audio, longer sounds, or more parameters?

To avoid storing huge values in memory, Nyquist uses lazy evaluation. Sounds are more like promises to deliver samples when asked, or you can think of a sound as an object with the *potential* to compute samples. Samples are computed only when they are needed. Nyquist Sounds can contain either samples or the potential to deliver samples, or some combination.

2.1.3 *Unit Generator Implementation*

What is inside a Unit Generator and how do we access it? If sounds have the potential to deliver audio samples on demand, sounds must encapsulate some information, so sounds in Nyquist are basically represented by the unit generators that produce them. If a unit generator has inputs, the sound (represented by a unit generator) will also have references to those inputs. Unit generators are implemented as objects that contain internal state such as the phase and frequency of an oscillator. This state is used to produce samples when the unit generator is called upon.

Although objects are used in the implementation, programs in Nyquist do not have access to the internal state of these objects. You can pass sounds as arguments to other unit generator functions and you can play sounds or write sounds to files, but you cannot access or modify these sound objects. Thus, it is more correct to think of sounds as *values* rather than objects. "Object" implies state and the possibility that the state can change. In contrast, a sound in Nyquist represents a long stream of samples that might eventually be computed and whose values are predetermined and immutable.

Other languages often expose unit generators as mutable objects and expose connections between unit generators as "patches" that can be modified. In this model, sound is computed by making a pass over the graph of interconnected unit generators, computing either one sample or a small block of samples. By making repeated passes over the graph, sound is incrementally computed.

While this incremental block-by-block computation sounds efficient (and it is), this is exactly what happens with Nyquist, at least in typical applications. In Nyquist, the `play` command demands a block of samples, and all the Nyquist sounds do some computation to produce the samples, but they are "lazy" so they only compute incrementally. In most cases, intermediate results are all computed incrementally, used, and then freed quickly so that the total memory requirements are modest.

2.2 Storing Sounds or Not Storing Sounds

If you write:

`play` *sound-expression*

then *sound-expression* can be evaluated incrementally and after playing the samples, there is no way to access them, so Nyquist is able to free the sample memory immediately. The entire sound is never actually present in memory at once.

On the other hand, if you write:

```
set var = sound-expression
```

then initially `var` will just be a reference to an object with the *potential* to compute samples. However, if you `play var`, the samples must be computed. And since `var` retains a reference to the samples, they cannot be deleted. Therefore, as the sound plays, the samples will build up in memory.

In general, you should *never assign sounds to global variables* because this will prevent Nyquist from efficiently freeing the samples.

2.2.1 Functional Programming in Nyquist

Programs are expressions! As much as possible, Nyquist programs should be constructed in terms of functions and values rather than variables and assignment statements.

Avoid sequences of statements and use nested expressions instead. Compose functions to get complex behaviors rather than performing sequential steps. An example of composing a nested expression is:

```
f(g(x), h(x))
```

An exception is this: Assigning expressions to local variables can make programs easier to read by keeping expressions shorter and simpler. However, you should *only assign values to local variables once*. For example, the previous nested expression could be expanded using local variables as follows (in SAL):

```
;; rewrite exec f(g(x), h(x))
begin with gg, hh ;; local variables
  set gg = g(x)
  set hh = h(x)
  exec f(gg, hh)
end
```

2.2.2 Eliminating Global Variables

What if you want to use the same sound twice? Wouldn't you save it in a variable?

Generally, this is a bad idea, because, as mentioned before, storing a sound in a variable can cause Nyquist to compute the sound and keep it in memory. There are other technical reasons not to store sounds in variables—mainly, sounds have an internal start time, and sounds are immutable, so if you compute a sound at time zero and store it in a variable, then try to use it later, you will have to write some extra code to derive a new sound at the desired starting time.

Instead of using global variables, you should generally use (global) functions. Here is an example of something to avoid:

```
;; this is NOT GOOD STYLE
set mysound = pluck(c4)
;; attempt to play mysound twice
;; this expression has problems but it might work
play seq(mysound, mysound)
```

Instead, you should write something like this:

```
;; this is GOOD STYLE
function mysound() return pluck(c4)
play seq(mysound(), mysound())
```

Now, `mysound` is a *function* that *computes* samples rather than storing them. You *could* complain that now `mysound` will be computed twice and in fact some randomness is involved so the second sound will not be identical to the first, but this version is preferred because it is more memory efficient and more "functional".

2.3 Non-Sinusoidal Waveforms

Our next example will be presented in several steps. Nyquist's `osc` function implements the table-lookup oscillator algorithm we saw in Section 1.2.5, and produces a sinusoid waveform by default. Our goal is to create a different sound using a wavetable consisting of several harmonics as opposed to a simple sinusoid. We begin with an explanation of harmonics. Then, in order to build a table, we will use a function that adds harmonics to form a wavetable.

2.3.1 Terminology – Harmonics, etc.

The shape of a wave, the *waveform*, is directly related to its spectral content, or the particular frequencies, amplitudes, and phases of its components. Spectral content is the primary factor in our perception of timbre or tone color. We are familiar with the fact that white light, when properly refracted, can be broken down into component colors, as in the rainbow. So too with a complex sound wave, which is the composite shape of multiple frequencies.

So far, we have made several references to sine waves, so called because they follow the plotted shape of the mathematical sine function. A perfect sine wave or its cosine cousin will produce a single frequency known as the fundamental. Once any deviation is introduced into the sinus shape (but not its basic period), other frequencies, known as harmonic partials are produced.

Partials are any additional frequencies but are not necessarily harmonic. Harmonics or harmonic partials are integer (whole number) multiples of the fundamental frequency (*f*) (*1f, 2f, 3f, 4f* ...). Overtone refers to any partial above the fundamental.[1] For convention's sake, we usually refer to the fundamental as partial #1. The first few harmonic partials are the fundamental frequency, octave above, octave plus perfect fifth above, 2 octaves above, two octaves and a major 3rd, two octaves and a major fifth, as pictured in Figure 2.4 for the pitch "A". After the eighth partial, the pitches begin to grow ever closer and do not necessarily correspond closely to equal-tempered pitches, as shown in the chart. In fact, even the fifths and thirds are slightly off their equal-tempered frequencies. You may note that the first few pitches correspond to the harmonic nodes of a violin (or any vibrating) string.

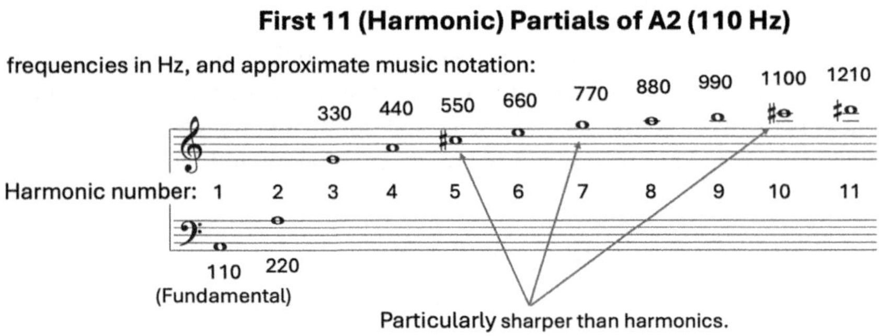

Figure 2.4: Relating harmonics to musical pitches. Equal temperament pitches C#4, G and C#5 are more than 10 cents (0.1 semitone) sharp relative to harmonics 5, 7, and 10, respectively. The 11th harmonic is approximately one quarter tone sharper than D6.

2.3.2 *Creating a Waveform by Summing Harmonics*

In the example below, the function `mkwave` calls upon `build-harmonic` to generate a total of four harmonics with amplitudes 0.5, 0.25, 0.125, and 0.0625. These are scaled and added (using +) to create a wavetable which is bound temporarily to `wave`.

A complete Nyquist wavetable specification is a list consisting of a sound, a pitch, and `#t`[2], indicating a periodic waveform. The pitch gives the nominal pitch of the sound. (This is implicit in a single cycle wave table, but a sampled sound may have many periods of the fundamental.) Pitch is expressed in half-steps, where middle C is 60 steps, as in MIDI pitch numbers. The list of sound, pitch, and T is formed in the last line of `mkwave`: since build-harmonic computes signals

[1]Overtone is not well-defined, so physicists use "partial" instead. Not all partials are harmonics, but all harmonics are partials.

[2]SAL for "true"; you can also write `t`, which is another way to write "true".

with a duration of one second, the fundamental is 1 Hz, and the `hz-to-step` function converts to pitch (in units of steps) as required.

```
define function mkwave()
  begin
    with wave = 0.5 * build-harmonic(1, 2048) +
                0.25 * build-harmonic(2, 2048) +
                0.125 * build-harmonic(3, 2048) +
                0.0625 * build-harmonic(4, 2048)
    set *mytable* = list(wave, hz-to-step(1.0), #t)
  end
```

Now that we have defined a function, the next step of this example is to build the wavetable. The following code calls `mkwave`, which sets `*mytable*` as a side effect:

```
exec mkwave()
```

2.3.3 Wavetable Variables

When Nyquist starts, several wavetables are created and stored in global variables for convenience. They are: `*sine-table*`, `*saw-table*`, and `*tri-table*`, implementing sinusoid, sawtooth, and triangle waves, respectively. The variable `*table*` is initialized to `*sine-table*`, and it is `*table*` that forms the default wave table for many Nyquist oscillator behaviors. If you want a proper, band-limited wavetable, you should construct it yourself, but if you do not understand this sentence and/or you do not mind a bit of aliasing, give `*saw-table*` and `*tri-table*` a try.

Note that in Lisp and SAL, global variables often start and end with asterisks (`*`). These are not special syntax, they just happen to be legal characters for names, and their use is purely a convention. As an aside, it is the possibility of using "`*`", "`+`" and "`-`" in variables that forces SAL to require spaces around operators. "`a * b`" is an expression using multiplication, while "`a*b`" is simply a variable.

2.3.4 Using Wavetables

Now you know that `*table*` is a global variable, and if you set it, `osc` will use it, but this will change *every* use of `osc`:

```
exec mkwave() ;; defined above
set *table* = *mytable*  ;; not recommended! read on...
play osc(c4)
```

In most cases, you will want to compute or select a wavetable, use it for one sound, and then compute or select another wavetable for the next sound. Using the global default wavetable `*table*` is awkward.

A *much* better way is to pass the wavetable directly to `osc` as its optional third parameter. Here is an example to illustrate:

```
;; redefine mkwave to set *mytable* instead of *table*
exec mkwave() ;; run the code to build *mytable*

play osc(c4, 1.0, *mytable*) ;; use *mytable*

;; note that osc(c4, 1.0) will still generate a sine tone
;;   because the default *table* is still *sine-table*
```

Now, you should be thinking, "wait a minute, you said to avoid setting global variables to sounds, and now you are doing just that with these wavetable examples. What a hypocrite!" Wavetables are a bit special because they are:

- typically short, so they do not claim much memory,
- typically used many times, so there can be significant savings by computing them once and saving them,
- not used directly as sounds but only as parameters to oscillators.

You do not have to save wavetables in variables, but it is common practice, in spite of the general advice to keep sounds out of global variables.

2.4 Piecewise Linear Functions: pwl

It is often convenient to construct signals in Nyquist using a list of (time, value) breakpoints which are linearly interpolated to form a smooth signal. The `pwl` function takes a list of parameters which denote (time, value) pairs. There is an implicit initial (time, value) pair of (0, 0), and an implicit final value of 0. There should always be an odd number of parameters, since the final value (but not the final time) is implicit. Thus, the general form of `pwl` looks like:

```
pwl(t1, v1, t2, v2, ..., tn)
```

and this results in a signal as shown in Figure 2.5.

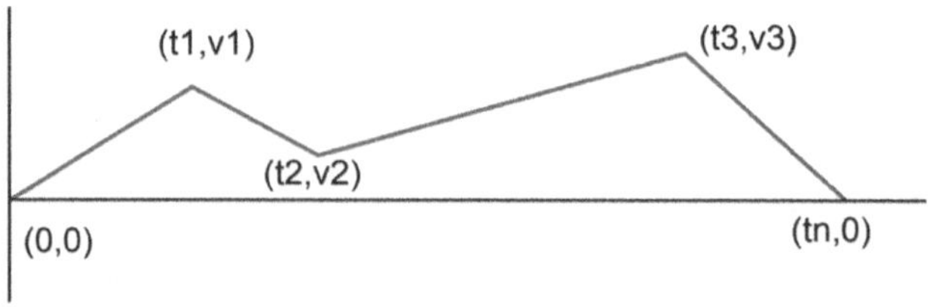

Figure 2.5: Piecewise Linear Functions.

Here are some examples of `pwl`:

```
; symmetric rise to 10 (at time 1) and fall back to 0 (at time 2):
;
pwl(1, 10, 2)

; a square pulse of height 10 and duration 5.
; Note that the first pair (0, 10) overrides the default initial
; point of (0, 0). Also, there are two points specified at time 5:
; (5, 10) and (5, 0). (The last 0 is implicit). The conflict is
; automatically resolved by pushing the (5, 10) breakpoint back to
; the previous sample, so the actual time will be 5 - 1/sr, where
; sr is the sample rate.
;
pwl(0, 10, 5, 10, 5)

; a constant function with the value zero over the time interval
; 0 to 3.5. This is a very degenerate form of pwl. Recall that there
; is an implicit initial point at (0, 0) and a final implicit value of
; 0, so this is really specifying two breakpoints: (0, 0) and (3.5, 0):
;
pwl(3.5)

; a linear ramp from 0 to 10 and duration 1.
; Note the ramp returns to zero at time 1. As with the square pulse
; above, the breakpoint (1, 10) is pushed back to the previous
; sample.
;
pwl(1, 10, 1)

; If you really want a linear ramp to reach its final value at the
; specified time, you need to make a signal that is one sample longer.
; The RAMP function does this:
;
ramp(10)  ; ramp from 0 to 10 with duration 1 + one sample
; period. RAMP is based on PWL; it is defined in nyquist.lsp.
```

2.4.1 Variants of pwl

Sometimes, you want a signal that does not start at zero or end at zero. There is also the option of interpolating between points with exponential curves instead of linear interpolation. There is also the option of specifying time intervals rather than absolute times. These options lead to many variants, for example:

`pwlv`(*v0, t1, v1, t2, v2, ..., tn, vn*) – “v” for “value first” is used for signals with non-zero starting and ending points

`pwev`(*v1, t2, v2, ..., tn, vn*) – exponential interpolation, $vi > 0$

`pwlr`(*i1, v1, i2, v2, ..., in*) – relative intervals rather than absolute times

See the *Nyquist Reference Manual* for more variants and combinations.

2.4.2 The Envelope Function: env

Envelopes created by env are a special case of the more general piecewise linear functions created by pwl. The form of env is:

env(*t1*, *t2*, *t4*, *L1*, *L2*, *L3*, *dur*)

(duration given by *dur* is optional). One advantage of env over pwl is that env

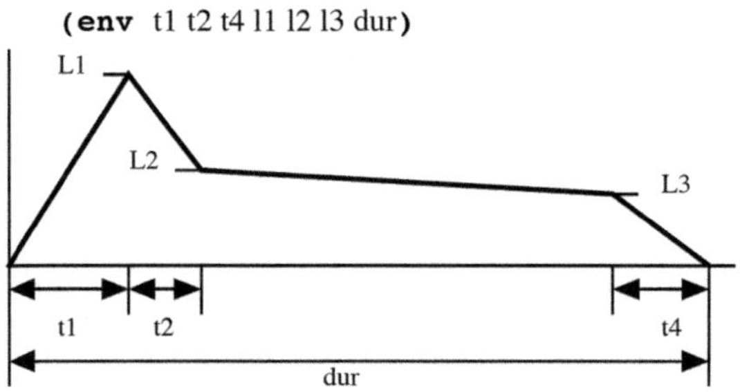

Figure 2.6: Envelope function env.

allows you to give fixed *attack* and *decay* times that do not stretch with duration. In contrast, the default behavior for pwl is to stretch each segment in proportion when the duration changes. (We have not really discussed duration in Nyquist, but we will get there later.)

2.5 Basic Wavetable Synthesis

Now, you have seen examples of using the oscillator function (or unit generator) osc to make tones and various functions (unit generators) to make envelopes or smooth control signals. All we need to do is multiply them together to get tones with smooth onsets and decays. Here is an example function to play a note:

```
; env-note produces an enveloped note. The duration
;   defaults to 1.0, but stretch can be used to change the duration.
;   Uses mkwave, second version defined above, to create *mytable*.

exec mkwave() ;; run the code to build *mytable*

function env-note(p)
  return osc(p, 1.0, *mytable*) *
         env(0.05, 0.1, 0.5, 1.0, 0.5, 0.4)

; try it out:
;
play env-note(c4)
```

This is a basic synthesis algorithm called wavetable synthesis. The advantages are:

- simplicity – one oscillator, one envelope,
- efficiency – oscillator samples are generated by fast table lookup and (usually) linear interpolation,
- direct control – you can specify the desired envelope and pitch.

Disadvantages are:

- the spectrum (strength of harmonics) does not change with pitch or time as in most acoustic instruments.

Often filters are added to change the spectrum over time, and we will see many other synthesis algorithms and variations of wavetable synthesis to overcome this problem.

2.6 Introduction to Scores

So far, we have seen how simple functions can be used in Nyquist to create individual *sound events*. We prefer this term to *notes*. While a sound event might be described as a note, the term *note* usually implies a single musical tone with a well-defined pitch. A *note* is conventionally described by:

- pitch – from low (bass) to high,
- starting time (notes begin and end),
- duration – how long is the note,
- loudness – sometimes called *dynamics*,
- timbre – everything else such as the instrument or sound quality, softness, harshness, noise, vowel sound, etc.

while *sound event* captures a much broader range of possible sound. A *sound event* can have:

- pitch, but may be unpitched noise or combinations,
- time – sound events begin and end,
- duration – how long is the event,
- loudness – also known as *dynamics*,
- potentially many evolving qualities.

Now, we consider how to organize sound events in time using *scores* in Nyquist. What is a *score*? Authors write books. Composers write *scores*. Figure 2.7 illustrates a conventional score. A score is basically a graphical display of music intended for conductors and performers. Usually, scores display a set of notes including their pitches, timing, instruments, and dynamics. In computer music, we define *score* to include computer readable representations of sets of notes or sound events.

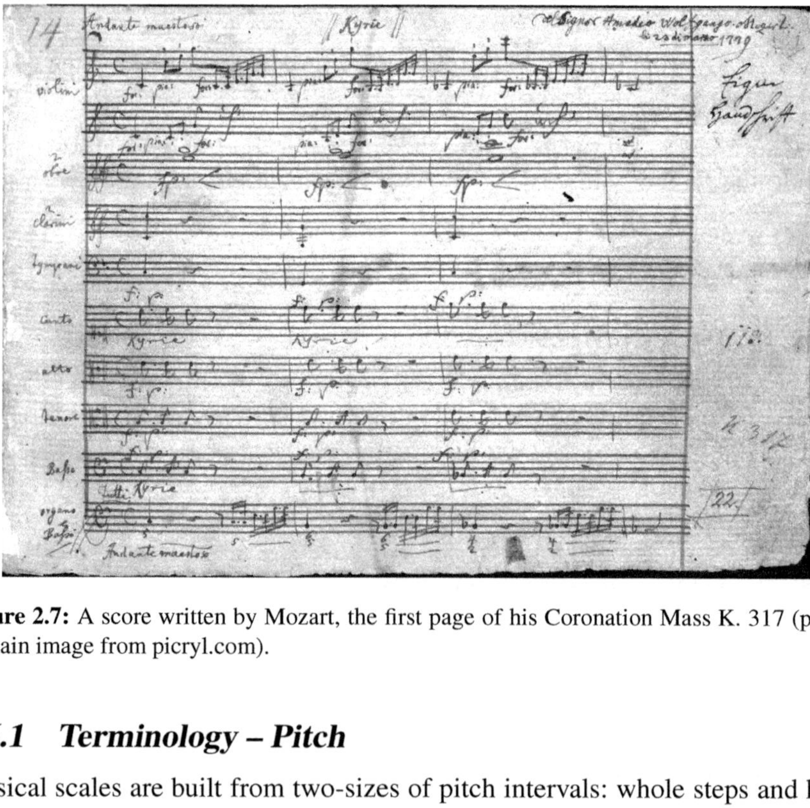

Figure 2.7: A score written by Mozart, the first page of his Coronation Mass K. 317 (public domain image from picryl.com).

2.6.1 Terminology – Pitch

Musical scales are built from two-sizes of pitch intervals: whole steps and half-steps, where a whole step represents about a 12% change in frequency, and a half-step is about a 6% change. A whole step is exactly two half-steps. Therefore, the basic unit in Western music is the half-step, but this is a bit wordy, so in Nyquist, we call these *steps*.[3]

Since Western music more-or-less uses integer numbers of half-steps for pitches, we represent pitches with integers. Middle C (ISO C4) is arbitrarily represented

[3]Physicists have the unit *Hertz* to denote cycles per second. Wouldn't it be great if we had a special name to denote half-steps? How about the *Bach* since J. S. Bach's Well-Tempered Clavier is a landmark in the development of the fixed-size half-step, or the *Schoenberg*, honoring Arnold's development of 12-tone music. Wouldn't it be cool to say 440 Hertz is 69 Bachs? Or to argue whether it's "Bach" or "Bachs?" But I digress ....

by 60. Nyquist pre-defines a number of convenient variables to represent pitches symbolically. We have `c4` = 60, `cs4` (C# or C-sharp) = 61, `cf4` (Cb or C-flat) = 59, `b3` (B natural, third octave) = 59, `bs3` (B# or B-sharp, 3rd octave) = 60, etc. **Note:** In Nyquist, we can use non-integers to denote detuned or microtonal pitches: 60.5 is a quarter step above 60 (`C4`).

Some other useful facts: Steps are logarithms of frequency, and frequency doubles every 12 steps, thus each half-step (or "step" in Nyquist terminology) represents a frequency ratio of $\sqrt[12]{2}$. Doubling frequency (or halving) is called an interval of an *octave*.

2.6.2 Lists

Scores are constructed from lists, so let's learn about lists.

2.6.2.1 Lists in Nyquist

Lists in Nyquist are represented as standard *singly-linked* lists. Every element cell in the list contains a link to the value and a link to the next element. The last element links to *nil*, which can be viewed as pointing to an empty list. Nyquist uses *dynamic typing* so that lists can contain any types of elements or any mixture of types; types are not explicitly declared before they are used. Also, a list can have nested lists within it, which means you can make any binary tree structure through *arbitrary nesting* of lists.

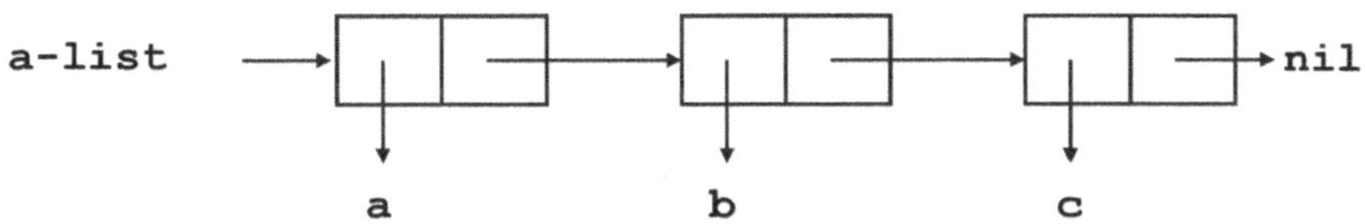

Figure 2.8: A list in Nyquist.

2.6.2.2 Notation

Although we can manipulate pointers directly to construct lists, this is frowned upon. Instead, we simply write expressions for lists. In SAL, we use curly brace notations for literal lists, e.g., `{a b c}`. Note that the three elements here are literal symbols, not variables (no evaluation takes place, so these symbols denote themselves, not the values of variables named by the symbols). To construct a list from variables, we call the `list` function with an arbitrary number of parameters, which are the list elements, e.g., `list(a, b, c)`. These parameters are evaluated as expressions in the normal way and the values of these expressions become list elements.

2.6.2.3 Literals, Variables, Quoting, Cons

Consider the following:

```
set a = 1, b = 2, c = 3
print {a b c}
```

This prints: `{a b c}`. Why? Remember that the brace notation {} does not evaluate anything, so in this case, a list of the *symbols* `a`, `b` and `c` is formed. To make a list of the *values* of `a`, `b`, and `c`, use `list`, which evaluates its arguments:

```
print list(a, b, c)
```

This prints: `{1 2 3}`.

What about numbers? Consider:

```
print list(1, 2, 3)
```

This prints: `{1 2 3}`. Why? Because *numbers are evaluated immediately by the Nyquist (SAL or Lisp) interpreter as the numbers are read. They become either integers (known as type FIXNUM) or floating point numbers (known as type FLONUM).* When a number is used as an expression (as in this example), or a subexpression, the number evaluates to itself.

What if you want to use `list` to construct a list of symbols?

```
print list(quote(a),  quote(b), quote(c))
```

This prints: `{a b c}`. The `quote()` form can enclose any expression, but typically just a symbol. The `quote()` form returns the symbol without evaluation.

If you want to add an element to a list, there is a special function, `cons`:

```
print cons(1, {b})
```

This prints: `{1 b}`. Study this carefully; the first argument becomes the first element of a new list. The *elements* of the second argument (a list) form the remaining elements of the new list.

In contrast, here is what happens with `list`:

```
print list(1, {b c d})
```

This prints: `{1 {b c d}}`. Study this carefully too; the first argument becomes the first element of a new list. The second argument becomes the second *element* of the new list, so the new list has two elements.

2.7 Scores

In Nyquist, scores are represented by lists of data. The form of a Nyquist score is the following:

```
{ sound-event-1
  sound-event-2
  ...
  sound-event-n }
```

where a *sound event* is also a list consisting of the event time, duration, and an expression that can be evaluated to compute the event. The expression, when evaluated, must return a sound:

```
{ {time-1 dur-1 expression-1}
  {time-2 dur-2 expression-2}
  ...
  {time-n dur-n expression-n} }
```

Each expression consists of a function name (sometimes called the *instrument*) and a list of keyword-value style parameters:

```
{ {time-1 dur-1 {instrument-1 pitch: 60}}
  {time-2 dur-2 {instrument-2 pitch: 62}}
  ...
  {time-n dur-n {instrument-n pitch: 62 vel: 100}} }
```

Here is an example score:

```
{ {0 1 {note pitch: 60 vel: 100}}
  {1 1 {note pitch: 62 vel: 110}}
  {2 1 {note pitch: 64 vel: 120}} }
```

Important things to note (pardon the pun) are:

- Scores are data. You can compute scores by writing code and using the list construction functions from the previous section (and see the *Nyquist Reference Manual* for many more).
- Expressions in scores are *lists*, not SAL expressions. The first element of the list is the function to call. The remaining elements form the parameter list.
- Expressions use keyword-style parameters, never positional parameters. The rationale is that keywords label the values, allowing us to pass the same score data to different *instruments*, which may implement some keywords, ignore others, and provide default values for missing keywords.
- Keyword parameters also allow us to treat scores as data. For example, Nyquist has a built-in function to find all the `pitch:` parameters and transpose them. If positional parameters were used, the transpose func-

tion would have to have information about each instrument function to find the pitch values (if any). Keyword parameters are more self-defining.

- In SAL, keyword parameters end with a colon, e.g., `pitch:`. In Lisp, keyword parameters *begin* with a colon, e.g., `:pitch`. The SAL compiler translates `pitch:` to `:pitch`, even when `pitch:` is used between braces. However, when you *print* a list with keywords, there is no reverse-translation, so `print {pitch: 40}` will display `{:pitch 40}`!

2.7.1 The score-begin-end "instrument" Event

Sometimes it is convenient to give the entire score a begin time and an end time because the *logical* time span of a score may include some silence. This information can be useful when splicing scores together. To indicate start and end times of the score, insert a *sound event* of the form:

```
{0 0 {score-begin-end 1.2 6}}
```

In this case, the score occupies the time period from 1.2 to 6 seconds.

For example, if we want the previous score, which nominally ends at time 3 to contain an extra second of silence at the end, we can specify the time span of the score is from 0 to 4 as follows:

```
{ {0 0 {score-begin-end 0 4}}
  {0 1 {note pitch: 60 vel: 100}}
  {1 1 {note pitch: 62 vel: 110}}
  {2 1 {note pitch: 64 vel: 120}} }
```

2.7.2 Playing a Score

To interpret a score and produce a sound, we use the `timed-seq()` function. The following plays the previous score:

```
set myscore = {
  {0 0 {score-begin-end 0 4}}
  {0 1 {note pitch: 60 vel: 100}}
  {1 1 {note pitch: 62 vel: 110}}
  {2 1 {note pitch: 64 vel: 120}} }
play timed-seq(myscore)
```

2.7.3 Making an Instrument

Now you know all about how Nyquist scores are represented and interpreted. The previous example will work because `note` is a built-in function in Nyquist that uses a built-in piano synthesizer. But it might be helpful to see a custom instrument definition, making the connection between scores and the wavetable synthesis examples we saw earlier. In the next example, we define a new instrument function that calls on our existing `env-note` instrument. The reason for making a new function to be our instrument is we want to use keyword parameters. Then, we modify `myscore` to use `myinstr`. (See Algorithm 3.)

Algorithm 3 Defining an instrument, using it in a Nyquist score, and playing the score.

```
variable *mytable* ;; declaration avoids parser warnings

function mkwave()
  begin
    set *mytable* = 0.5 * build-harmonic(1, 2048) +
                    0.25 * build-harmonic(2, 2048) +
                    0.125 * build-harmonic(3, 2048) +
                    0.0625 * build-harmonic(4, 2048)
    set *mytable* = list(*mytable*, hz-to-step(1.0), #t)
  end

exec mkwave()

function env-note(p)
  return osc(p, 1.0, *mytable*) *
         env(0.05, 0.1, 0.5, 1.0, 0.5, 0.4)

;; define the "instrument" myinstr that uses keyword parameters
;; this is just a stub, env-note() does most of the work...
function myinstr(pitch: 60, vel: 100)
  return env-note(pitch) * vel-to-linear(vel)

set myscore = {
  {0 0 {score-begin-end 0 4}}
  {0 1 {myinstr pitch: 60 vel: 50}}
  {1 1 {myinstr pitch: 62 vel: 70}}
  {2 1 {myinstr pitch: 64 vel: 120}} }

play timed-seq(myscore)
```

Note that in `myinstr` we scale the amplitude of the output by `vel-to-linear(vel)` to get some loudness control. "vel" is short for "velocity" which refers to the velocity of piano keys—higher numbers mean faster, which means louder. The "vel" scale is nominally 1 to 127 (as in the MIDI standard) and `vel-to-linear()` converts this to a scale factor. We will learn more about amplitude later.

2.7.4 Making a Score

Besides giving complete control over instruments, parameters, and timing, the really exciting thing about scores is the possibility of *computing them* rather than writing them by hand, which is obviously very tedious. In the next example, we use list functions to embed data into a score and play it. Our goal is to create a sequence of 32 notes with pitches taken randomly from a list and velocities that increase to the mid-point, then decrease to the end. (Later, we will learn some more elegant ways to do this, but for now, we will take the "brute force" approach of constructing the score from list nodes.)

Let us begin by initializing an empty list and writing a loop that iterates 32 times. Note that we use a second `for` expression to generate a new start time for each note:

```
set pitches = {bf3 c4 cs4 ds4 fs4 g5}
set myscore = nil ;; an empty list
loop
  for i from 0 below 32  ; iterate 32 times
  for start from 0 by 0.25  ; start times are every 0.25 s
  ... make and append a note here ...
end
```

Now, to create each sound event, we can use nested calls to `list`:

```
set pitch = nth(random(length(pitches)), pitches)
set vel = 40 + 5 * #?(i < 16, i, 32 - i)
set event = list(start, 1.5, list(quote(note),
                 keyword(pitch), pitch, keyword(vel), vel))
```

A number of details are illustrated here: The `nth` function returns the (zero-based) n^{th} element of a list. To compute `vel`, a *conditional expression* (with `#?`) is used to create an increasing sequence up to `i` = 16, then a decreasing function beyond that. The *duration* of each event (note) is 1.5 seconds. A typical event is `{4 1.5 {note pitch: c4 vel: 84}}`. You might be tempted to write `list(start, 1.5, list(note, pitch:, pitch, vel:, vel))`, but this will fail for two reasons: First, `note` is a variable reference, but *we want the symbol* itself. Write `quote(note)` to denote the symbol `note`. Secondly, SAL interprets `pitch:` to be a keyword, but we also want `pitch:` as a symbol. Writing `quote(pitch:)` will not work because `quote` does not take keyword parameters. Instead, you can write `keyword(pitch)` to *construct a keyword symbol*. Unlike the `{...}` notation, `list` is a function that evaluates each parameter expression, and expressions must be *separated by commas*.

We need to build a list from individual sound events. SAL has an "insert-at-end" operator, so `set myscore &= event` will do the job. Finally, we can put this all together into a program to compute `myscore`. The program is shown below. In this example, one additional trick is used: As explained earlier, Lisp keywords are denoted by an initial colon, and SAL's `pitch:` is translated to Lisp's `:pitch`, so our goal is really to insert the symbol `:pitch` into our list. Lisp convention is that symbols that begin with colon are automatically initialized to their own symbol name, as if LISP automatically executes something like:

```
set :pitch = keyword(pitch)
```

These Lisp keywords are accessible in SAL, so instead of writing the wordy expression `keyword(pitch)` to construct a keyword, we can simply write `:pitch` as a variable and it will be evaluated to its own name, the *symbol* `:pitch`! Compare the code above, using `keyword(pitch)` and `keyword(vel)` to the code below, using `:pitch` and `:vel`.

For more detailed examples on list manipulation and SAL programming in general, see Chapter 3 "Introduction to SAL" of *Algorithmic Composition: A Guide to Composing Music with Nyquist* (87).

Algorithm 4 Creating and playing a Nyquist score using list functions.

```
set pitches = {bf4 c5 cs5 ds5 fs5 g5}
set myscore = nil  ; an empty list
loop with pitch, vel, event
  for i from 0 below 32  ; iterate 32 times
  for start from 0 by 0.25  ; start times are every 0.25 s
  set pitch = nth(random(length(pitches)), pitches)
  set vel = 10 + 6 * #?(i < 16, i, 32 - i)
  set event = list(start, 1.5, list(quote(note),
                      :pitch, pitch, :vel, vel))
  set myscore &= event
end
play timed-seq(myscore)
```

2.8 Summary

Now you should know how to build a simple wavetable instrument with the waveform consisting of any set of harmonics and with an arbitrary envelope controlled by `pwl` or `env`. You can also write or compute scores containing many instances of your instrument function organized in time, and you can synthesize the score using `timed-seq`. You might experiment by creating different waveforms, different envelopes, using non-integer pitches for microtuning, or notes overlapping in time to create chords or clusters.

Chapter 3

Sampling Theory Introduction

Topics Discussed: Sampling Theory, Analog to/from Digital Conversion, Fourier Synthesis, Aliasing, Quantization Noise, Amplitude Modulation

The principles which underlie almost all digital audio applications and devices, be they digital synthesis, sampling, digital recording, or CD or iPod playback, are based on the basic concepts presented in this chapter. New forms of playback, file formats, compression, synthesis, processing and storage of data are all changing on a seemingly daily basis, but the underlying mechanisms for converting real-world sound into digital values and converting them back into real-world sound has not varied much since Max Mathews developed MUSIC I in 1957 at Bell Labs (57).

The theoretical framework that enabled musical pioneers such as Max Mathews to develop digital audio programs stretches back over a century. The groundbreaking theoretical work done at Bell Labs in the mid-20th century is worth noting. Bell Labs was concerned with transmitting larger amounts of voice data over existing telephone lines than could normally be sent with analog transmissions, due to bandwidth restrictions. Many of the developments pertaining to computer music were directly related to work on this topic.

Harry Nyquist, a Swedish-born physicist laid out the principles for sampling analog signals at even intervals of time and at twice the rate of the highest frequency so they could be transmitted over telephone lines as digital signals (67), even though the technology to do so did not exist at the time. Part of this work is now known as the Nyquist theorem. Nyquist worked for AT&T, then Bell Labs. Twenty years later, Claude Shannon, mathematician and early computer scientist,

DOI: 10.1201/9781003782711-3

also working at Bell Labs and then M.I.T., developed a proof for the Nyquist theory.[1] The importance of their work to information theory, computing, networks, digital audio, digital photography, and computer graphics (images are just signals in 2D!) cannot be overstated. Pulse Code Modulation (PCM), a widely used method for encoding and decoding binary data, such as that used in digital audio, was invented by Alec Reeves (5), and further developed at Bell Labs in work attributed to John R. Pierce, a brilliant engineer in many fields, including computer music.

In this chapter, we will learn the basic theory of *sampling*, or representing continuous functions with discrete data.

3.1 Intuitive Approach

The world is continuous. Time marches on and on, and there are plenty of things that we can measure at any instant. For example, weather forecasters might keep an ongoing record of the temperature or barometric pressure. If you are in the hospital, the nurses might be keeping a record of your temperature, your heart rate, or your brain waves. Any of these records gives you a function $f(t)$ where, at a given time t, $f(t)$ is the value of the particular thing that interests you.

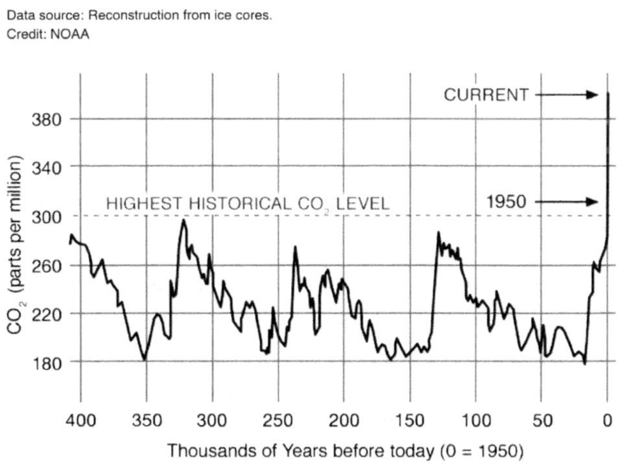

Figure 3.1: Carbon dioxide concentration data from climate.nasa.gov.

[1]The Shannon Theorem (86), a pioneering work in information theory, should not be confused with the Shannon Juggling Theory of the same author, in which he worked out the mathematics of juggling numerous objects ((F+D)H=(V+D)N, where F is the time an object spends in the air, D is the time a object spends in a hand, V is the time a hand is vacant, N is the number of objects juggled, and H is the number of hands)—he was an avid juggler as well.

Figure 3.1 represents a continuous function of time. What we mean by "continuous" is that at any instant of time the function takes on a well-defined value, so that it makes a squiggly line graph that could be traced without the pencil ever leaving the paper. This might also be called an analog function. Of course, the time series that interest us are those that represent sound. In particular, we want to take these time series, stick them on the computer, and play with them!

Now, if you've been paying attention, you may realize that at this moment we're in a bit of a bind: sound is a continuous function. That is, at every instant in time, we could write down a number that is the value of the function at that instant—how much your eardrum has been displaced, the instantaneous air pressure, voltage from a microphone, and so on. But such a continuous function would provide an infinite list of numbers (any one of which may have an infinite expansion, like $\pi = 3.1415...$), and no matter how big your computer is, you're going to have a pretty tough time fitting an infinite collection of numbers on your hard drive.

So how do we do it? How can we represent sound as a finite collection of numbers that can be stored efficiently, in a finite amount of space, on a computer, and played back and manipulated at will? In short, how do we represent sound digitally? That's the problem that we'll investigate in this chapter.

Somehow we have to come up with a finite list of numbers that does a good job of representing our continuous function. We do it by sampling the original function at some predetermined rate, called the *sampling rate*, recording the value of the function at that moment. For example, maybe we only record the temperature every 5 minutes. The graph in Figure 3.1 really comes from discrete samples obtained from ice cores, so this is also an example of *sampling* to represent a continuous function using discrete values. For sound we need to go a lot faster, and we often use a special device that grabs instantaneous amplitudes at rapid, audio rates (called an analog to digital converter, or ADC).

A continuous function is also called an analog function, and, to restate the problem, we have to convert analog functions to lists of samples, in binary, which is the fundamental way that computers store information. In computers, think of a digital sound as a function of location in computer memory. That is, sounds are stored as lists of numbers, and as we read through them we are basically creating a discrete function of time of individual amplitude values.

In analog to digital conversions, continuous functions (for example, air pressures, sound waves, or voltages) are sampled and stored as numerical values. (See Figure 3.2.) In digital to analog conversions, numerical values are interpolated by the converter to force some continuous system (such as amplifiers, speakers, and subsequently the air and our ears) into a continuous vibration. Interpolation just means smoothly transitioning between the discrete numerical values.

Figure 3.2: A pictorial description of the recording and playback of sounds through an ADC/DAC.

3.1.1 Analog Versus Digital

The distinction between analog and digital information is fundamental to the realm of computer music (and in fact computer anything!). In this section, we'll offer some analogies, explanations, and other ways to understand the difference more intuitively.

Imagine watching someone walking along, bouncing a ball. Now imagine that the ball leaves a trail of smoke in its path. What does the trail look like? (See Figure 3.3.) Probably some sort of continuous zigzag pattern, right?

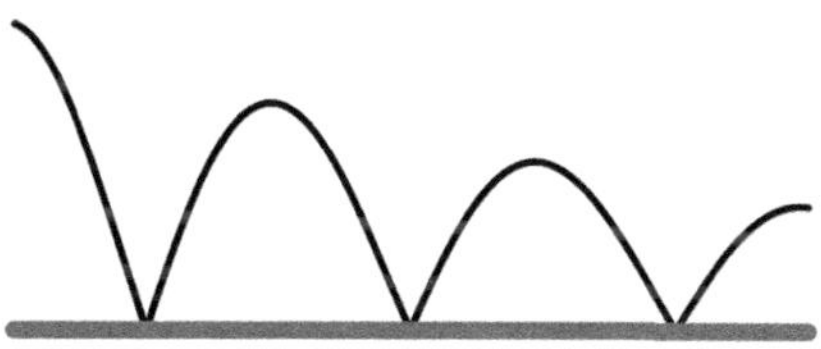

Figure 3.3: The path of a bouncing ball.

OK, keep watching, but now blink repeatedly. What does the trail look like now? Because we are blinking our eyes, we're only able to see the ball at discrete moments in time. It's on the way up, we blink, now it's moved up a bit more, we blink again, now it may be on the way down, and so on. We'll call these snapshots samples because we've been taking visual samples of the complete trajectory that the ball is following. (See Figure 3.4.) The rate at which we obtain these samples (blink our eyes) is called the sampling rate.

It's pretty clear, though, that the faster we sample, the better chance we have of getting an accurate picture of the entire continuous path along which the ball has been traveling.

What's the difference between the two views of the bouncing ball: the blinking and the nonblinking? Each view pretty much gives the same picture of the ball's path. We can tell how fast the ball is moving and how high it's bouncing. The only

Figure 3.4: The same path, but sampled by blinking.

real difference seems to be that in the first case the trail is continuous, and in the second it is broken, or discrete. That's the main distinction between analog and digital representations of information: analog information is continuous, while digital information is not.

3.1.2 Analog and Digital Waveform Representations

Now let's take a look at two time-domain representations of a sound wave, one analog and one digital, in Figure 3.5.

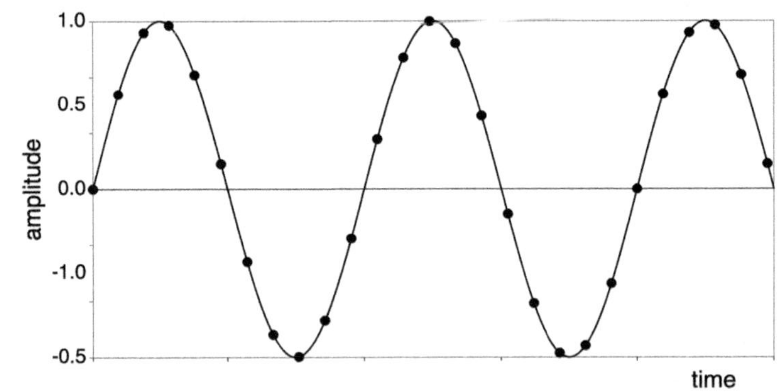

Figure 3.5: An analog waveform and its digital cousin: the analog waveform has smooth and continuous changes, and the digital version of the same waveform consists only of points along the curve. The black circles are the actual samples taken by the computer. Note that nothing in between those points is stored in the computer.

Figure 3.5 emphasizes the point that digitally recorded waveforms are apparently missing some original information from analog sources. The continuous curve between the samples (black circles) is "missing". However, by increasing the number of samples taken each second (the sample rate), as well as increasing the accuracy of those samples (the resolution), an extremely accurate recording can be made. In fact, we can prove mathematically that discrete samples can represent certain continuous functions *without any loss of information*! And in practice, we can use this theory to record audio with imperceptible loss or distortion.

3.2 Sampling Theory

So now we know that we need to sample a continuous waveform to represent it digitally. We also know that the faster we sample it, the better. But this is still a little vague. How often do we need to sample a waveform in order to achieve a good representation of it?

The answer to this question is given by the Nyquist sampling theorem, which states that to represent a signal well, the sampling rate (or sampling frequency – not to be confused with the frequency content of the sound) needs to be at least twice the highest frequency contained in the sound.

3.2.1 Frequency Content

We'll be giving a much more precise description of the frequency domain later, but for now we can simply think of sounds as combinations of more basic sounds that are distinguished according to their rate of vibration, called *frequency*. Perceptually, higher frequencies are associated with higher *pitch height* and higher brightness.

As we learned earlier, the basic sound is called a sinusoid, the general term for sine-like waveforms. The term *pitch height* refers to our perception of these components *if* we could hear them separately, but ordinarily, we cannot. To summarize, sounds can be decomposed into the sum of basic sinusoidal components, each of which has a frequency.

All sound can be viewed as a combination of these sinusoids with varying amplitudes. It's sort of like making soup and putting in a bunch of basic spices: the flavor will depend on how much of each spice you include, and you can change things dramatically when you alter the proportions. The sinusoids are our basic sound spices! The complete description of how much of each of the frequencies is used is called the spectrum of the sound.

Since sounds change over time, the proportions of each of the sinusoids changes too. Just like when you spice up that soup, as you let it boil the spice proportion may be changing as things evaporate.

3.2.2 Highest Frequency in a Sound

Consider Figure 3.6. The graph at the top is our usual time-domain graph, or audiogram, of the waveform created by a five-note whistled melody. Time is on the x-axis, and amplitude is on the y-axis.

The bottom graph is the same melody, but this time we are looking at a time-frequency representation. The idea here is that if we think of the whistle as made up of contiguous small chunks of sound, then over each small time period the sound is composed of differing amounts of various pieces of frequency. The

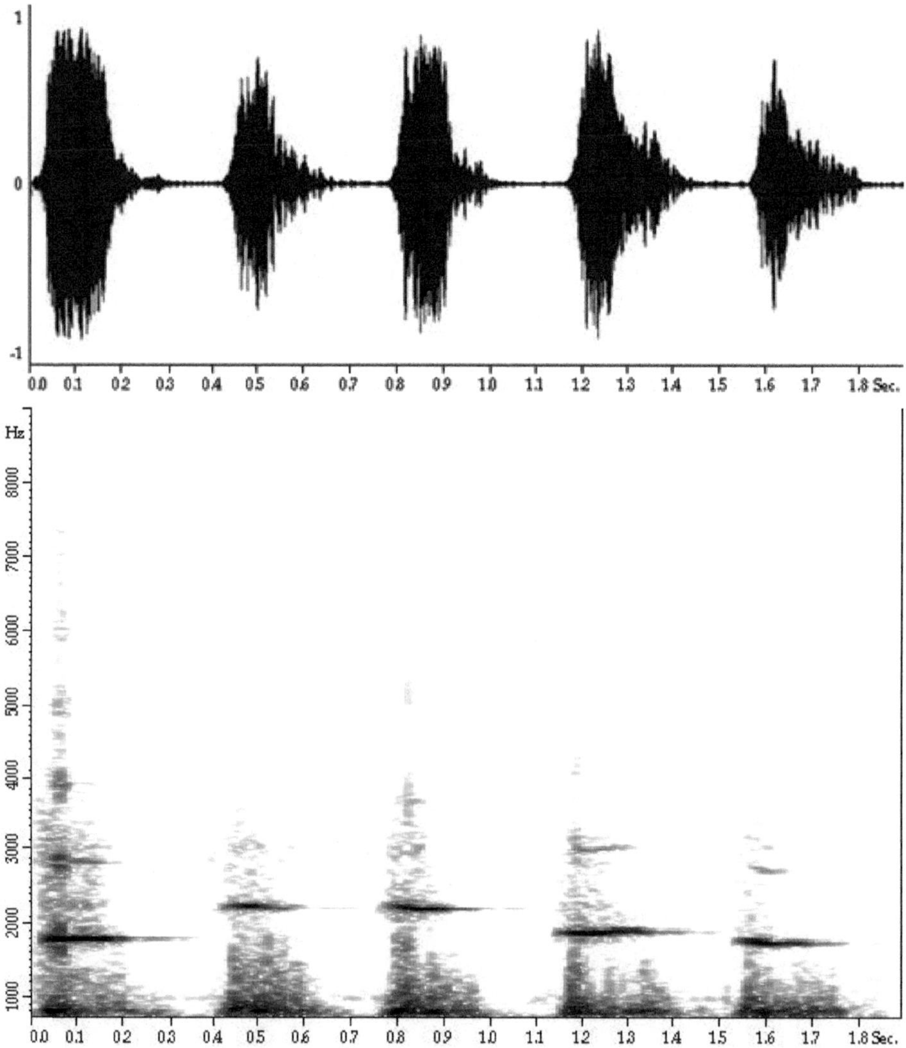

Figure 3.6: Two graphical representations of sound.

amount of frequency y at time t is encoded by the brightness of the pixel at the coordinate (t, y). The darker the pixel, the more of that frequency at that time. For example, if you look at time 0.4 you see a band of white, except near 2,500, showing that around that time we mainly hear a pure tone of about 2,500 Hz, while at 0.8 seconds, there are contributions all around from about 0 Hz to 5,500 Hz, but stronger ones at about 2,500 Hz and 200 Hz.

It looks like the signal only contains frequencies up to 8,000 Hz. If this were the case, we would need to sample the sound at a rate of 16,000 Hz (16 kHz) in order to accurately reproduce the sound. That is, we would need to take sound bites (bytes?!) 16,000 times a second.

In the next section, when we talk about representing sounds in the frequency domain (as a combination of various amplitude levels of frequency components, which change over time) rather than in the time domain (as a numerical list of sample values of amplitudes), we'll learn a lot more about the ramifications of the Nyquist theorem for digital sound. For example, since the human ear only responds to sounds up to about 20,000 Hz, we need to sample sounds at least 40,000 times a second, or at a rate of 40,000 Hz, to represent these sounds for human consumption. You may be wondering why we even need to represent sonic frequencies that high (when the piano, for instance, only goes up to the high 4,000 Hz range in terms of *pitches* or repetition rate). The answer is timbral, particularly spectral. Those higher frequencies do exist and fill out the descriptive sonic information.

Just to review: We measure frequency in cycles per second (cps) or Hertz (Hz). The frequency range of human hearing is usually given as 20 Hz to 20,000 Hz, meaning that we can hear sounds in that range. Knowing that, if we decide that the highest frequency we're interested in is 20 kHz, then according to the Nyquist theorem, we need a sampling rate of at least twice that frequency, or 40 kHz.

3.3 The Frequency Domain

Earlier, we talked about the basic atoms of sound—the sine wave, and about the function that describes the sound generated by a vibrating tuning fork. In this section we're talking a lot about the frequency domain. If you remember, our basic units, sine waves, only had two parameters: amplitude and frequency. It turns out that these dull little sine waves are going to give us the fundamental tool for the analysis and description of sound, and especially for the digital manipulation of sound. That's the frequency domain: a place where lots of little sine waves are our best friends.

But before we go too far, it's important to fully understand what a sine wave is, and it's also wonderful to know that we can make these simple little curves ridiculously complicated, too. And it's useful to have another model for generating these functions. That model is called a phasor.

3.3.1 Description of a Phasor

Think of a bicycle wheel suspended at its hub. We're going to paint one of the spokes bright red, and at the end of the spoke we'll put a red arrow. We now put some axes around the wheel—the x-axis going horizontally through the hub, and the y-axis going vertically. We're interested in the height of the arrowhead relative to the x-axis as the wheel—our phasor—spins around counterclockwise. (See Figure 3.7.)

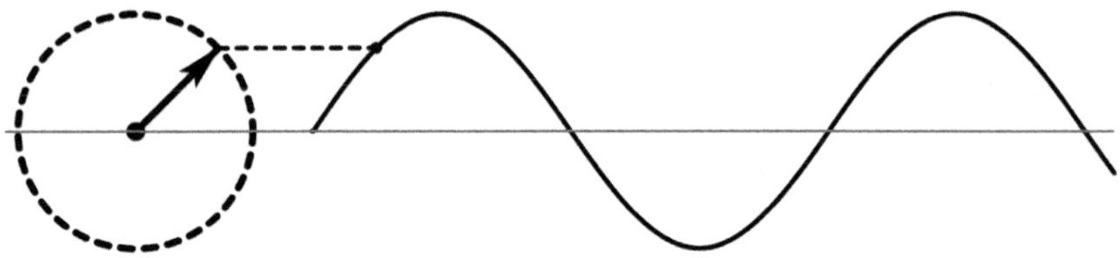

Figure 3.7: Sine waves and phasors. As the sine wave moves forward in time, the arrow goes around the circle at the same rate. The height of the arrow (that is, how far it is above or below the x-axis) as it spins around in a circle is described by the sine wave.

In other words, if we trace the arrow's location on the circle and measure the height of the arrow on the y-axis as our phasor goes around the circle, the resulting curve is a sine wave!

As time goes on, the phasor goes round and round. At each instant, we measure the height of the dot over the x-axis. Let's consider a simple example first. Suppose the wheel is spinning at a rate of one revolution per second. This is its frequency (and remember, this means that the period is 1 second/revolution). This is the same as saying that the phasor spins at a rate of 360 degrees per second, or better yet, 2π radians per second (if we're going to be mathematicians, then we have to measure angles in terms of radians). So 2π radians per second is the angular velocity of the phasor.

This means that after 0.25 seconds the phasor has gone $\pi/2$ radians (90 degrees), and after 0.5 seconds it's gone π radians or 180 degrees, and so on. So, we can describe the amount of angle that the phasor has gone around at time t as a function, which we call $\theta(t)$.

Now, let's look at the function given by the height of the arrow as time goes on. The first thing that we need to remember is a little trigonometry.

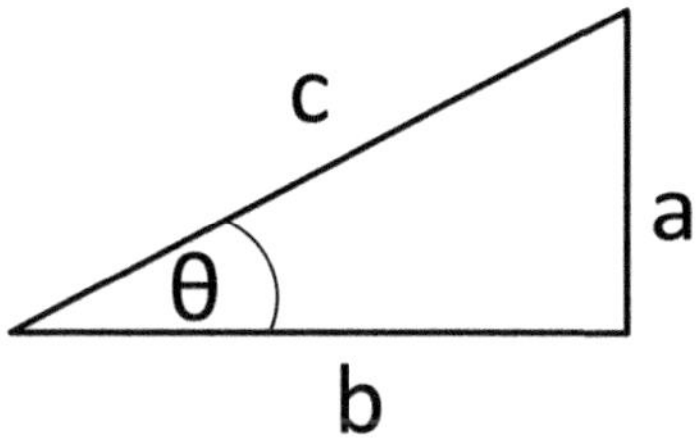

Figure 3.8: Triangle.

The sine and cosine of an angle are measured using a right triangle. For our right triangle, the sine of θ, written $sin(\theta)$ is given by the equation: $sin(\theta) = a/c$ (See Figure 3.8.)

This means that: $a = c \times sin(\theta)$

We'll make use of this in a minute, because in this example a is the height of our triangle.

Similarly, the cosine, written $cos(\theta)$, is: $cos(\theta) = b/c$

This means that: $b = c \times cos(\theta)$. This will come in handy later, too.

Now back to our phasor. We're interested in measuring the height at time t, which we'll denote as $h(t)$. At time t, the phasor's arrow is making an angle of $\theta(t)$ with the x-axis. Our basic phasor has a radius of 1, so we get the following relationship: $h(t) = sin(\theta(t)) = sin(2\pi t)$. We also get this nice graph of a function, which is our favorite old sine curve.

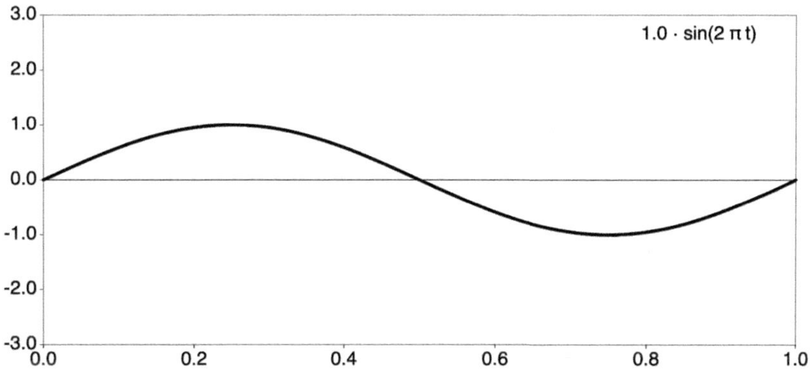

Figure 3.9: Basic sinusoid.

Now, how could we change this curve? Well, we could change the amplitude—this is the same as changing the length of our arrow on the phasor. We'll keep the frequency the same and make the radius of our phasor equal to 3. Then we get: $h(t) = 3 \times sin(2\pi t)$. Then we get the nice curve in Figure 3.10, which is another kind of sinusoid (bigger!).

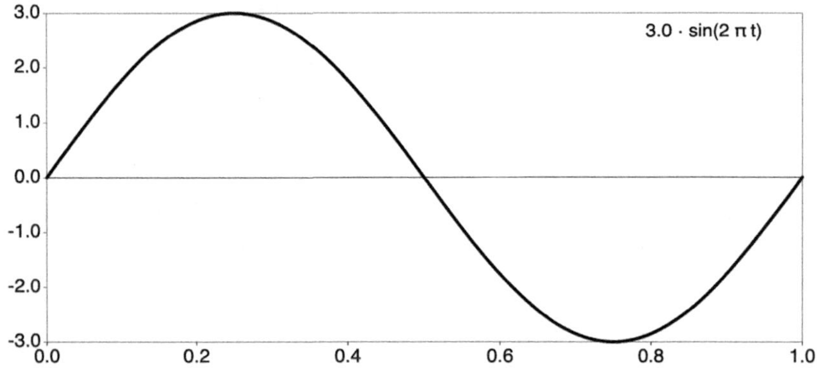

Figure 3.10: Bigger sine curve.

Now let's start messing with the frequency, which is the rate of revolution of the phasor. Let's ramp it up a notch and instead start spinning at a rate of five revolutions per second. Now: $\theta(t) = 5 \times (2\pi t) = 10\pi t$. This is easy to see since after 1 second we will have gone five revolutions, which is a total of 10π radians. Let's suppose that the radius of the phasor is 3. Again, at each moment we measure the height of our arrow (which we call $h(t)$), and we get: $h(t) = 3 \times sin(\theta(t)) = 3 \times sin(10\pi t)$. Now we get the sinusoid in Figure 3.11.

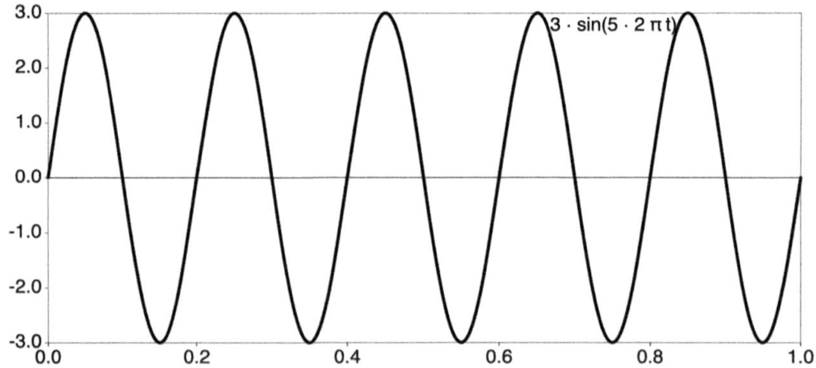

Figure 3.11: Bigger, faster sine curve.

In general, if our phasor is moving at a frequency of v revolutions per second and has radius A, then plotting the height of the phasor is the same as graphing this sinusoid: $h(t) = A \times sin(v \times 2\pi t)$. Now we're almost done, but there is one last thing we could vary: we could change the place where we start our phasor spinning. For example, we could start the phasor moving at a rate of five revolutions per second with a radius of 3, but start the phasor at an angle of $\pi/4$ radians, instead.

Now, what kind of function would this be? Well, at time t = 0 we want to be taking the measurement when the phasor is at an angle of $\pi/4$, but other than that, all is as before. So the function we are graphing is the same as the one above, but with a phase shift of $\pi/4$. The corresponding sinusoid is: $h(t) = 3 \times sin(10\pi t + \pi/4)$, which is shown in Figure 3.12.

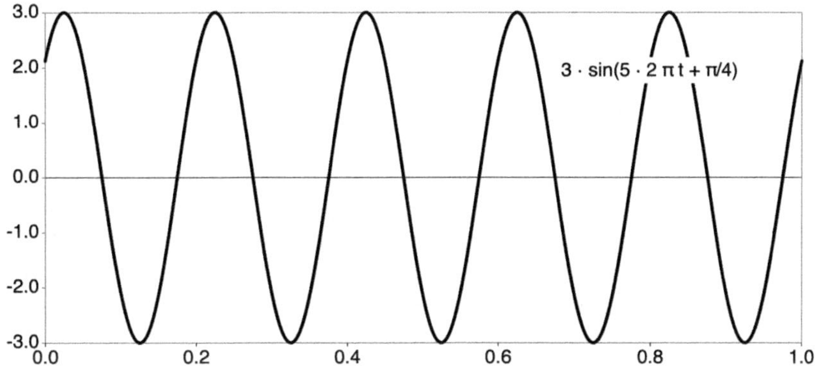

Figure 3.12: Changing the phase.

Our most general sinusoid of amplitude A, frequency v, and phase shift ϕ has the form: $h(t) = A \times sin(v \times 2\pi t + \phi)$, which is more commonly expressed with frequency ω in *radians per second* instead of frequency v in *cycles per second*: $h(t) = A \times sin(\omega t + \phi)$.

A particularly interesting example is what happens when we take the phase shift equal to 90 degrees, or $\pi/2$ radians. Let's make it nice and simple, with frequency equal to one revolution per second and amplitude equal to 1 as well. Then we get our basic sinusoid, but shifted ahead $\pi/2$. Does this look familiar? This is the graph of the cosine function! (Figure 3.13)

You can do some checking on your own and see that this is also the graph that you would get if you plotted the displacement of the arrow from the y-axis. So now we know that a cosine is a phase-shifted sine!

3.3.2 Fourier Analysis

Now we know that signals can be decomposed into a (possibly infinite) sum of phasors or partials or sinusoids—however you want to look at it. But how do we determine this sum?

The Fourier transform, named for French scientist and mathematician Jean Baptiste Fourier (1768–1830), is a surprisingly simple and direct formula to write

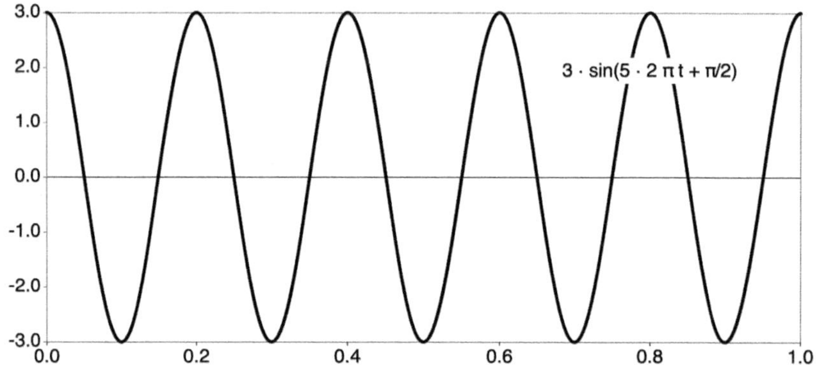

Figure 3.13: 90-degree phase shift (cosine).

this infinite sum. Since we have to deal with phase somehow, we will begin with an expression of the Fourier transform that keeps the sine and cosine parts separate. The signal we want to analyze is $f(t)$. The result of the analysis will be two functions. $R(\omega)$ is a function of frequency (in radians per second) that gives us the amplitude of a cosine at that frequency, and $X(\omega)$ is a function of frequency that gives us the amplitude of a sine at that frequency.

$$R(\omega) = \int_{-\infty}^{\infty} f(t)cos(\omega t)dt$$

$$X(\omega) = -\int_{-\infty}^{\infty} f(t)sin(\omega t)dt$$

Why the minus sign when computing X? It relates to whether the positive direction of rotation is considered clockwise or counterclockwise. You would think the convention would be based on the simplest form (so drop the minus sign), but the Fourier transform is closely related to the Inverse Fourier transform (how do we construct a time-domain signal from its frequency-domain representation?), and one or the other transform has to have a minus sign, so this is the convention.

Note that this is all *continuous* math. We will get back to sampling soon, but if we want to understand what sampling does to a continuous signal, we have to deal with continuous functions.

Note also, *and this is very important*, that we are "integrating out" all time. The functions R and X are functions of frequency. It does not make sense (at this point) to say "What is the Fourier transform of the signal at time t?"—instead, we transform infinite functions of time ($f(t)$) into infinite functions of frequency, so all notions of time are absorbed into frequencies.

3.3.2.1 What About Phase?

We saw in the previous section how cosine is simply a sine function that is "phase shifted", and we can achieve any phase by some combination of sine and cosine at the same frequency. Thus, we get to choose: Do we want to talk about sinusoids with frequency, amplitude, and phase? Or do we want to talk about cosines and sines, each with just frequency and amplitude? The two are equivalent, so we started with cosines and sines. Once we have the cosine $R(\omega)$ and sine $X(\omega)$ parts, we can derive a representation in terms of phase. For any given ω of interest, we have:

$$R(\omega) \times cos(\omega t) + X(\omega) \times sin(\omega t) =$$
$$\sqrt{R(\omega)^2 + X(\omega)^2} \times sin(\omega t + arctan(X(\omega)/R(\omega)))$$

In other words, we can write the partial with frequency ω as $A(\omega) \times sin(\omega t + \theta(\omega))$ where:

$$A(\omega) = \sqrt{R(\omega)^2 + X(\omega)^2}$$

and

$$\theta(\omega) = arctan(X(\omega)/R(\omega))$$

3.3.2.2 Complex Representation

Rather than separating the sine and cosine parts, we can use complex numbers because, among other properties, each complex number has a real part and an imaginary part. We can think of a phasor as rotating in the complex plane, so a single complex number can represent both amplitude and phase:

$$F(\omega) = R(\omega) + j \cdot X(\omega)$$

Here, j represents $\sqrt{-1}$. You probably learned to use i for imaginary numbers, but i is also the electrical engineering symbol for *current* (usually in units of Amperes), and since digital signal processing falls largely into the domain of electrical engineering, we go along with the EE's and replace i by j.

Now things get interesting... Recall Euler's formula:[2]

$$e^{jx} = cos(x) + j \cdot sin(x)$$

If we rewrite the pair, R,X as $R + j \cdot X$, and use Euler's formula, we can derive:

$$F(\omega) = \int_{-\infty}^{\infty} f(t) e^{-j\omega t} dt$$

[2]Which one is Euler's formula? There are no less than seven formulas named for Euler, not to mention conjectures, equations, functions, identities, numbers, theorems and laws. This is the one in complex analysis. Euler invented so much mathematics that many things are named for the first person that *proved* Euler's original idea, just to spread the fame a little. There's a whole article in Wikipedia named "List of things named after Leonhard Euler", but I digress ....

3.3.2.3 Example Spectrum

The result of a Fourier transform is a continuous function of frequency sometimes called the *frequency spectrum* or just *spectrum*. Figure 3.14 shows the spectrum measured from a gamelan tone. You can see there is energy in a wide range of frequencies, but also some peaks that indicate strong sinusoidal partials here and there.

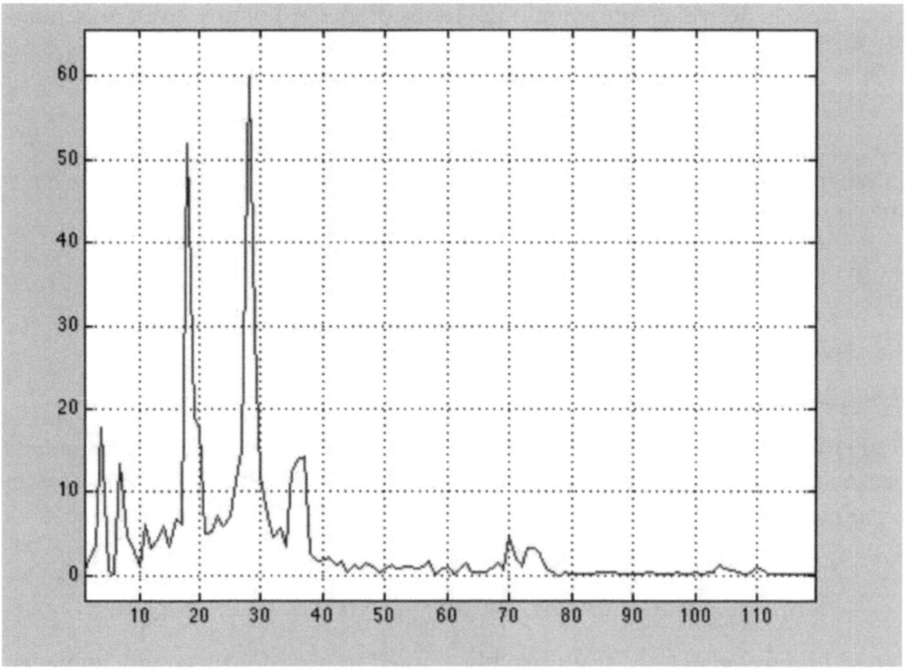

Figure 3.14: FFT plot of a gamelan instrument.

3.3.3 Fourier and the Sum of Sines

In this section, we'll try to give some intuition into the spectrum, building on the previous section.

A long time ago, Fourier proved the mathematical fact that any periodic waveform can be expressed as the sum of an infinite set of sine waves. The frequencies of these sine waves must be integer multiples of some fundamental frequency.

In other words, if we have a trumpet sound at middle A (440 Hz), we know by Fourier's theorem that we can express this sound as a summation of sine waves: 440 Hz, 880 Hz, 1,320 Hz, 1,760 Hz..., or 1, 2, 3, 4... times the fundamental, each at various amplitudes. This is rather amazing, since it says that for every periodic waveform, if we know the repetition rate, we basically know the frequencies of

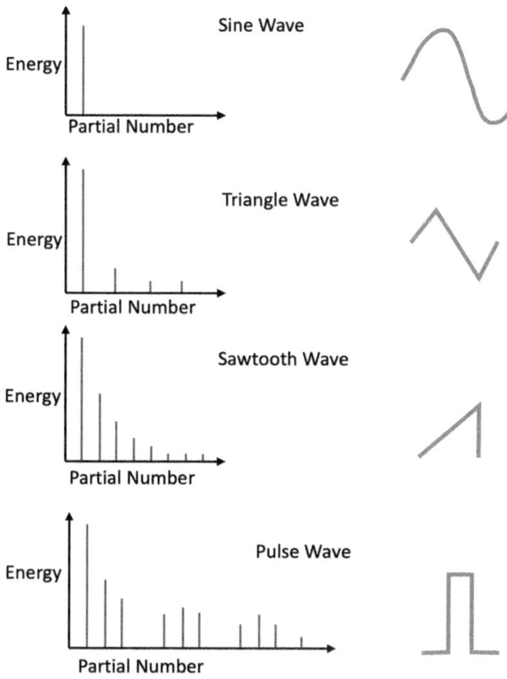

Figure 3.15: The spectrum of the sine wave has energy only at one frequency. The triangle wave has energy at odd-numbered harmonics (meaning odd multiples of the fundamental), with the energy of each harmonic decreasing as 1 over the square of the harmonic number ($1/N^2$). In other words, at the frequency that is N times the fundamental, we have $1/N^2$ as much energy as in the fundamental.

all of its partials. (Keep in mind however, that no trumpet player will ever play an infinitely long, steady tone, and no real-life tone is truly periodic if the periodicity comes to an end. We will not worry about this for now.)[3]

Figure 3.15 shows some periodic waveforms and their associated spectra. The partials in the sawtooth wave decrease in energy in proportion to the inverse of the harmonic number ($1/N$). Pulse (or rectangle or square) waveforms have energy over a broad area of the spectrum.

[3]By the way, periodic waveforms generally have clear pitches. In evolutionary terms, periodicity implies an energy source to sustain the vibration, and pitch is a good first-order feature that tells us whether the energy source is big enough to be a threat or small enough to be food. Think lion roar vs. goat bleat. It should not be too surprising that animals—remember we are the life forms capable of running away from danger and chasing after food—developed a sense of hearing, including pitch perception, which at the most basic level serves to detect energy sources and estimate size.

3.3.3.1 Real, Imaginary, Amplitude, Phase

In these drawings, we are carelessly forgetting about phase. Generally, we cannot hear phase differences, but we are very adept at hearing amplitudes at different frequencies. Therefore, we usually plot just the amplitude of the signal when we plot the spectrum, and we ignore the phase. Recall that in terms of real and imaginary parts, the amplitude is just the square root of the sum of squares:

$$A(\omega) = \sqrt{R(\omega)^2 + X(\omega)^2}$$

3.4 Sampling and the Frequency Domain

Now that we understand something about the Fourier transform, we return to our problem of understanding sampling. What does sampling do to a signal? In the continuous math world, we can model sampling as a simple multiplication of two time-domain signals, as shown in Figure 3.16.

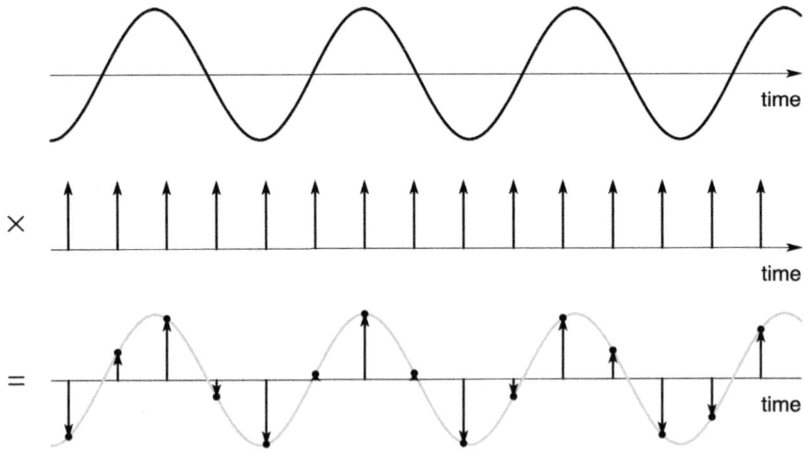

Figure 3.16: Sampling is effectively multiplication in the time domain: We multiply by 1 (or more properly an instantaneous but infinite impulse whose integral is 1) wherever we capture samples, and we remove the rest of the signal by multiplying by zero.

This gets quite interesting in the frequency domain. Multiplying by a series of impulses in the time domain (Figure 3.16) is equivalent to copying and shifting the spectrum in the frequency domain (Figure 3.17). The copies are shifted by the *sampling rate*, which of course is a frequency.

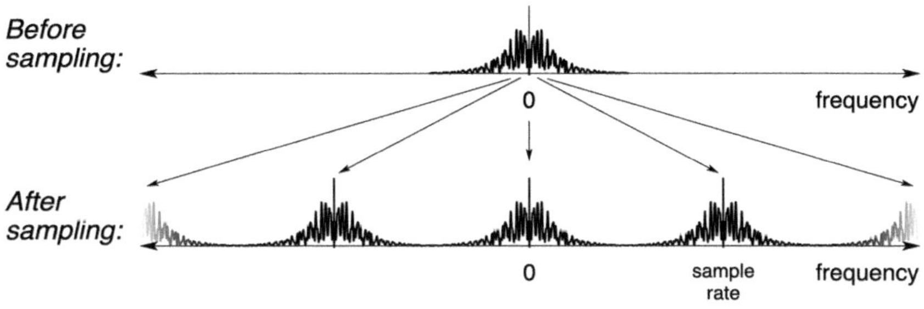

Figure 3.17: Sampling in the time domain gives rise to shifted spectral copies in the frequency domain. The spectral copies are shifted by multiples of the sample rate.

3.4.1 Negative Frequencies

Looking at Figure 3.17, you should be wondering why the spectrum is shown with negative as well as positive frequencies. You can consider negative frequencies to be just the result of the formulas for the Fourier transform. While "negative 440 Hertz" may sound like nonsense, in mathematical terms, it is just a question of writing $sin(\omega t)$ or $sin(-\omega t)$, but $sin(-\omega t) = sin(\omega t + \pi)$, so we are really talking about certain phase shifts. Since we mostly ignore phase anyway, we often plot only the positive frequencies. In the case of sampling theory, we show both negative and positive frequencies of the spectrum.

3.4.2 Aliasing

Notice in Figure 3.17 that after sampling, the copies of the spectrum come close to overlapping. What would happen if the spectrum contained higher frequencies. Figure 3.18 illustrates a broader spectrum.

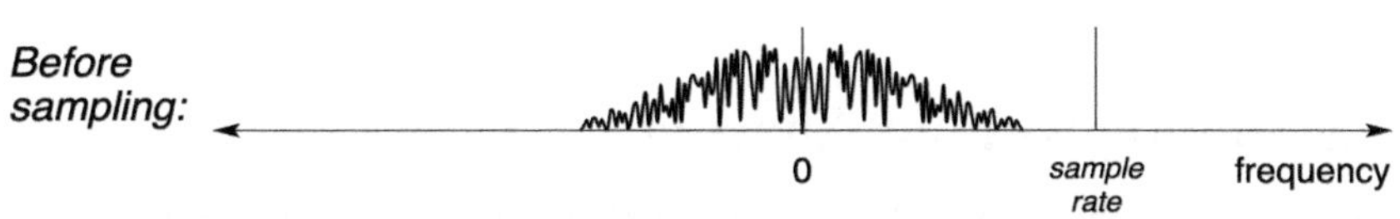

Figure 3.18: A broader spectrum (contains higher frequencies) before sampling.

Figure 3.19 illustrates the signal after sampling. What a mess! The copies of the spectrum now overlap. The Nyquist frequency (one-half the sampling rate, and one half the amount by which copies are shifted) is shown by a vertical dotted line. Notice that there is a sort of mirror symmetry around that line: the original spectrum extending above the Nyquist frequency is "folded" to become new frequencies below the Nyquist frequency.

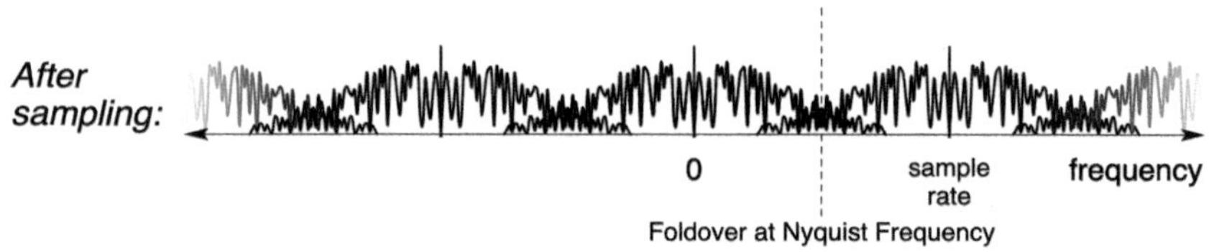

Figure 3.19: A broader spectrum (contains higher frequencies) after sampling. While shown as separate overlapping copies here, the copies are in fact summed into a single spectrum.

This is really bad because new frequencies are introduced and *added* to the original spectrum. Although drawn in the figure as overlapping lines, in reality there should be one line representing the sum of the spectra (and furthermore, the signals contain both phase and amplitude, so their sum is not a simple addition of only amplitudes.). The overlapping frequencies are called *aliases* of the frequencies above the Nyquist frequency. To avoid aliasing, it is necessary to sample at higher than twice the highest frequency of the original signal.

In the time domain, aliasing is a little more intuitive, at least if we consider the special case of a sinusoid. Figure 3.20 shows a fast sinusoid at a frequency more than half the sample rate. This frequency is "folded" to become a lower frequency below half the sample rate. Note that both sinusoids pass perfectly through the available samples, which is why they are called aliases. They have the same "signature" in terms of samples.

To summarize, *the frequency range (bandwidth) of a sampled signal is determined by the sample rate.* We can only capture and represent frequencies below half the sample rate, which is also called the *Nyquist frequency*. Alternatively, we can say to capture a given signal bandwidth, we must sample at twice the bandwith, which is also called the *Nyquist rate*.

3.5 Sampling without Aliasing

In practice, we seldom have the luxury of controlling the bandwidth of our analog signals. How do you tell the triangle player to make those tinkly sounds, but don't go above 22 kHz? The real world is full of high frequencies we cannot hear, but which can become audible as aliases if we are not careful. The solution and standard practice is to *filter* out the high frequencies *before* sampling, as shown in Figure 3.21.

3.5.1 Converting Back to Analog

A similar process is used to convert digital signals back to analog. If we were to simply output a train of impulses based on the digital samples, the spectrum would look like that in the lower half of Figure 3.17, with lots of very high frequencies (in fact, these are aliases of all the sinusoids in the original spectrum). We remove these unwanted parts of the signal with another filter as shown in Figure 3.22.

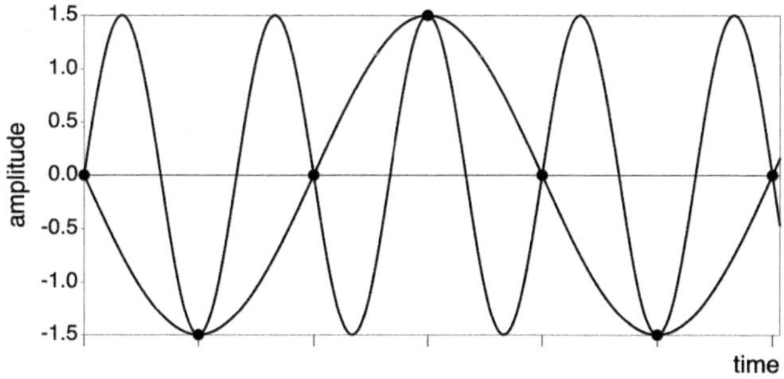

Figure 3.20: Aliasing, or foldover, happens when we sample a frequency that is more than half the sampling rate. When the frequency we want to sample is too high, we *undersample* and get an unwanted lower-frequency that is created by the sampling process itself. Here, samples are shown as small black circles. Samples of the higher-frequency sinusoid create an alias, the lower-frequency sinusoid, which passes through the same points.

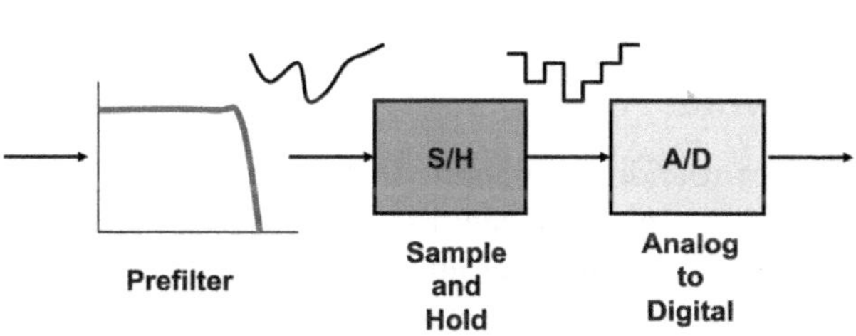

Figure 3.21: Aliasing is avoided by removing frequencies above the Nyquist frequency (half the sample rate) using a prefilter (sometimes called an *anti-aliasing filter*).

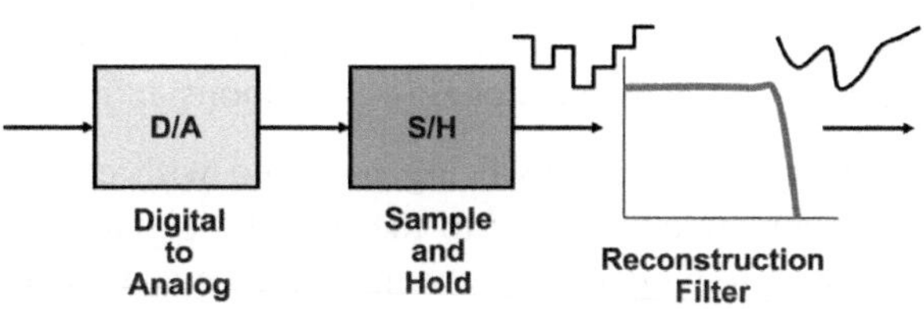

Figure 3.22: To convert a digital signal to analog, we need to *remove* the artifacts of sampling. This is accomplished by sending the output of the digital-to-analog converter first into a sample-and-hold circuit that holds the signal steady while the converter is transitioning to the next sample value, then through a *reconstruction filter*, which removes high frequencies above the Nyquist frequency. In theory, the signal sent to the filter should consist of instantaneous pulses rather than the "stairsteps" shown here, and often short pulses are used as a better approximation to instantaneous pulses (69).

3.6 Imperfect Sampling

So far, we have described sampling as if samples were real numbers obtained without error. What happens in the imperfect real world, and what happens to rounding errors, since real samples are actually integers with finite precision?

3.6.1 *How to Describe Noise*

To describe error in audio, we need a way to measure it. Since our hearing basically responds to audio in a logarithmic manner, the important thing is not the absolute error but the ratio between the signal and the error. We call errors in audio "noise", and we measure the *signal-to-noise ratio*.

Ratio is so important in audio, and the range of signals and noise is so large, that we use a special unit, the dB or decibel to represent ratios, or more precisely logarithms of ratios. Given an amplitude ratio A, we can compute decibels as $dB = 20\log_{10}(A)$. More details on bels and decibels will be covered starting in Section 10.2.2.5. A handy constant to remember is a factor of 2 in amplitude is about 6 dB, so a factor of 4 is about 12 dB. What can you hear? A change of 1 dB is barely noticeable. A change of 10 dB is easily noticeable, and your range of hearing is about 10 of these big steps (around 100 dB).

3.6.2 *Quantization Noise*

What is the effect of rounding? Imagine that there is significant signal change between each pair of samples and the true value of the signal we are capturing has no preference for any value over any other. In that case, we can expect the signal to fall randomly between two integer sample values. If we round to the nearest value, the rounding error will be a uniformly distributed random number between –0.5 and 0.5 (considering samples to be integers).

Figure 3.23 illustrates a signal being captured and the resulting rounding error. Note that the samples must fall on the grid of discrete time points and discrete integer sample values, but the actual signal is continuous and real-valued.

Rather than thinking of the signal as being recorded with error, consider this: If we could add the quantization error to the original signal, then the original signal would pass through integer sample values and we could capture the signal perfectly! Thus, the effect of quantization error is to add random values in the range –0.5 to +0.5 to the original signal before sampling.

It turns out that uniform random samples are white noise, so calling error "noise" is quite appropriate. How loud is the noise? The resulting signal-to-noise ratio, given M-bit samples, is $6.02M + 1.76$ dB. This is very close to saying "the signal-to-noise ratio is 6 dB per bit". You only get this signal-to-noise ratio if the signal uses the full range of the integer samples. In real life, you always record with some "headroom", so you probably lose 6 to 12 dB of the best possible signal. There is also a limit to how many bits you can use—remember that the bits are coming from analog hardware, so how quiet can you make circuits, and how accurately can you measure voltages? In practice, 16-bit converters offering a theoretical 98 dB signal-to-noise ratio are readily available and widely used. 20- and 24-bit converters (and even some described as "32-bit") are used in high-end equipment, but these are not accurate to the least-significant bit, so the true signal-to-noise ratio cannot be estimated merely by counting bits.

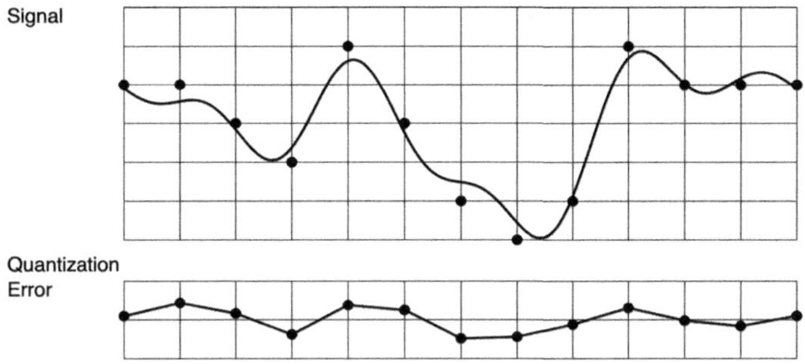

Figure 3.23: When a signal is sampled, the real-valued signal must be rounded at each sample to the nearest integer sample value. The resulting error is called *quantization error*.

3.7 Sampling Summary

One amazing result of sampling theory is that if the signal being sampled has a finite bandwidth, then we can sample the signal at discrete time points and *completely recover* the original continuous signal. It seems too good to be true that all those infinitely many values between samples are not really necessary!

Aside from this startling theoretical finding, we learned that the sample rate should be at least double that of the highest frequency of the signal. Also, error is introduced by rounding samples to integers, an unavoidable step in the real world, but the signal-to-noise ratio is about 6 dB per bit, so with 16 bits or more, we can make noise virtually imperceptible.

3.8 Special Topics in Sampling

3.8.1 *Dither*

When we described quantization noise, we assumed that rounding error was random. Now consider the case where the signal is a pure sine tone with amplitude from –1.4 to +1.4. It should be clear that after rounding, this signal will progress through sample values of –1, 0, 1, 0, –1, 0, 1, 0, ... (possibly repeating each of these values, depending on frequency). This is anything but random, and this non-random rounding will inject higher, possibly audible frequencies into the recorded signal rather than noise. To avoid this unpleasant phenomenon, it is common to actually add noise *on purpose* before sampling. The added noise "randomizes" the rounding so that more audible artifacts are avoided.

This process of adding noise is called *dithering*. Dithering is also used in computer graphics, photography, and printing to avoid "posterized" effects when rendering smooth color gradients. Another, more sophisticated way to use dithering, also called *noise shaping*, is to design the spectrum of the added dither noise to optimize the perceived signal-to-noise ratio. Since we are more sensitive to some frequencies than others, when we add noise to a signal, it is a good idea to include more hard-to-hear frequencies in the noise than easy-to-hear noise. With this trick, we can make the apparent quality of 16-bit audio *better* than 16-bits in some frequency regions where we are most sensitive, by sacrificing the signal-to-noise ratio at frequencies (especially high ones) where we do not hear so well.

3.8.2 *Oversampling*

Another great idea in sampling is oversampling. A problem with high-quality digital audio conversion is that we need anti-aliasing filters and reconstruction filters that are: (1) analog and (2) have very difficult to achieve requirements, namely that the filter passes everything without alteration right up to the Nyquist frequency, then suddenly cuts out everything above that frequency. Filters, typically have a smooth transition from passing signal to cutting signals, so anti-aliasing filters and reconstruction filters used to be marvels of low-noise audio engineering and fabrication.

With oversampling, the idea is to sample at a very high sample rate to avoid stringent requirements on the analog anti-aliasing filter. For example, suppose your goal is to capture frequencies up to 20 kHz. Using a sample rate of 44.1 kHz means your anti-aliasing filter must pass 20 kHz and reject everything above 22.05 kHz (half of 44.1 kHz). This requires an elaborate and expensive filter. Instead, suppose you (over)sample at 176.4 kHz so you can capture up to 88.2 kHz. Now, your analog filter can pass everything up to 20 kHz and does not need to reject everything until 88.2 kHz, so there are about 2 octaves to make that transition, a much easier filter to build in practice.

But, now you have a 176.4 kHz sample rate, and some frequencies between 20 kHz and 88.2 kHz leaked through your cheap filter. No problem! We can implement another filter in the digital domain to get rid of everything above 20 kHz and then simply drop 3 out of 4 samples to get down to the desired 44.1 kHz sample rate.

Similarly, we can digitally up-sample from 44.1 kHz to 176.4 kHz just before digital-to-analog conversion so that the high output frequencies start above 88.2 kHz, making it easy to build a high-quality, low-noise reconstruction (smoothing) filter.

Oversampling was invented by Paul Lansky, a computer music composer at Princeton, and first published as a letter to *Computer Music Journal.* Paul did not patent his invention or anticipate that it would be used in billions of digital audio devices.

3.9 Amplitude Modulation

Time-domain representations show us a lot about the amplitude of a signal at different points in time. Amplitude is a word that means, more or less, "how much of something", and in this case it might represent pressure, voltage, some number that measures those things, or even the in-out deformation of the eardrum.

For example, the time-domain picture of the trumpet waveform in Figure 3.24 starts with the attack of the note, where you see a rapid increase in amplitude. The signal continues on to the steady-state portion (sustain) of the note. In this case, you see some amplitude variation with an overall decreasing trend. The signal ends with a more rapid decay (release). We sometimes call the attack and decay *transients* because the signal is changing rapidly, but as you can see in this example, acoustic signals are often changing throughout, even during the "sustain" period. We also use the word transient, perhaps more typically, to describe timbral fluctuations during the sound that are irregular or singular and to distinguish those kinds of sounds from the steady state. Notice also that there are very regular pulses in the signal at about 260 Hz. These are the individual periods of vibration, and their periodicity is perceived as a steady pitch.

From the typical sound event shown in Figure 3.24, we can tell something about how the sound's amplitude develops over time (what we call its amplitude envelope).

3.9.1 Envelopes in Sound Synthesis

In sound synthesis, we often start with a steady tone such as a periodic waveform and multiply by an envelope function to create an artificial amplitude envelope.

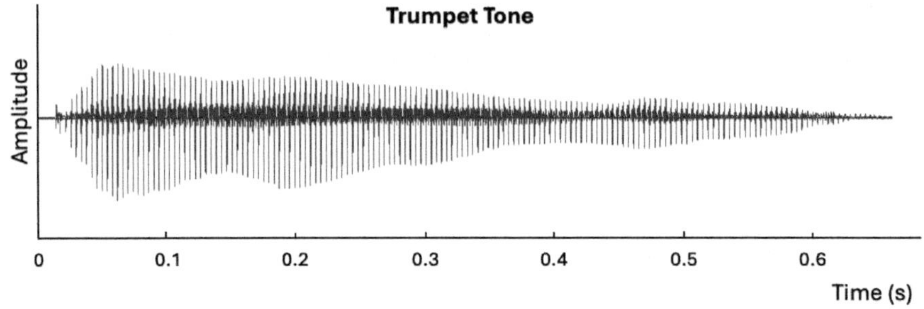

Figure 3.24: A time-domain waveform of a single trumpet tone. It is easy to see variations of amplitude in this time-domain representation. If you connected the peaks, the result would give you the amplitude envelope. More typically, the amplitude would be computed as $sqrt(x(t)^2)$ with some local averaging to smooth out the peaks.

In Nyquist (the programming language), we write this using the multiply (*) operator in expressions that typically look like:

steady-signal-expression * *envelope-expression*

In Nyquist, you can use the `pwl` or `env` functions, for example, to make envelopes, as we have seen before.

Another type of amplitude modulation is amplitude vibrato, often called *tremolo*[4], where we want a wavering amplitude. One way to create this effect is to vary the amplitude using a low-frequency oscillator (LFO). However, be careful not to simply multiply by the LFO. Figure 3.25 shows what happens to a signal multiplied by `lfo(6)`.

To get a more typical vibrato, offset the `lfo` signal so that it does not go through zero. Figure 3.26 shows an example. You can play the expressions from Figures 3.25 and 3.26 and hear the difference. To further test your understanding, explain how Figure 3.25 appears to have 3 periods of oscillation in 0.25 s, while Figure 3.26 appears to have only 1.5 periods of oscillation, even though the LFO for both figures has a frequency of 6 Hz.

[4]Often, electronic musicians define *vibrato* to mean periodic frequency variation (only), and *tremolo* to mean periodic amplitude variation, but *vibrato* in acoustic instruments and voice, as named and produced by musicians, consists of variations in amplitude, frequency, and relative strengths of partials. Furthermore, musicians use *tremolo* to mean a rapid repetition of notes at the same pitch. I use the terms "amplitude vibrato", "frequency vibrato", and "spectral vibrato", or just "vibrato" if the meaning is clear, and I avoid the overloaded term "tremolo".

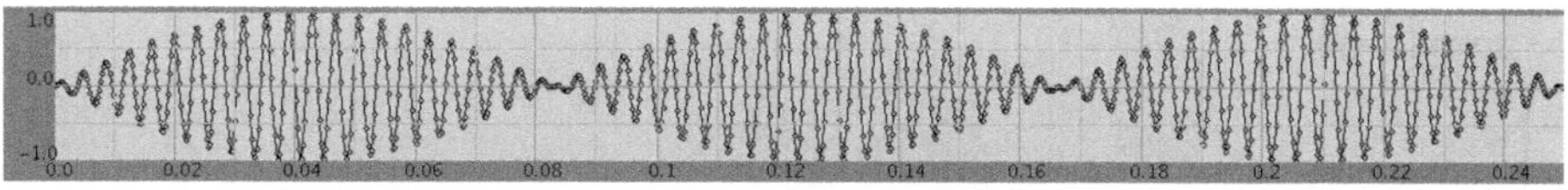

Figure 3.25: The output from `osc(c4) * lfo(6)`. The signal has extreme pulses at twice the LFO rate because `osc(6)` crosses through zero twice for each cycle. Only 1/4 second is plotted.

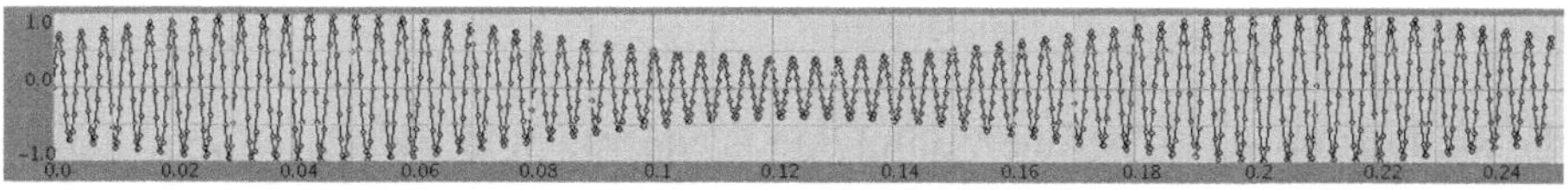

Figure 3.26: The output from `osc(c4) * (0.7 + 0.3 * lfo(6))`. The signal vibrates at 6 Hz and does not diminish to zero because the vibrato expression contains an offset of 0.7.

3.9.2 Amplitude Modulation by Audible Frequencies

If the modulation rate shown in Figure 3.25 is increased from 6 Hz into the audible range, some very interesting things happen. In the frequency domain, the original spectrum is shifted up and down by the modulation frequency. So a rapidly modulated sinusoid becomes two sinusoids, and there is no energy at the original frequency—it is all shifted. Figure 3.27 shows the modulation of an 880 Hz signal by a 220 Hz modulation.

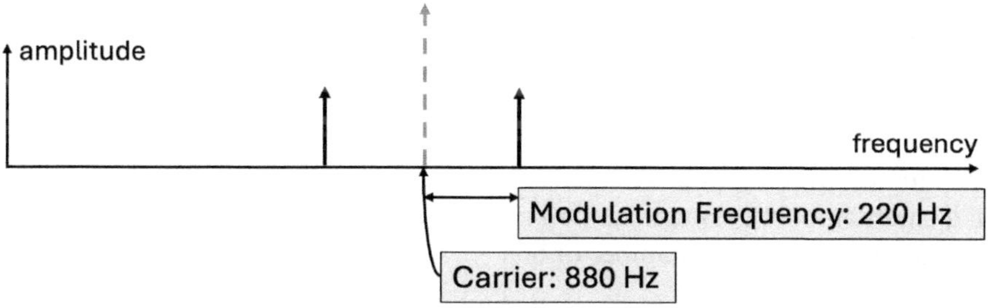

Figure 3.27: The result of modulating (multiplying) one sinusoid at 880 Hz by another at 220 Hz.

In more general terms, an entire complex signal can be transformed by amplitude modulation. Figure 3.28 shows the effect of modulating a complex signal indicated by the trapezoidal-shaped spectrum. The original spectrum (dotted lines) is shifted up and down. This effect is also known as *ring modulation*. It has a characteristic metallic sound because shifted harmonic spectra are no longer harmonic.

The modulation need not be a pure sinusoid. If the sinusoid is offset (as in Figure 3.26), the original frequencies will be retained. This is a direct result of the distributive property of multiplication over addition, which says adding an offset to

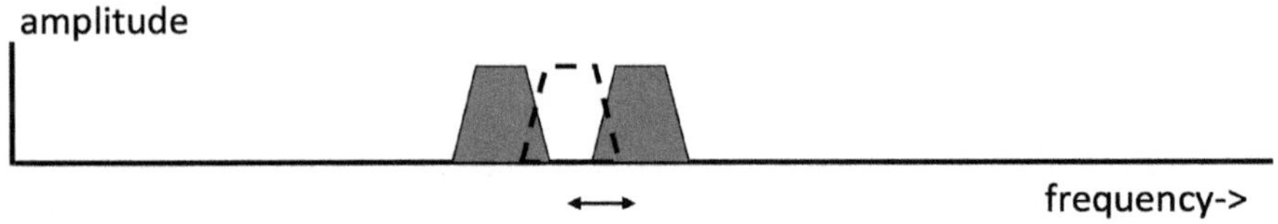

Figure 3.28: The result of modulating (multiplying) a complex signal (illustrated by the trapezoidal spectrum in dotted lines) by a sinusoidal modulator. The original spectrum is shifted up and down by the frequency of the modulator.

the modulation signal before multiplying is equivalent to adding the signal after multiplying:

$$signal \times (modulation + 1) = signal \times modulation + signal \times 1$$

Adding a constant offset (with a frequency of 0 Hz) is just a special case of modulation signals with multiple frequencies. The result of using a rich modulation spectrum is the original signal shifted up and down by each frequency contained in the modulation. For a more formal and complete text on this and other signal processing topics, see *Discrete-Time Signal Processing* (68).

3.10 Summary

Sampling obtains a discrete digital representation of a continuous signal. Although intuition suggests that the information in a continuous signal is infinite, this is not the case in practice. Limited bandwidth (or the fact that we only care about a certain bandwidth) means that we can capture all frequencies of interest with a finite sampling rate. The presence of noise in all physical systems means that a small amount of quantization noise is not significant, so we can represent each sample with a finite number of bits.

Dither and noise shaping can be applied to signals before quantization occurs to reduce any artifacts that might occur due to non-random rounding—typically this occurs in low amplitude sinusoids where rounding errors can become periodic and audible. Another interesting technique is oversampling, where digital low-pass filtering performs some of the work typically done by a hardware low-pass filter to prevent aliasing.

Amplitude modulation at low frequencies is a fundamental operation used to control loudness in mixing and to shape notes and other sound events in synthesis. We typically scale the signal by a factor from 0 to 1 that varies over time to create envelopes and vibrato effects. On the other hand, periodic amplitude modulation at audible frequencies acts to shift frequencies up and down by the modulating frequency. This can be used as a form of distortion, for synthesis, and other effects.

Chapter 4

Frequency Modulation and Behaviors

Topics Discussed: Frequency Modulation, Behaviors and Transformations in Nyquist

Frequency modulation (FM) is a versatile and efficient synthesis technique that is widely implemented in software and hardware. By understanding how FM works, you will be able to design parameter settings and control strategies for your own FM instrument designs.

4.1 Introduction to Frequency Modulation

Frequency modulation occurs naturally. It is rare to hear a completely stable steady pitch. Some percussion instruments are counter-examples, e.g., a piano tone or a tuning fork or a bell, but most instruments and the human voice tend to have at least some natural frequency change.

4.1.1 Examples

Common forms of frequency variation in music include:

- Voice inflection, natural jitter, and vibrato in singing.
- Vibrato in instruments. Vibrato is a small and quasi-periodic variation of pitch (accompanied by amplitude and spectral variations), often around 6 Hz and spanning a fraction of a semitone.

DOI: 10.1201/9781003782711-4

- Instrumental effects, e.g., electric guitars sometimes have "whammy bars" that stretch or relax all the strings to change their pitch. Guitarists can "bend" strings by pushing the string sideways across the fretboard.
- Many tones begin low and come up to pitch.
- Loose vibrating strings go sharp (higher pitch) as they get louder. Loose plucked strings get flatter (lower pitch), especially during the initial decay.
- The slide trombone, Theremin, voice, violin, etc. create melodies by changing pitch, so melodies on these instruments can be thought of as examples of frequency modulation (as opposed to, say, pianos, where melodies are created by selecting from fixed pitches).

4.1.2 FM Synthesis

Normally, vibrato is a slow variation created by musicians' muscles. With electronics, we can increase the vibrato rate into the audio range, where interesting things happen to the spectrum. The effect is so dramatic, we no longer refer to it as vibrato but instead call it *FM Synthesis*.

Frequency modulation (FM) is a synthesis technique based on the simple idea of periodic modulation of the signal frequency. That is, the frequency of a carrier sinusoid is modulated by a modulator sinusoid. The peak frequency deviation, also known as *depth of modulation*, expresses the strength of the modulator's effect on the carrier oscillator's frequency.

FM synthesis was invented by John M. Chowning (9) and became very popular due to its ease of implementation and computationally low cost, as well as its (somewhat surprisingly) powerful ability to create realistic and interesting sounds.

4.2 Theory of FM

Let's look at the equation for a simple frequency controlled sine oscillator. Often, this is written:

$$y(t) = A\sin(2\pi\phi t) \tag{4.1}$$

where ϕ (phi) is the frequency in Hz. Note that if ϕ is in in Hz (cycles per second), the frequency in radians per second is $2\pi\phi$. At time t, the phase will have advanced from 0 to $2\pi\phi t$, which is the integral of $2\pi\phi$ over a time span of t. We can express what we are doing in detail as:

$$y(t) = A\sin(2\pi\int_0^t \phi dx) \tag{4.2}$$

To deal with a time-varying frequency modulation, we will substitute frequency *function* $f(\cdot)$ for ϕ:

$$y(t) = A\sin(2\pi \int_0^t f(x)dx) \tag{4.3}$$

Frequency modulation uses a rapidly changing function:

$$f(t) = C + D\sin(2\pi Mt) \tag{4.4}$$

where C is the carrier, a frequency offset that in many cases is the fundamental or "pitch". D is the depth of modulation that controls the amount of frequency deviation (called modulation), and M is the frequency of modulation in Hz. Plugging this into Equation 4.3 and simplifying gives the equation for FM:

$$y(t) = A\sin(2\pi \int_0^t C + D\sin(2\pi Mx)dx) \tag{4.5}$$

Note that the integral of sin is cos, but the only difference between the two is phase. By convention, we ignore this detail and simplify Equation 4.5 to get this equation for an FM oscillator:

$$y(t) = A\sin(2\pi Ct + I\sin(2\pi Mt)) \tag{4.6}$$

$I = D/M$ is known as the index of modulation. When $D \neq 0$, sidebands appear in the spectra of the signal above and below the carrier frequency C, at multiples of $\pm M$. In other words, we can write the set of frequency components as $C \pm kM$, where k=0,1,2,.... The number of significant components increases with I, the index of modulation.

4.2.1 Negative Frequencies

According to these formulas, some frequencies will be negative. This can be interpreted as merely a phase change: $\sin(-x) = -\sin(x)$ or perhaps not even a phase change: $\cos(-x) = \cos(x)$. Since we tend to ignore phase, we can just ignore the sign of the frequency and consider negative frequencies to be positive. We sometimes say the negative frequencies "wrap around" (zero) to become positive. The main caveat here is that when frequencies wrap around and add to positive frequencies of the same magnitude, the components may not add in phase. The effect is to give FM signals a complex evolution as the index of modulation increases and adds more and more components, both positive and negative.

4.2.2 Harmonic Ratio

The human ear is very sensitive to harmonic vs. inharmonic spectra. Perceptually, harmonic spectra are very distinctive because they give a strong sense of pitch.

The harmonic ratio Barry Truax (94) is the ratio of the modulating frequency to the carrier frequency, such that $H = M/C$. If H is a rational number, the spectrum is harmonic; if it is irrational, the spectrum is inharmonic.

4.2.3 Rational Harmonic Ratio

If $H = 1$ the spectrum is harmonic and the carrier frequency is also the fundamental, i.e., $F_0 = C$. To show this, remember that the frequencies will be $C \pm kM$, where $k = 0,1,2,...$, but if $H = 1$, then $M = C$, so the frequencies are $C \pm kC$, or simply kC. This is the definition of a harmonic series: multiples of some fundamental frequency C.

When $H = 1/m$, and m is a positive integer, C instead becomes the mth component (harmonic) because the spacing between harmonics is $M = C/m$, which is also the fundamental: $F_0 = M = C/m$.

With $H = 2$, we will get sidebands at $C \pm 2kC$ (where $k = 0,1,2,...$), thus omitting all even harmonics — which is a characteristic of cylindrical woodwinds such as the clarinet.

4.2.4 Irrational Harmonic Ratio

If H is irrational, the negative frequencies that wrap around at 0 Hz tend to land between the positive frequency components, thus making the spectrum denser. If we make H much less than 1 (M much less than C), and if H is irrational (or at least not a simple fraction such as $1/n$), the FM-generated frequencies will cluster around C (the spacing between components will be relatively small); yielding sounds that have no distinct pitch and that can mimic drums and gongs.

4.2.5 FM Spectra and Bessel Functions

The sidebands infused by FM are governed by Bessel functions of the first kind and n^{th} order; denoted $J_n(I)$, where I is the index of modulation. The Bessel functions determine the magnitudes and signs of the frequency components in the FM spectrum. These functions look a lot like damped sine waves, as can be seen in Figure 4.1.

Here are a few insights that help explain why FM synthesis sounds the way it does:

- $J_0(I)$ gives the amplitude of the carrier.
- $J_1(I)$ gives the amplitude of the first upper and lower sidebands.
- Generally, $J_n(I)$ governs the amplitudes of the nth upper and lower sidebands.

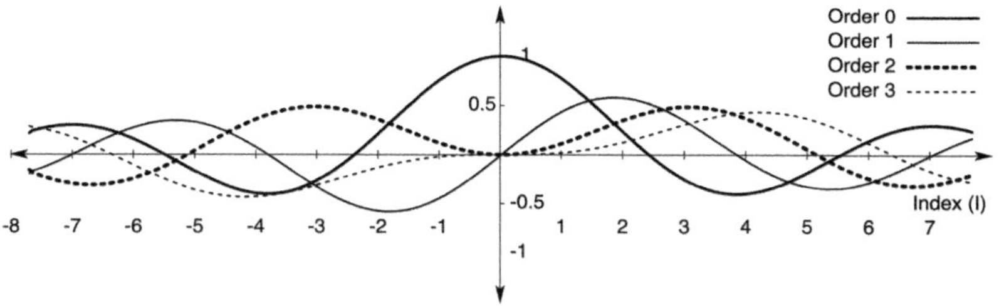

Figure 4.1: Bessel functions of the first kind, orders 0 to 3. The x axis represents the index of modulation in FM.

- Higher-order Bessel functions start from zero and increase more and more gradually, so higher-order sidebands only have significant energy when I is large.
- The spectral bandwidth increases with I. The upper and lower sidebands represent the higher and lower frequencies, respectively. The larger the value of I, the more significant sidebands you get.
- As I increases, the energy of the sidebands vary much like a damped sinusoid.

4.2.6 Index of Modulation

The index of modulation, $I = D/M$, allows us to relate the depth of modulation, D, the modulation frequency, M, and the index of the Bessel functions. In practice, this means that if we want a spectrum that has the energy of the Bessel functions at some index I, with frequency components separated by M, then we must choose the depth of modulation according to the relation $I = D/M$ (62). As a "rule of thumb", the number of sidebands is roughly $I + 1$. That is, if $I = 10$ we get $10 + 1 = 11$ sidebands above, and 11 sidebands below the carrier frequency. In theory, there are infinitely many sidebands at $C \pm kM$, where k = 0, 1, 2, ... if the modulation is non-zero, but the intensity of sidebands falls rapidly toward zero as k increases, and this rule considers only significant sidebands. (Note that this formula fails at $I = 0$: it predicts the carrier plus 1 side band above and one below, but there are no side bands in this case.)

Figure 4.1 allows us to compare this rule of thumb to exact values. For example, if $I = 1$, the rule says to expect 2 sidebands. At $I = 1$ in the figure, we see J_0 ("Order 0") and J_1 ("Order 1") are strong. The second sideband J_2 ("Order 2") is significantly lower at 0.11, or about –19 dB. The rule says not to expect a third upper sideband. J_3 ("Order 3") is in fact at 0.02, or about –34 dB. You can also see in the figure that the higher-order Bessel functions rise from zero at higher indices of modulation, and this general trend explains the rule. In addition, the functions are not monotonically increasing. The variation of the Bessel functions makes it very hard to achieve a particular spectrum even if we have a rough expectation of the number of sidebands.

4.2.7 Time-Varying Parameters

For music applications, constant values of A, C, D, and M would result in a rock-steady tone of little interest. In practice, we usually vary all of these parameters, replacing them with $A(t), C(t), D(t)$, and $M(t)$. *Usually*, these parameters change slowly compared to carrier and modulator frequencies, so we assume that all the analysis here still applies and allows us to make predictions about the short-time spectrum. FM is particularly interesting because we can make very interesting changes to the spectrum with just a few control parameters, primarily $D(t)$, and $M(t)$.

4.2.8 Examples of FM Signals

Figures 4.2 and 4.3 show examples of FM signals. The X-axes on the plots represent time—here denoted in multiples of π.

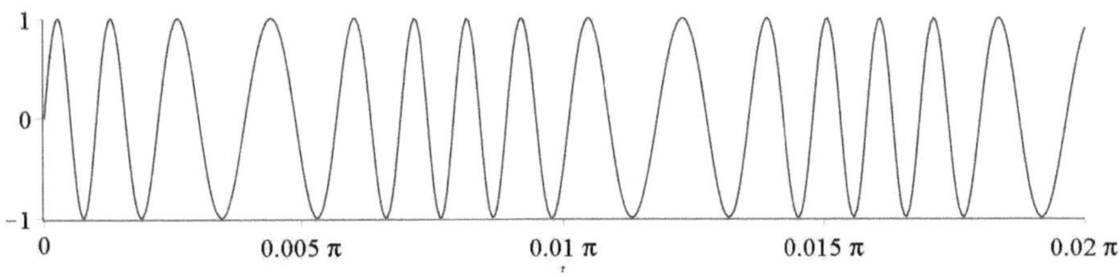

Figure 4.2: A = 1, C = 242 Hz, D = 2, M = 40 Hz.

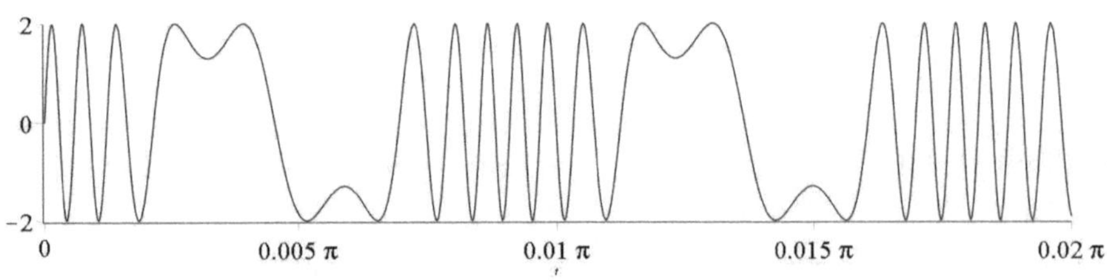

Figure 4.3: A = 2, C = 210 Hz, D = 10, M = 35 Hz.

4.3 Frequency Modulation with Nyquist

Now that you have a grasp of the theory, let's use it to make some sound.

4.3.1 Basic FM

The basic FM oscillator in Nyquist is the function `fmosc`. The signature for `fmosc` is:

`fmosc(`*basic-pitch*`,` *modulation* `[,` *table* `[,` *phase* `]])`

Let's break that down:

- *basic-pitch* is the carrier frequency, expressed in steps. If there is no modulation, this controls the output frequency. Remember this is in steps, so if you put in a number like 440 expecting Hz, you will actually get `step-to-hz(440)`, which is about 0.9 *terahertz*![1] Use `A4` instead, or write something like `hz-to-step(441.0)` if you want to specify frequency in Hertz.
- *modulation* is the modulator. The *amplitude* of the modulator controls the *depth* of modulation—how much does the frequency deviate from the nominal carrier frequency based on *basic-pitch*? An amplitude of 1 (the nominal output of (osc) for example), gives a frequency deviation of ± 1. If you have been paying attention, you will realize that 1 gives a *very* low index of modulation (1/M)—you probably will not hear anything but a sine tone. (Note that Nyquist's implementation is close to Equation 4.5—Nyquist performs the integral, so the scale factor really is the *depth D*.) Typically,
    - you will use a large number for modulation, and
    - you will also scale *modulation* by some kind of envelope. By varying the depth of modulation, you will vary the spectrum, which is typical in FM synthesis.

  The *frequency* of *modulation* is just the modulation frequency. It can be the same as the carrier frequency if you want the C:M ratio to be 1:1. This parameter is where you control the C:M ratio.
- *table* is optional and allows you to replace the default sine waveform with any waveform table. The table data structure is exactly the same one you learned about earlier for use with the `osc` function.
- *phase* is also optional and gives the initial phase. Generally, changing the initial phase will not cause any perceptible changes.

[1] Need we point out this is somewhat higher than the Nyquist frequency?

4.3.2 Index of Modulation Example

Produce a harmonic sound with about 10 harmonics and a fundamental of 100 Hz. We can choose $C = M = 100$, which gives $C : M = 1$ and is at least one way to get a harmonic spectrum. Since the number of harmonics is 10, we need the carrier plus 9 sidebands, and so $I + 1 = 9$ or $I = 8$. $I = D/M$ so $D = IM$, $D = 8 \times 100 = 800$. Finally, we can write:

```
fmosc(hz-to-step(100), 800 * hzosc(100)).
```

4.3.3 FM Example in Nyquist

The following plays a characteristic FM sound in Nyquist:

```
play fmosc(c4, pwl(1, 4000, 1) * osc(c4)) ~ 10
```

Since the modulation comes from `osc(c4)`, the modulation frequency matches the carrier frequency (given by `fmosc(c4, ...)`, so the C:M ratio is 1:1. The *amplitude* of modulation ramps from 0 to 4000, giving a final index of modulation of $I = 4000/$ *steptohz*(*C*4) = 15.289. Thus, the spectrum will evolve from a sinusoid to a rich spectrum with the carrier and around $I + 1$ sidebands, or about 17 harmonics. Try it!

For a musical tone, you should multiply the `fmosc` signal by an envelope. Otherwise, the output amplitude will be constant. Also, you should replace the `pwl` function with an envelope that increases and then decreases, at least if you want the sound to get brighter in the middle.

4.4 Behavioral Abstraction

We now continue our introduction to fundamental concepts and structures in Nyquist. Think about the concept of "piano note". Piano notes can have a wide range of pitches, loudnesses, and durations, yet it still makes sense to think of "piano note" as a concept that describes the set of all of these instances. It also makes sense to talk about transformations such as longer, higher, or louder notes. In Nyquist, we use *behaviors* to describe classes of sounds, gestures, and even sequences of sub-behaviors (such as melodies), and we use ordinary functions (in the programming language sense) to model behaviors.

In Nyquist, all functions are subject to transformations. You can think of transformations as additional parameters to every function, and functions are free to use these additional parameters in any way. The set of transformation parameters is captured in what is referred to as the transformation environment. (Note that the term *environment* is heavily overloaded in computer science. This is yet another usage of the term.)

Behavioral abstraction is the ability of functions to adapt their behavior to the transformation environment. This environment may contain certain abstract notions, such as loudness, stretching a sound in time, etc. These notions will mean different things to different functions. For example, an oscillator should produce more periods of oscillation in order to stretch its output. An envelope, on the other hand, might only change the duration of the sustain portion of the envelope in order to stretch. Stretching recorded audio could mean resampling it to change its duration by the appropriate amount.

Thus, transformations in Nyquist are not simply operations on signals. For example, if I want to stretch a note, it does not make sense to compute the note first and then stretch the signal. Doing so would cause a drop in the pitch. Instead, a transformation modifies the transformation environment in which the note is computed. Think of transformations as making requests to functions. It is up to the function to carry out the request. Since the function is always in complete control, it is possible to perform transformations with "intelligence"; that is, the function can perform an appropriate transformation, such as maintaining the desired pitch and stretching only the "sustain" portion of an envelope to obtain a longer note.

4.4.1 Behaviors

Nyquist sound expressions denote a whole class of behaviors. The specific sound computed by the expression depends upon the environment. There are a number of transformations, such as `stretch` and `transpose` that alter the environment, and hence the behavior.

The most common transformations are `shift` and `stretch`, but remember that these do not necessarily denote simple time shifts or linear stretching: When you play a longer note, you don't simply stretch the signal! The behavior concept is critical for music.

4.4.2 Evaluation Environment

To implement the behavior concept, all Nyquist expressions evaluate within an *environment*.

The transformation environment is implemented in a simple manner. The environment is simply a set of special global variables. These variables should not be read directly and should never be set directly by the programmer. Instead, there are functions to read them, and they are automatically set and restored by transformation operators, which will be described below. The Nyquist environment includes: starting time, stretch factor, transposition, legato factor, loudness, sample rates, and more.

4.4.3 Manipulating the Environment Example

A very simple example of a transformation affecting a behavior is the stretch operator (~):

```
pluck(c4) ~ 5
```

This example can be read as "evaluate `pluck` in an environment that has been stretched by 5 relative to the current environment".

4.4.4 Transformations

Many transformations are relative and can be nested. Stretch does not just set the stretch factor; instead, it *multiplies* the stretch factor by a factor, so the final stretch factor in the new environment is relative to the current one.

Nyquist also has "absolute" transformations that override any existing value in the environment. For example,

```
function tone2() return osc(c4) ~~ 2
```

returns a 2 second tone, even if you write:

```
play tone2() ~ 100  ; 2 second tone
```

because the "absolute stretch" (~~) overrides the stretch operator ~. Even though `tone2` is called with a stretch factor of 100, its absolute stretch transformation overrides the environment and sets it to 2.

Also, note that once a sound is computed, it is immutable. The following use of a global variable to store a sound is not recommended, but serves to illustrate the immutability aspect of sounds:

```
set mysnd = osc(c4)  ; compute sound, duration = 1
play mysnd ~ 2  ; plays duration of 1
```

The stretch factor of 2 in the second line has no effect because `mysnd` evaluates to an immutable sound. Transformations only apply to functions[2] (which we often call *behaviors* to emphasize they behave differently in different contexts) and expressions that call on functions to compute sounds. Transformations do not affect sounds once they are computed.

4.4.4.1 *An Operational View*

You can think about this operationally: When Nyquist evaluates *expr* ~ 3, the ~ operator is not a function in the sense that expressions on the left and right are evaluated and passed to a function where "stretching" takes place. Instead, it is better to think of ~ as a control construct that:

[2]This is a bit of a simplification. If a function merely returns a pre-computed value of type SOUND, transformations will have no effect.

- changes the environment by tripling the stretch factor
- evaluates *expr* in this new environment
- restores the environment
- returns the sound computed by *expr*.

Thus, if *expr* is a *behavior* that computes a sound, the computation will be affected by the environment. If *expr* is a *sound* (or a variable that stores a sound), the sound is already computed and evaluation merely returns the sound with no transformation.

Transformations are described in detail in the *Nyquist Reference Manual* (find "Transformations" in the index). In practice, the most critical transformations are `at` (`@`) and `stretch` (`~`), which control when sounds are computed and how long they are.

4.5 Sequential Behavior (seq)

Consider the simple expression:

```
play seq(my-note(c4, q), my-note(d4, i))
```

The idea is to create the first note at time 0, and to start the next note when the first one finishes. This is all accomplished by manipulating the environment. In particular, `*warp*` is modified so that what is locally time 0 for the second note is transformed, or warped, to the logical stop time of the first note.

One way to understand this in detail is to imagine how it might be executed: first, `*warp*` is set to an initial value that has no effect on time, and `my-note(c4, q)` is evaluated. A sound is returned and saved. The sound has an ending time, which in this case will be `1.0` because the duration q is `1.0`. This ending time, `1.0`, is used to construct a new `*warp*` that has the effect of shifting time by `1.0`. The second note is evaluated, and will start at time `1.0`. The sound that is returned is now added to the first sound to form a composite sound, whose duration will be `2.0`. Finally, `*warp*` is restored to its initial value.

Notice that the semantics of `seq` can be expressed in terms of transformations. To generalize, the operational rule for `seq` is: evaluate the first behavior according to the current `*warp*`. Evaluate each successive behavior with `*warp*` modified to shift the new note's starting time to the ending time of the previous behavior. Restore `*warp*` to its original value and return a sound which is the sum of the results.

In the Nyquist implementation, audio samples are only computed when they are needed, and the second part of the `seq` is not evaluated until the ending time (called the logical stop time) of the first part. It is still the case that when the second part is evaluated, it will see `*warp*` bound to the ending time of the first part.

A language detail: Even though Nyquist defers evaluation of the second part of the `seq`, the expression can reference variables according to ordinary Lisp/SAL scope rules. This is because the `seq` captures the expression in a *closure*, which retains all of the variable bindings.

4.6 Simultaneous Behavior (sim)

Another operator is `sim`, which invokes multiple behaviors at the same time. For example,

```
play 0.5 * sim(my-note(c4, q), my-note(d4, i))
```

will play both notes starting at the same time.

The operational rule for `sim` is: evaluate each behavior at the current `*warp*` and return the sum of the results. (In SAL, the `sim` function applied to sounds is equivalent to adding them with the infix + operator.)

4.7 Logical Stop Time

We have seen that the default behavior of `seq` is to cause sounds to begin at the end of the previous sound in the sequence. What if we want to play a sequence of short sounds separated by silence? One possibility is to insert silence (see `s-rest`), but what if we want to play equally spaced short sounds? We have to know how long each short sound lasts in order to know how much silence to insert. Or what if sounds have long decays and we want to space them equally, requiring some overlap?

All of these cases point to an important music concept: We pay special attention to the beginnings of sounds, and the time interval between these onset times (often called *IOI* for "Inter-Onset Interval") is usually more important than the specific duration of the sound (or note). Thus, spacing notes according to their duration is not really a very musical idea.

Instead, we can try to separate the concepts of duration and IOI. In music notation, we can write a quarter note, meaning "play this sound for one beat", but put a dot over it, meaning "play this sound short, but it still takes a total of one beat". (See Figure 4.4.) It is not too surprising that music notation and theory would have rather sophisticated concepts regarding the organization of sound in time.

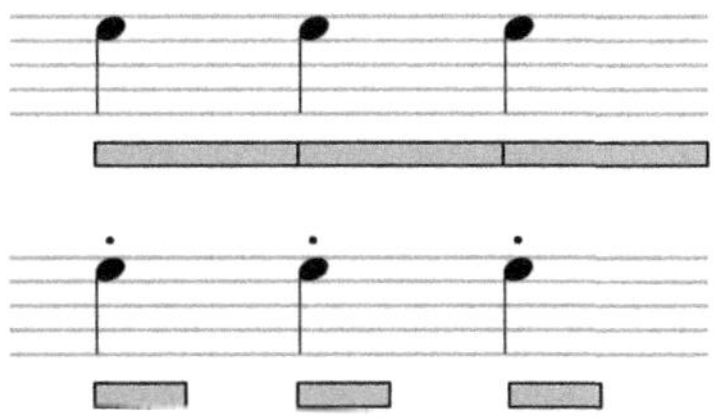

Figure 4.4: Standard quarter notes nominally fill an entire beat. Staccato quarter notes, indicated by the dots, are played shorter, but they still occupy a time interval of one beat. The "on" and "off" time of these short passages is indicated graphically below each staff of notation.

Nyquist incorporates this musical thinking into its representation of sounds. A sound in Nyquist has one start time, but there are effectively two "stop" times. The *signal* stop is when the sound samples end. After that point, the sound is considered to continue forever with value of zero. The *logical* stop marks the "musical" or "rhythmic" end of the sound. If there is a sound after it (e.g., in a sequence computed by `seq`), the next sound begins at this *logical stop* time of the sound.

The logical stop is usually the signal stop by default, but you can change it with the `set-logical-stop` function. For example, the following will play a sequence of 3 plucked-string sounds with durations of 2 seconds each, but the IOI, that is, the time between notes, will be only 1 second.

```
play seq(set-logical-stop(pluck(c4) ~ 2, 1),
         set-logical-stop(pluck(c4) ~ 2, 1),
         set-logical-stop(pluck(c4) ~ 2, 1))
```

4.8 Sequential and Simultaneous Iteration

Just as procedural languages have constructs such as `for` loops that iterate blocks of code, usually with a loop *index* variable that takes on values of 0, 1, 2, ... $n - 1$, Nyquist has special forms to instantiate n behaviors simultaneously or sequentially. Try the following two examples to play a chord and an *arpeggio* using `simrep` and `seqrep`:

```
play simrep(i, 6, piano-note(3, c4 + i * 5, 100))
play seqrep(i, 6, piano-note(0.3, c4 + i * 5, 100))
```

In these little programs, the variable `i` takes on values 0, 1, 2, 3, 4, and 5, producing pitches 60, 65, 70, 75, 80, and 85. (Note that if we name the loop variable `i`, it will "hide" the global binding of `i` which represents the eIghth note duration of 0.5.) See the *Nyquist Reference Manual* for more about `simrep` and `seqrep`.

4.9 Scores in Nyquist

Scores in Nyquist (introduced in Section 2.7) indicate "sound events", which consist of functions to call and parameters to pass to them. For each sound event there is also a start time and a "duration", which is really a Nyquist stretch factor. When you render a score into a sound (usually by calling `timed-seq` or executing the function `sound-play`), each sound event is evaluated by adjusting the environment according to the time and duration as if you wrote

sound-event(parameters) ~ *duration* @ *time*

The resulting sounds are then summed to form a single sound.

4.10 Summary

In this unit, we covered frequency modulation and FM synthesis. Frequency modulation refers to anything that changes pitch within a sound. Frequency modulation at audio rates can give rise to many partials, making FM Synthesis a practical, efficient, and versatile method of generating complex evolving sounds with a few simple control parameters.

All Nyquist sounds are computed by *behaviors* in an environment that can be modified with *transformations*. Functions describe behaviors. Each behavior can have explicit parameters as well as implicit environment values, so behaviors represent classes of sounds (e.g., piano tones), and each instance of a behavior can be different. Being "different" includes having different start times and durations, and some special constructs in Nyquist, such as `sim`, `seq`, `at` (`@`) and `shift` (~) use the environment to organize sounds in time. These concepts are also used to implement *scores* in Nyquist.

Chapter 5

Spectral Analysis and Nyquist Patterns

Topics Discussed: Short-Time Fourier Transform, Spectral Centroid, Patterns, Algorithmic Composition

In this chapter, we dive into the *Fast Fourier Transform* (FFT) for spectral analysis and use it to compute the *spectral centroid*. Then, we learn about some *Nyquist* functions that make interesting sequences of numbers and how to incorporate those sequences as note parameters in scores. Finally, we consider a variety of algorithmic composition techniques.

5.1 The Short-Time Fourier Transform and FFT

In practice, the Fourier transform cannot be used computationally because the input is infinite and the signals are continuous. Therefore, we use the *Discrete Short-Time Fourier Transform* (DSTFT), where the continuous *integral* becomes a *summation* of discrete time points (samples), and where the summation is performed over a finite time interval, typically around 50 to 100 ms. The so-called discrete short-time Fourier transform (DSTFT, or just DFT) equations are shown in Figure 5.1. Note the similarity to the Fourier transform integrals we saw earlier. Here, R_k represents the real coefficients and X_k are the imaginary coefficients (68).

The *Fast Fourier Transform* (FFT) is simply a fast algorithm for computing the DFT. FFT implies DFT, but rather than directly implementing the equations in Figure 5.1, which has a run time proportional to N^2, the FFT uses a very clever $N \log N$ algorithm to transform N samples.

DOI: 10.1201/9781003782711-5

$$R_k = \sum_{i=0}^{N-1} x_i \cos(2\pi ki / N)$$

$$X_k = -\sum_{i=0}^{N-1} x_i \sin(2\pi ki / N)$$

Figure 5.1: Equations for the short-time discrete Fourier transform. Each R_k, X_k pair represents a different frequency in the spectrum.

An FFT of a time-domain signal takes the samples and gives us a new set of numbers representing the frequencies, amplitudes, and phases of the sine waves that make up the sound we have analyzed. It is these data points that are displayed in the sonograms we looked at earlier.

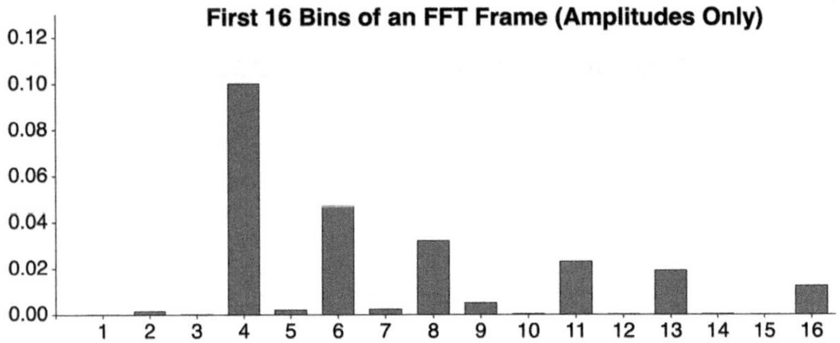

Bin	Bin Frequency (Hz)	Amplitude
0	0	(omitted from plot)
1	43	0.00003
2	86	0.0015
3	129	0.0001
4	172	0.1
5	215	0.002
6	258	0.047
7	301	0.0023
8	345	0.032
9	388	0.005
10	431	0.00026
11	474	0.023
12	517	0.0001
13	560	0.019
14	603	0.00013
15	646	0.00005
16	689	0.0123

Figure 5.2: Graph and table of spectral components.

Figure 5.2 illustrates some FFT data. It shows the first 16 bins of a typical FFT analysis after the conversion is made from real and imaginary numbers to amplitude/phase pairs. We left out the phases, because, well, it was too much trouble to just make up a bunch of arbitrary phases between 0 and 2π. In a lot of cases, you might not need them (and in a lot of cases, you would!). In this case, the sample rate is 44.1 kHz and the FFT size is 1,024, so the bin width (in frequency) is the sample rate (44,100) divided by the FFT size, or about 43 Hz.

We confess that we just sort of made up the numbers; but notice that we made them up to represent a sound that has a simple, more or less harmonic structure with a fundamental somewhere in the 66 Hz to 88 Hz range (you can see its harmonics at around 2, 3, 4, 5, and 6 times its frequency, and note that the harmonics decrease in amplitude more or less like they would in a sawtooth wave).

One important consequence of the FFT (or equivalently, DFT) is that we only "see" the signal during a short period. We pretend that the spectrum is stable, at least for the duration of the analysis window, but this is rarely true. Thus, the FFT tells us something about the signal over the analysis window, but we should always keep in mind that the FFT changes with window size and the concept of a spectrum at a point in time is not well defined. For example, harmonics of periodic signals usually show up in the FFT as peaks in the spectrum with some spread rather than single-frequency spikes, even though a harmonic intuitively has a single specific frequency.

5.1.1 How to Interpret a Discrete Spectrum

Just as we divide signals over time into discrete points (called samples), the DFT divides the spectrum into discrete points we call *frequency bins*. The DFT captures all of the information in the analysis window, so if you analyze N samples, you should have N degrees of freedom in the DFT. Since each DFT bin has an amplitude and phase, we end up with about $N/2$ bins. The complete story is that there are actually $N/2+1$ bins, but one represents zero frequency where only the real term is non-zero (because $sin(0)$ is 0), and one bin represents the Nyquist frequency where again, only the real term is non-zero (because $sin(2\pi ki/N)$ is zero).[1]

These $N/2+1$ bins are spaced across the frequency range from 0 to the Nyquist frequency (half the sample rate), so the spacing between bins is the sample rate divided by the number of bins:

bin frequency spacing = sample rate / number of samples

We can also relate the frequency spacing of bins to the duration of the analysis window:

[1]With each bin having 2 dimensions (real and imaginary), $N/2+1$ bins implies the result of the transform has $N+2$ dimensions. That should set off some alarms: How can you transform N input dimensions (real-valued samples) into $N+2$ output dimensions? This apparent problem is resolved when you realize that the first and last imaginary terms are zero, so there are really only N output dimensions that carry any information. Without this property, the DFT would not be invertible.

number of samples = analysis duration × sample rate, so
bin frequency spacing =
sample rate / (analysis duration × sample rate), so
bin frequency spacing = 1 / analysis duration

5.1.2 Frame or Analysis Window Size

So let's say that we decide on a frame size of 1,024 samples. This is a common choice because most FFT algorithms in use for sound processing require a number of samples, that is, a power of two, and it's important not to get too much or too little of the sound.

A frame size of 1,024 samples gives us 512 frequency bands. If we assume that we're using a sample rate of 44.1 kHz, we know that we have a frequency range (remember the Nyquist theorem) of 0 kHz to 22.05 kHz. To find out how wide each of our frequency bins is, we use one of the formulas above, e.g., sample rate / number of samples, or 44100 / 1024, or about 43 Hz. Remember that frequency perception is logarithmic, so 43 Hz gives us worse resolution at the low frequencies and better resolution (at least perceptually) at higher frequencies.

By selecting a certain frame size and its corresponding bandwidth, we avoid the problem of having to compute an infinite number of frequency components in a sound. Instead, we just compute one component for each frequency band.

5.1.3 Time/Frequency Trade-off and the Uncertainty Principle

A drawback of the FFT is the trade-off that must be made between frequency and time resolution. The more accurately we want to measure the frequency content of a signal, the more samples we have to analyze in each frame of the FFT. Yet there is a cost to expanding the frame size—the larger the frame, the less we know about the temporal events that take place within that frame. This trade-off is captured in the expression:

bin frequency spacing = 1 / analysis duration.

Small frequency spacing is good, but so is a short duration, and they are inversely proportional! We simply can't have it both ways. See Figure 5.3 for an illustration.

This time/frequency trade-off in audio analysis is mathematically identical to the Heisenberg Uncertainty Principle, which states that you can never simultaneously know the exact position and the exact speed of an object.

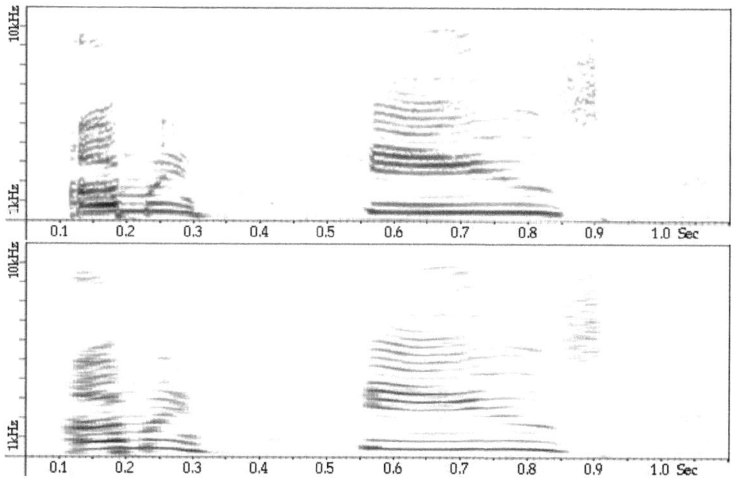

Figure 5.3: Selecting an FFT size involves making trade-offs in terms of time and frequency accuracy. Basically it boils down to this: The more accurate the analysis is in one domain, the less accurate it will be in the other. This figure illustrates what happens when we choose different frame sizes. In the first illustration, we used an FFT size of 512 samples, giving us pretty good time resolution. In the second, we used 2,048 samples, giving us pretty good frequency resolution. As a result, frequencies are smeared vertically in the first analysis, while time is smeared horizontally in the second. What's the solution to the time/frequency uncertainty dilemma? Compromise.

5.1.4 Magnitude or Amplitude Spectrum

Figure 5.1 shows that we get real (cosine) and imaginary (sine) numbers from the DFT or FFT. Typically, we prefer to work with amplitude and phase (in fact, we often ignore the phase part and just work with amplitude). You can think of real and imaginary as Cartesian coordinates, and amplitude and phase as radius and angle in polar coordinates. The amplitude components A_i are easily computed from the real R_i and imaginary X_i components using the formula:

$$A_i = \sqrt{R_i^2 + X_i^2}$$

For an N-point FFT (input contains N samples), the output will have $N/2+1$ bins, and therefore $N/2+1$ amplitudes. The first amplitude corresponds to 0 Hz, the second to (sample rate / N), etc., up to the last amplitude that corresponds to the frequency (sample rate / 2).

5.2 Spectral Centroid

Music cognition researchers and computer musicians commonly use a measure of sounds called the *spectral centroid*. The spectral centroid is a measure of the

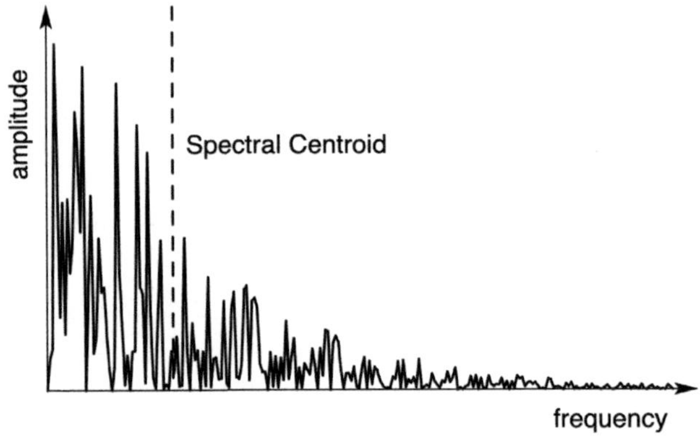

Figure 5.4: A magnitude spectrum and its spectral centroid (dashed line). If you were to cut out the spectrum shape from cardboard, it would balance on the centroid. The spectral centroid is a good measure of the overall placement of energy in a signal from low frequencies to high.

"brightness" of a sound, and it turns out to be extremely important in the way we compare different sounds. If two sounds have a radically different centroid, they are generally perceived to be timbrally distant (sometimes this is called a *spectral metric*).

Basically, the spectral centroid can be considered the average frequency component (taking into consideration the amplitude of all the frequency components), as illustrated in Figures 5.4 and 5.5. The formula for the spectral centroid of one FFT frame of a sound is:

$$c = \frac{\sum f_i a_i}{\sum a_i}, \text{where } f_i \text{ is the frequency of the } i^{\text{th}} \text{ bin and } a_i \text{ is the amplitude.}$$

5.3 Patterns

Nyquist offers pattern objects that generate data streams. For example, the `cycle-class` of objects generate cyclical patterns such as "1 2 3 1 2 3 1 2 3 ...", or "1 2 3 4 3 2 1 2 3 4 ...". Patterns can be used to specify pitch sequences, rhythm, loudness, and other parameters.

In this section, we describe a variety of pattern objects. These patterns are pretty abstract, but you might think about how various types of sequences might be applied to music composition. In the following section, we will see how to incorporate patterns into the generation of scores for Nyquist, using a very powerful macro called `score-gen`.

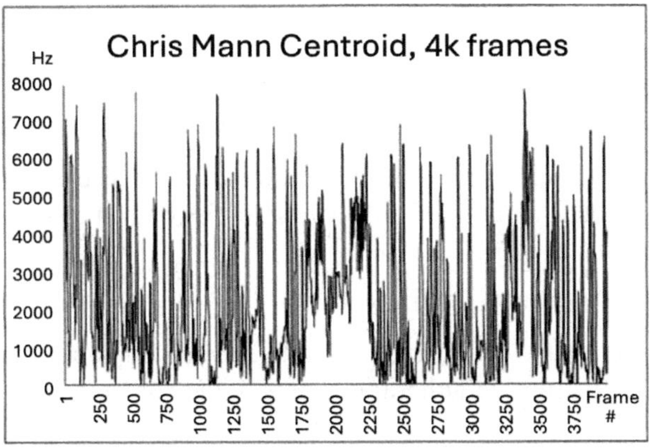

Figure 5.5: The centroid curve of a sound over time. This curve is of a rapidly changing voice (Australian sound poet Chris Mann). Each point in the horizontal dimension represents a new spectral frame. Note that centroids tend to be rather high and never the fundamental (this would only occur if our sound is a pure sine wave).

Pattern functions are automatically loaded when you start Nyquist. To use a pattern object, you first create the pattern, e.g.,

```
set pitch-source = make-cycle(list(c4, d4, e4, f4))
```

In this example, `pitch-source` is an object of class `cycle-class` which inherits from `pattern-class`.[2]

After creating the pattern, you can access it repeatedly with `next` to generate data, e.g.,

```
play seqrep(i, 13, pluck(next(pitch-source), 0.2))
```

This will create a sequence of notes with the following pitches: c, d, e, f, c, d, e, f, c, d, e, f, c. If you evaluate this again, the pitch sequence will continue, starting on d.

It is very important not to confuse the creation of a sequence with its access. Consider this example:

```
play seqrep(i, 13, pluck(next(make-cycle(
                         list(c4, d4, e4, f4))), 0.2))
```

[2]Because SAL is not an object-oriented language, these classes and their methods are not directly accessible from SAL. Instead, Nyquist defines a functional interface, e.g., `make-cycle` creates an instance of `cycle-class`, and the `next` function, introduced below, retrieves the next value from any instance of `pattern-class`. Using LISP syntax, you can have full access to the methods of all objects.

This looks very much like the previous example, but it only repeats notes on middle-C. The reason is that every time `pluck` is evaluated, `make-cycle` is called and creates a new pattern object. After the first item of the pattern is extracted with `next`, the cycle is not used again, and no other items are generated.

To summarize this important point, there are two steps to using a pattern. First, the pattern is created and stored in a variable. Second, the pattern is accessed (multiple times) using `next`.

`next(`*pattern-object* `[,#t ])`

`next` returns the next element from a pattern generator object. If the optional second argument is true (default value is false), then an entire period is returned as a list.

5.3.1 Pattern Examples

The following descriptions cover the basic ideas of the Nyquist pattern library. In most cases, details and optional parameters are not described here to keep the descriptions short and to emphasize the main purpose of each type of pattern. For complete descriptions, see the *Nyquist Reference Manual*, or better yet, just read the manual instead of these summaries.

5.3.1.1 Heap

The `heap-class` selects items in random order from a list without replacement, which means that all items are generated once before any item is repeated. For example, two periods of `make-heap({a b c})` might be `(C A B) (B A C)`. Normally, repetitions can occur even if all list elements are distinct. This happens when the last element of a period is chosen first in the next period. To avoid repetitions, the `max:` keyword argument can be set to 1. If the main argument is a pattern instead of a list, a period from that pattern becomes the list from which random selections are made, and a new list is generated every period. (See Section 5.3.2 on nested patterns.)

5.3.1.2 Palindrome

The `palindrome-class` repeatedly traverses a list forwards and then backwards. For example, two periods of `make-palindrome({a b c})` would be `(A B C C B A) (A B C C B A)`. The `elide:` keyword parameter controls whether the first and/or last elements are repeated:

```
make-palindrome(a b c, elide: nil)
        ;; generates A B C C B A A B C C B A ...

make-palindrome(a b c, elide: t)
        ;; generates A B C B A B C B ...
```

```
make-palindrome(a b c, elide: :first)
        ;; generates A B C C B A B C C B ...

make-palindrome(a b c, elide: :last)
        ;; generates A B C B A A B C B A ...
```

5.3.1.3 Random

The `random-class` generates items at random from a list. The default selection is uniform random with replacement, but items may be further specified with a weight, a minimum repetition count, and a maximum repetition count. Weights give the relative probability of the selection of the item (with a default weight of one). The minimum count specifies how many times an item, once selected at random, will be repeated. The maximum count specifies the maximum number of times an item can be selected in a row. If an item has been generated n times in succession, and the maximum is equal to n, then the item is disqualified in the next random selection. Weights (but not currently minima and maxima) can be patterns. The patterns (thus the weights) are recomputed every period.

5.3.1.4 Line

The `line-class` is similar to the cycle class, but when it reaches the end of the list of items, it simply repeats the last item in the list. For example, two periods of `make-line({a b c})` would be `(A B C) (C C C)`.

5.3.1.5 Accumulation

The `accumulation-class` takes a list of values and returns the first, followed by the first two, followed by the first three, etc. In other words, for each list item, return all items from the first through the item. For example, if the list is `(A B C)`, each generated period is `(A A B A B C)`.

5.3.1.6 Copier

The `copier-class` makes copies of periods from a sub-pattern. For example, three periods of `make-copier( make-cycle({a b c}, for: 1), repeat: 2, merge: t)` would be `(A A) (B B) (C C)`. Note that entire periods (not individual items) are repeated, so in this example the `for:` keyword was used to force periods to be of length one so that each item is repeated by the `repeat:` count.

5.3.1.7 Length

The `length-class` generates periods of a specified length from another pattern. This is similar to using the `for:` keyword, but for many patterns, the `for:` parameter alters the points at which other patterns are generated. For example, if the palindrome pattern has an `elide:` pattern parameter, the value will be computed every period. If there is also a `for:` parameter with a value of 2, then elide: will be recomputed every 2 items. In contrast, if the palindrome (without a `for:` parameter) is embedded in a *length* pattern with a length of 2, then the periods will all be of length 2, but the items will come from default periods of the palindrome, and therefore the `elide:` values will be recomputed at the beginnings of default palindrome periods.

5.3.1.8 Window

The `window-class` groups items from another pattern by using a sliding window. If the *skip* value is 1, each output period is formed by dropping the first item of the previous period and appending the next item from the pattern. The *skip* value and the output period length can change every period. For a simple example, if the period length is 3 and the *skip* value is 1, and the input pattern generates the sequence A, B, C, ..., then the output periods will be (A B C), (B C D), (C D E), (D E F), ...

5.3.2 Nested Patterns

Patterns can be nested, that is, you can write patterns of patterns. In general, the `next` function does not return patterns. Instead, if the next item in a pattern is a (nested) pattern, next recursively gets the next item of the nested pattern.

While you might expect that each call to `next` would advance the top-level pattern to the next item, and descend recursively if necessary to the inner-most nesting level, this is not how `next` works. Instead, `next` remembers the last top-level item, and if it was a pattern, `next` continues to generate items from that same inner pattern until the end of the inner pattern's *period* is reached. The next paragraph explains the concept of the *period*.

5.3.2.1 Periods

The data returned by a pattern object is structured into logical groups called *periods*. You can get an entire period (as a list) by calling `next(pattern, t)`. For example:

```
set pitch-source = make-cycle(list(c4, d4, e4, f4))
print next(pitch-source, t)
```

This prints the list `(60 62 64 65)`, which is one period of the cycle.

You can also get explicit markers that delineate periods by calling `send(pattern, :next)`. In this case, the value returned is either the next item of the pattern, or the symbol `+eop+` if the end of a period has been reached.

What determines a period? This is up to the specific pattern class, so see the documentation for specifics. You can override the "natural" period by using the keyword `for:`, e.g.,

```
set pitch-source =
        make-cycle(list(c4, d4, e4, f4), for: 3)
print next(pitch-source, t)
print next(pitch-source, t)
```

This prints the lists `(60 62 64) (65 60 62)`. Notice that these periods just restructure the stream of items into groups of 3.

Nested patterns are probably easier to understand by example than by specification. Here is a simple nested pattern of cycles:

```
set cycle-1 = make-cycle({a b c})
set cycle-2 = make-cycle({x y z})
set cycle-3 = make-cycle(list(cycle-1, cycle-2))
loop
  repeat 9
  exec format(t, "~A ", next(cycle-3))
end
```

This will print "A B C X Y Z A B C". Notice that the inner-most cycles `cycle-1` and `cycle-2` generate a period of items before the top-level `cycle-3` advances to the next pattern.

5.3.3 Summary of Patterns

Pattern generators are a bit like unit generators in that they represent sequences or streams of values, they can be combined to create complex computations, they encapsulate state on which the next output depends, and they can be evaluated incrementally. Patterns produce streams of numbers intended to become parameters for algorithmic compositions, while unit generators produce samples.

Patterns can serve as parameters to other pattern objects, enabling complex behaviors to run on multiple time scales. Since patterns are often constructed from lists (e.g., cycle, random, heap, copier, line, palindrome patterns), the output of each pattern is structured into groupings called *periods*, and pattern generators have parameters (especially *for:*) to control or override period lengths. Even period lengths can be controlled by patterns!

5.4 Score Generation and Manipulation

A common application of pattern generators is to specify parameters for notes. (It should be understood that "notes" in this context means any Nyquist behavior, whether it represents a conventional note, an abstract sound object, or even some micro-sound event that is just a low-level component of a hierarchical sound organization. Similarly, "score" should be taken to mean a specification for a sequence of these "notes".) The `score-gen` macro establishes a convention for representing scores and for generating them using patterns.

The `timed-seq` macro already provides a way to represent a score as a list of expressions. We can go a bit further by specifying that *all notes are specified by an alternation of keywords and values, where some keywords have specific meanings and interpretations.* By insisting on this keyword/value representation, we can treat scores as self-describing data, as we will see below.

To facilitate using *patterns* to create *scores*, we introduce the `score-gen` construct, which looks like a function but is actually a *macro*. The main difference is that a *macro* does not evaluate every parameter immediately, but instead can operate on parameters as expressions. The basic idea of `score-gen` is you provide a template for notes in a score as a set of keywords and values. For example,

```
set pitch-pattern = make-cycle(list(c4, d4, e4, f4))
score-gen(dur: 0.4, name: quote(my-sound),
          pitch: next(pitch-pattern), score-len: 9)
```

Generates a score of 9 notes as follows:

```
((0 0 (SCORE-BEGIN-END 0 3.6))
 (0 0.4 (MY-SOUND :PITCH 60))
 (0.4 0.4 (MY-SOUND :PITCH 62))
 (0.8 0.4 (MY-SOUND :PITCH 64))
 (1.2 0.4 (MY-SOUND :PITCH 65))
 (1.6 0.4 (MY-SOUND :PITCH 60))
 (2 0.4 (MY-SOUND :PITCH 62))
 (2.4 0.4 (MY-SOUND :PITCH 64))
 (2.8 0.4 (MY-SOUND :PITCH 65))
 (3.2 0.4 (MY-SOUND :PITCH 60)))
```

The use of keywords like `:PITCH` helps to make scores readable and easy to process without specific knowledge about the functions called in the score. For example, one could write a transpose operation to transform all the `:pitch` parameters in a score without having to know that pitch is the first parameter of `pluck` and the second parameter of `piano-note`. Keyword parameters are also used to give flexibility to note specification with `score-gen`. Since this approach requires the use of keywords, the next section is a brief explanation of how to define functions that use keyword parameters.

5.4.1 Keyword Parameters

Keyword parameters are parameters whose presence is indicated by a special symbol, called a keyword, followed by the actual parameter. Keyword parameters in SAL have default values that are used if no actual parameter is provided by the caller of the function.

To specify that a parameter is a keyword parameter, use a keyword symbol (one that ends in a colon) followed by a default value. For example, here is a function that accepts keyword parameters and invokes the `pluck` function:

```
define function k-pluck(pitch: 60, dur: 1)
  return pluck(pitch, dur)
```

Notice that within the body of the function, the actual parameter value for keywords `pitch:` and `dur:` are referenced by writing the keywords without the colons (`pitch` and `dur`) as can be seen in the call to `pluck`. Also, keyword parameters have default values. Here, they are 60 and 1, respectively.

Now, we can call k-pluck with keyword parameters. A function call would look like:

```
k-pluck(pitch: c3, dur: 3)
```

Usually, it is best to give keyword parameters useful default values. That way, if a parameter such as `dur:` is missing, a reasonable default value (1) can be used automatically. It is never an error to omit a keyword parameter, but the called function can check to see if a keyword parameter was supplied or not. Because of default values, we can call `k-pluck(pitch: c3)` with no duration, `k-pluck(dur: 3)` with only a duration, or even `k-pluck()` with no parameters.

5.4.2 Using score-gen

The `score-gen` macro computes a score based on keyword parameters. Some keywords have a special meaning, while others are not interpreted but merely placed in the score. The resulting score can be synthesized using `timed-seq`. The form of a call to `score-gen` is simply:

```
score-gen(k1: e1, k2: e2, ...)
```

where the *k*'s are keywords and the *e*'s are expressions. A score is generated by evaluating the expressions once for each note and constructing a list of keyword-value pairs. A number of keywords have special interpretations. The rules for interpreting these parameters will be explained through a set of "How do I ..." questions below.

How many notes will be generated? The keyword parameter `score-len:` specifies an upper bound on the number of notes. The keyword `score-dur:` specifies an upper bound on the starting time of the last note in the score. (To be more precise, the `score-dur:` bound is reached when the default starting time of the next note is greater than or equal to the `score-dur:` value. This definition is necessary because note times are not strictly increasing.) When either bound is reached, score generation ends. At least one of these two parameters must be specified or an error is raised. These keyword parameters are evaluated just once and are not copied into the parameter lists of generated notes.

What is the duration of generated notes? The keyword `dur:` defaults to 1 and specifies the nominal duration in seconds. Since the generated note list is compatible with `timed-seq`, the starting time and duration (to be precise, the stretch factor) are not passed as parameters to the notes. Instead, they control the Nyquist environment in which the note will be evaluated.

What is the start time of a note? The default start time of the first note is zero. Given a note, the default start time of the next note is the start time plus the inter-onset time, which is given by the `ioi:` parameter. If no `ioi:` parameter is specified, the inter-onset time defaults to the duration, given by `dur:`. In all cases, the default start time of a note can be overridden by the keyword parameter `time:`. So, in other words, to get the time of each note, compute the expression given as (time:). If there is no `time:` parameter, compute the time of the previous note plus the value of `ioi:`, and if there is no `ioi:`, then use `dur:`, and if there is no `dur:`, use 1.

When does the score begin and end? The behavior `SCORE-BEGIN-END` contains the beginning and ending of the score (these are used for score manipulations, e.g., when scores are merged, their begin times can be aligned.) When `timed-seq` is used to synthesize a score, the `SCORE-BEGIN-END` marker is not evaluated. The `score-gen` macro inserts an event of the form:

`(0 0 (SCORE-BEGIN-END` *`begin-time end-time`*`))`

with begin-time and end-time determined by the `begin:` and `end:` keyword parameters, respectively. (Recall that these `score-begin-end` events do not make sound, but they are used by score manipulation functions for splicing, stretching, and other operations on scores.) If the `begin:` keyword is not provided, the score begins at zero. If the `end:` keyword is not provided, the score ends at the default start time of what would be the next note after the last note in the score (as described in the previous paragraph). Note: if `time:` is used to compute note starting times, and these times are not increasing, it is strongly advised to use end: to specify an end time for the score, because the default end time may not make sense.

What function is called to synthesize the note? The name: parameter names the function. Like other parameters, the value can be any expression, including something like next(`fn-name-pattern`), allowing function names to be recomputed for each note. The default value is `note`.

Can I make parameters depend upon the starting time or the duration of the note? `score-gen` sets some handy variables that can be used in expressions that compute parameter values for notes:

- the variable `sg:start` accesses the start time of the note,
- `sg:ioi` accesses the inter-onset time,
- `sg:dur` accesses the duration (stretch factor) of the note,
- `sg:count` counts how many notes have been computed so far, starting at 0.

The order of computation is: `sg:count`, then `sg:start`, then `sg:ioi` and finally `sg:dur`; so, for example, an expression for `dur:` can depend on `sg:ioi`.

Can parameters depend on each other? The keyword `pre:` introduces an expression that is evaluated before each note, and `post:` provides an expression to be evaluated after each note. The `pre:` expression can assign one or more global variables which are then used in one or more expressions for parameters.

How do I debug score-gen expressions? You can set the `trace:` parameter to true (t) to enable a print statement for each generated note.

How can I save scores generated by `score-gen` *that I like?* If the keyword parameter `save:` is set to a symbol, the global variable named by the symbol is set to the value of the generated sequence. Of course, the value returned by `score-gen` is just an ordinary list that can be saved like any other value.

In summary, the following keywords have special interpretations in `score-gen`: `begin:`, `end:`, `time:`, `dur:`, `name:`, `ioi:`, `trace:`, `save:`, `score-len:`, `score-dur:`, `pre:`, `post:`. All other keyword parameters are expressions that are evaluated once for each note and become the parameters of the notes.

5.5 Introduction to Algorithmic Composition

There are many types and approaches to *machine-aided composition*, which is also called *algorithmic composition*, *computer-assisted composition*, *automatic composition*, and *machine generated music* (all of which have varying shades of meaning depending on the author that uses them and the context).

Some examples of approaches include:

- Use of music notation software, which is arguably computer-assisted, but rarely what we mean by "machine-aided composition".
- Cutting and pasting of music materials (notation or audio) in editors can be effective, but leaves all the decision-making to the composer, so again, this is not usually considered to be machine-aided composition.

- Editing macros and other high-level operations enable composers to (sometimes) delegate some musical decision-making to machines and perform high-level operations on music compositions.
- *Algorithmic composition* usually refers to simple numerical or symbolic algorithms to generate musical material, e.g., mapping the digits of π to pitches.
- Procedures + random numbers allow composers to create structures with randomized details.
- *Artificial intelligence* seeks to model music composition as search, problem solving, knowledge-directed decisions, or optimization.
- Music models attempt to formalize music theory or perhaps particular musical styles to enable examples to be generated computationally.
- *Machine learning* typically seeks to learn music models automatically from examples, often using sequence-learning techniques from other domains such as natural language processing.
- *Constraint solving and search* techniques allow composers to describe music in terms of properties or restrictions and then use computers to search for solutions that satisfy the composers' specifications.

The following sections describe a number of approaches that I have found useful. The list is by no means exhaustive. One thing you will discover is that there are few if any music generation systems that one can simply pick up and use. Almost every approach and software package offers a framework within which composers can adjust parameters or provide additional details to produce material which is often just the starting point in producing a complete piece of music. There is no free lunch!

For much more on algorithmic composition, see *Algorithmic Composition: A Guide to Composing Music with Nyquist* (87). This book contains many examples created with Nyquist.

5.5.1 Negative Exponential Distribution

Random numbers can be interesting, but what does it mean to be "random" in time? You might think that it would be useful to make the inter-onset interval (IOI) be a uniform random distribution, but this turns out to be not so interesting because the resulting sequence or rhythm is a little too predictable.

In the real world, we have random events in time such as atomic decay or something as mundane as the time points when a yellow car drives by. The inter-arrival time of these random events has a negative exponential distribution, as shown in

Figure 5.6. The figure shows that the probability of longer and longer intervals is less and less likely.

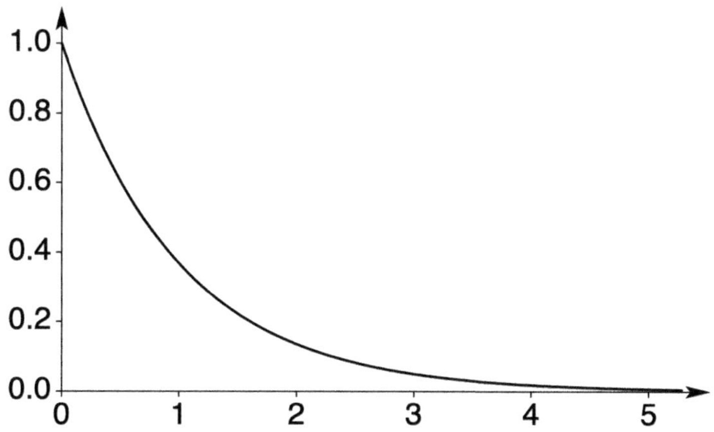

Figure 5.6: The negative exponential distribution.

See "Distributions" in the *Nyquist Reference Manual* for implementations. (The `exponential-dist` function can be used directly to compute `ioi:` values in `score-gen`. You might want to code upper and lower bounds to avoid the extremes of this infinite distribution.) Another way to generate something like a (negative) exponential distribution is, at every time point (e.g., every 16th note or every 10 ms), play a note with some low probability *p*. In this approach, IOI is not explicitly computed, but the distribution of IOI's will approximate the negative exponential shown in Figure 5.6.

Yet another way to achieve a negative exponential distribution is to choose time points uniformly within a time span (e.g., in Nyquist, the expression `rrandom() * dur` will return a random number in [0, `dur`).) Then, *sort* the time points into increasing order, and you will obtain points where the IOI has a negative exponential distribution.

Nyquist supports many other interesting probability distributions. See "Distributions" in the *Nyquist Reference Manual* for details.

5.5.2 Random Walk

What kinds of pitch sequences create interesting melodies? Melodies are mostly made up of small intervals, but a uniform random distribution creates many large intervals. Melodies often have fractal properties, with a mix of mainly small intervals, but occasional larger ones. An interesting idea is to randomly choose a direction (up or down) and interval size in a way that emphasizes smaller intervals over larger ones (99). Sometimes, this is called a "random walk", as illustrated in Figure 5.7.

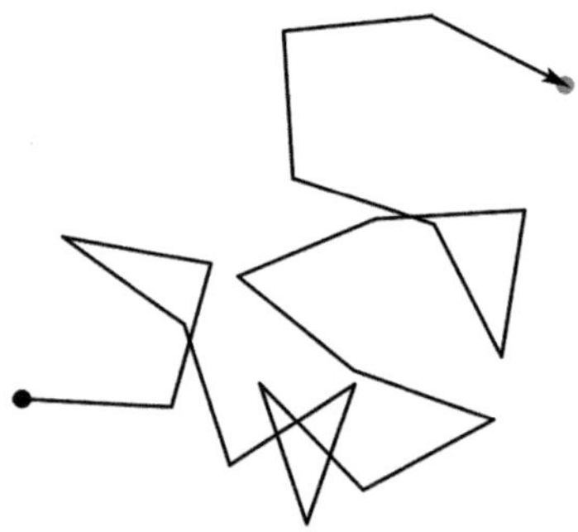

Figure 5.7: A random walk in two dimensions. Each step has the same length, but the direction is random.

5.5.3 *Markov Chains*

A Markov Chain is a formal model of random sequential processes that is widely used in many fields (27). A Markov Chain consists of a set of states (in music, these could be chords, for example). The output of a Markov Chain is a sequence of states. The probability of making a transition to a state depends *only* on the previous state. Figure 5.8 illustrates a Markov Chain. The three states represent chords, and each chord has transitions to itself and other chords labeled with probabilities.

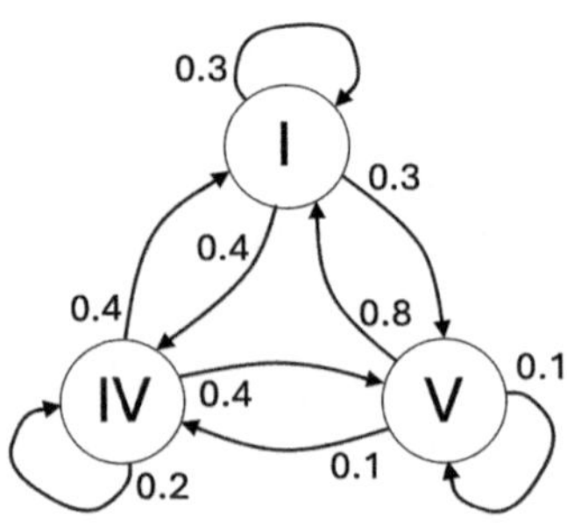

Figure 5.8: A Markov Chain for simple chord progressions with labeled transition probabilities. For example, the V chord is very likely (0.8) to transition to the I chord.

5.5.4 Rhythmic Pattern Generation

There are many techniques for rhythmic patterns. An interesting perceptual fact about rhythms is that almost any rhythm will make a certain amount of musical sense if it has at least two or three sound events, not so many sound events that we cannot remember the sequence, and *the rhythm is repeated.* Therefore, a simple but effective "random rhythm generator" is the following: Decide on a length. Generate this many random Boolean values in sequence. Make each element of the sequence represent an onset or a rest and play at least several repetitions of the resulting rhythm. For example, if each 0 or 1 represents a 16th note, and we play a sound on each "1", a clear structured rhythm will be heard:

01101110100 01101110100 01101110100 01101110100 ...

5.5.5 Serialism

At the risk of over-simplifying, serialism arose as an attempt to move beyond the tonal concepts that dominated Western musical thought through the beginning of the 20th century (98). Arnold Schoenberg created his 12-tone technique that organized music around "tone rows" which are permutations of the 12 pitch classes of the chromatic scale (namely, C, C#, D, D#, E, F, F#, G, G#, A, A#, B). Starting with a single permutation, the composer could generate new rows through transposition, inversion, and playing the row backwards (called retrograde). Music created from these sequences tends to be *atonal* with no favored pitch center or scale. Because of the formal constraints on pitch selection and operations on tone rows, serialism has been an inspiration for many algorithmic music compositions.

5.5.6 Fractals and Nature

Melodic contours are often fractal-like, and composers often use fractal curves to generate music data. Examples include Larry Austin's *Canadian Coastline*, based on the fractal nature of a natural coastline, and John Cage's *Atlas Eclipticalis*, based on positions of stars.

5.5.7 Grammars

Formal grammars, most commonly used in formal descriptions of programming languages, have been applied to music (78). Consider the formal grammar:

melody ::= intro middle ending
middle ::= phrase | middle phrase
phrase ::= A B C B | A C D A

which can be read as: "A *melody* is an *intro* followed by a *middle* followed by and *ending*. A *middle* is recursively defined as either a *phrase* or a *middle* followed by a *phrase* (thus, a *middle* is one or more *phrases*), and a *phrase* is the sequence A B C B or the sequence A C D A. We haven't specified yet what is an *intro* or *ending*.

Grammars are interesting because they give a compact description of many alternatives, e.g., the formal grammar for Java allows for all Java programs, and the music grammar above describes many possibilities as well. However, grammars give clear constraints—a Nyquist program is rejected by the grammar for Java, and music in the key of C# cannot be generated by the music grammar example above.

5.5.8 Pitch and Rhythm Grids

Traditional Western music is based on discrete pitch and time values. We build scales out of half steps that we often represent with integers, and we divide time into beats and sub-beats. One interesting and useful technique in algorithmic music is to compute parameters from continuous distributions, but then *quantize* values to fit pitches into conventional scales or round times and durations to the nearest sixteenth beat or some other rhythmic grid (87).

5.6 Tendency Masks

A problem with algorithmic composition is that the output can become static if the same parameters or probability distributions are used over and over. At some point, we recognize that even random music has an underlying probability distribution, so what is random becomes just a confirmation of our expectations.

One way to combat this perception of stasis is to create multi-level structures, e.g., patterns of patterns of patterns. A more direct way is to simply give the high-level control back to the composer. As early as 1970, Gottfried Michael Koenig used *tendency masks* to control the evolution of parameters in time in order to give global structure and control to algorithmic music composition. Barry Truax used tendency masks to control parameters for granular synthesis (discussed in the next chapter) (95). Figure 5.9 illustrates tendency masks for two parameters. The masks give a range of possible values for parameters. Note that the parameter values can be chosen between upper and lower bounds, and that the bounds change over time.

Figure 5.9: Tendency masks offer a way for composers to retain global control over the evolution of a piece even when the moment-by-moment details of the piece are generated algorithmically. Here, the vertical axis represents parameter values and the horizontal axis represents time. The two colored areas represent possible values (to be randomly selected) for each of two parameters used for music generation.

5.7 Summary

We have learned about a variety of approaches to algorithmic music generation. Nyquist supports algorithmic music generation especially through the `score-gen` macro, which iteratively evaluates expressions and creates note lists in the form of Nyquist scores. Nyquist also offers a rich pattern library for generating parameter values. These patterns can be used to implement many "standard" algorithmic music techniques such as serialism, random walks, Markov Chains, probability distributions, pitch and rhythmic grids, etc.

We began by learning details of the FFT and spectral centroid. The main reason to introduce these topics is to prepare you to extract spectral centroid data from one sound source and use it to control parameters of music synthesis. Hopefully, you can combine this sonic control with some higher-level algorithmic generation of sound events to create an interesting piece. Good luck!

Chapter 6

Nyquist Techniques and Granular Synthesis

Topics Discussed: Recursion, Duration Matching, Control Functions, and Granular Synthesis

6.1 Programming Techniques in Nyquist

One of the unusual things about Nyquist is the support for timing (temporal semantics), which is lacking in most programming languages. Nyquist also has signals as a fundamental data type. Here we introduce a number of different programming techniques related to timing and signals that are useful in Nyquist.

6.1.1 Recursive Sound Sequences

We first look at the idea of recursive sound sequences. The `seq` function delays evaluation of each behavior until the previous behavior is finished. There are other functions, including `timed-seq`, that work in a similar way. This delayed evaluation, a form of *lazy evaluation*, is important in practice because if sound computation can be postponed until needed, Nyquist can avoid storing large signals in memory. Lazy evaluation has another benefit, in that it allows you to express infinite sounds recursively. Consider a *drum roll* as an example. We define a drum roll recursively as follows: Start with one drum stroke and follow it with a drum roll!

The `drum-roll()` function below is a direct implementation of this idea. `drum-roll()` builds up a drum roll one stroke at a time, recursively, and re-

DOI: 10.1201/9781003782711-6

turns an infinite drum roll sound sequence. Even Google doesn't have that much disk space, so to avoid the obvious problem of storing an infinite sound, we can multiply `drum-roll()` by an envelope. In `limited-drum-roll()`, we make a finite drum roll by multiplying `drum-roll()` by `const(1, 2)`. `const(1, 2)` is a unit generator that returns a constant value of 1 until the duration of 2, then it drops to 0. Here, multiplying a limited sound by an infinite sound gives us a finite computation and result. Note that the multiplication operator in Nyquist is quite smart. It knows that when multiplying by 0, the result is always 0; and when a sound reaches its stop time, it remains 0 forever, thus Nyquist can terminate the recursion at the sound stop time.

```
define function drum-stroke()
  return noise() * pwev(1, 0.05, 0.1)

define function drum-roll()
  return seq(drum-stroke(), drum-roll())  ; recursion!

define function limited-drum-roll()
  return const(1, 2) * drum-roll()  ; duration=2

play limited-drum-roll()
```

Note that in this example, there is a risk that the "envelope" `const(1, 2)` might cut off a `drum-stroke` suddenly.[1] Here, `drum-stroke` happen to be 0.1 seconds long, which means a 2-second `drum-roll` has exactly 20 full `drum-stroke`, so a `drum-stroke` and the envelope will end exactly together. In general, either `seqrep` or an envelope that gives a smooth fadeout would be a better design.

6.1.2 Matching Durations

In Nyquist, sounds are considered to be functions of time, with no upper bound on time. Sounds *do* have a "stop time" after which the signal is considered to remain at zero forever. This means that you can easily combine sounds of different durations by mistake. For example, you can multiply a 1-second oscillator signal by a 2-second envelope, resulting in a 1-second signal that probably ends abruptly before the envelope goes to zero.

It is a "feature" of Nyquist that you can compose longer sounds from shorter sounds or multiply by short envelopes to isolate sections of longer sounds, but this leads to one of the most common errors in Nyquist: Combining sounds and controls with different durations by mistake.

[1] Recall that `const(1, 2)` is a control signal with the constant value 1 for 2 seconds. It cuts off instantly at 2 seconds.

Here is an example of this common error:

```
play pwl(0.5, 1, 10, 1, 13) *    ; 13-seconds duration
     osc(c4)  ; nominally 1-second duration
              ; final result: sound stops at 1 second(!)
```

Remember that Nyquist sounds are immutable. Nyquist will not and cannot go back and recompute behaviors to get the "right" durations—how would it know? There are two basic approaches to make durations match. The first is to make everything have a nominal length of 1 and use the *stretch* operator to change durations:

```
(pwl(0.1, 1, 0.8, 1, 1) * osc(c4)) ~ 13
```

Here we have changed `pwl` to have a duration of 1 rather than 13. This is the default duration of `osc`, so they match. Note also the use of parentheses to ensure that the stretch factor applies to both `pwl` and `osc`.

The second method is to provide duration parameters everywhere:

```
pwl(0.5, 1, 10, 1, 13) * osc(c4, 13)
```

Here, we kept the original 13-second long `pwl` function, but we explicitly set the duration of `osc` to 13. If you provide duration parameters everywhere, you will often end up passing duration as a parameter, but that's not always a bad thing, as it makes duration management more explicit.

6.1.3 Control Functions

Another useful technique in Nyquist is to carefully construct control functions. Synthesizing control is like synthesizing sound, and often control is even more important than waveforms and spectra in producing a musical result.

6.1.3.1 Smooth Transitions

Apply envelopes to almost everything. Even control functions can have control functions! A good example is vibrato. A "standard" vibrato function might look like `lfo(6) * 5`, but this would generate constant vibrato throughout a tone. Instead, consider `lfo(6) * 5 * pwl(0.3, 0, 0.5, 1, 0.9, 1, 1)` where the vibrato depth is controlled by an envelope. Initially, there is no vibrato, the vibrato starts to emerge at 0.3 and reaches the full depth at 0.5, and finally tapers rapidly from 0.9 to 1. Of course this might be stretched, so these numbers are relative to the whole duration. Thus, we not only use envelopes to get smooth transitions in amplitude at the beginnings and endings of notes, we can use envelopes to get smooth transitions in vibrato depth and other controls.

6.1.3.2 Composing Control Functions

The are a few main "workhorse" functions for control signals.

1. For periodic variation such as vibrato, the `lfo` function generates low-frequency sinusoidal oscillations. The default sample rate of `lfo` is 1/20 of the audio sample rate, so do not use this function for audio frequencies. If the frequency is not constant, the simplest alternative is `hzosc`, which allows its first argument to be a `SOUND` as well as a number.

2. For non-periodic but deterministic controls such as envelopes, `pwl` and the related family (including `pwlv` and `pwlev`) or the envelope function `env` are good choices.

3. For randomness, a good choice is `noise`. By itself, `noise` generates audio rate noise, which is not suitable for adding small random fluctuations to control signals. What we often use in this case is a random signal that ramps smoothly from one amplitude to the next, with a new amplitude every 100 ms or so. You can obtain this effect by making a very low sample rate `noise` signal. When this signal is added to or multiplied by a higher sample rate signal, the `noise` signal is linearly interpolated to match the rate of the other signal, thus achieving a smooth ramp between samples. The expression for this is `sound-srate-abs(10, noise())`, which uses the `sound-srate-abs` transform to change the environment for `noise` to a sample rate of 10 Hz. See Figure 6.1.

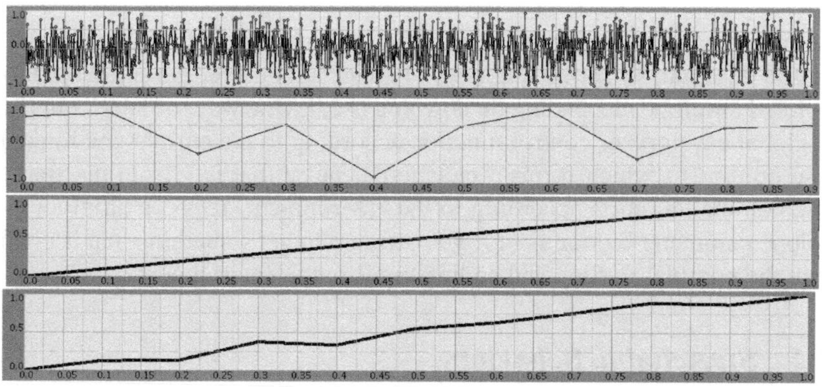

Figure 6.1: Plots of: `noise`, `sound-srate-abs(10, noise())`, `ramp()` and `sound-srate-abs(10, noise()) * 0.1 + ramp()`. The bottom plot shows how the `noise` function can be used to add jitter or randomness to an otherwise mathematically smooth control function. Such jitter or randomness occurs naturally, often due to minute natural human muscle tremors.

6.1.3.3 Global vs. Local Control Functions

Nyquist allows you to use control functions including envelopes at different levels of hierarchy. For example, you could synthesize a sequence of notes with individual amplitude envelopes, then multiply the whole sequence by an overarching envelope to give a sense of phrase. Figure 6.2 illustrates how global and "local" envelopes might be combined.

Figure 6.2: Hierarchical organization of envelopes.

In the simple case of envelopes, you can just apply the global envelope through multiplication after notes are synthesized. In some other cases, you might need to actually pass the global function as a parameter to be used for synthesis. Suppose that in Figure 6.2, the uppermost (global) envelope is required to control the index of modulation in FM synthesis. This effect cannot be applied after synthesis, so you must pass the global envelope as a parameter to each note. Within each note, you might expect the whole global envelope to somehow be shifted and stretched according to the note's start time and duration, but that does not happen. Instead, since the control function has already been computed as a `SOUND`, it is immutable and fixed in time. Thus, the note only "sees" the portion of the control function over the duration of the note, as indicated by the dotted lines in Figure 6.2.

In some cases, e.g., FM synthesis, the control function determines the note start time and duration, so `fmosc` might try to create a tone over the entire duration of the global envelope, depending on how you use it. One way to "slice" out a piece of a global envelope or control function according to the current environment is to use `const(1)` which forms a rectangular pulse that is 1 from the start time to the nominal duration according to the environment. If you multiply a global envelope parameter by `const(1)`, you are sure to get something that is confined within the nominal starting and ending times in the environment.

6.1.4 Stretchable Behaviors

An important feature of Nyquist is the fact that functions represent *classes* of behaviors that can produce signals at different start times, with different durations, and be affected by many other parameters, both explicit and implicit (17).

Nyquist has default stretch behaviors for all of its primitives, and we have seen this many times. Often, the default behavior does the "right thing", (see the discussion above about matching durations). But sometimes you need to customize what it means to "stretch" a sound. For example, if you stretch a melody, you make notes longer, but if you stretch a drum roll, you do not make drum strokes slower. Instead, you add more drum strokes to fill the time. With Nyquist, you can create your own abstract behaviors to model things like drum rolls, constant-rate trills, and envelopes with constant attack times, none of which follow simple default rules of stretching.

Here is an example where you want the number of things to increase with duration:

```
define function n-things()
  begin
    with dur = get-duration(1),
         n = round(dur / *thing-duration*)
   return seqrep(i, n, thing() ~~ 1)
end
```

The basic idea here is to first "capture" the nominal duration using:

```
get-duration(1)
```

Then, we compute `n` in terms of duration. Now, if we simply made `n` things in the current stretch environment (stretch by `dur`), we would create a sound with duration roughly `n` × `*thing-duration*` × `dur`, but we want to compute `thing()` without stretching. The `~~` operator, also called *absolute stretch*, resets the environment stretch factor to 1 when we call `thing()`, so now the total duration will be approximately `n` × `*thing-duration*`, which is about equal to `get-duration(1)` as desired.

Here is an example where you want an envelope to have a fixed rise time:

```
define function my-envelope()
  begin
    with dur = get-duration(1)
    return pwl(*rise-time*, 1, dur - *fall-time*,
               1, dur) ~~ 1
  end
```

As in the previous example, we "capture" duration to the variable `dur` and then compute within an *absolute stretch* (`~~`) of 1 so that all duration control is explicit and in terms of `dur`. We set the rise time to a constant, `*rise-time*` and compute the beginning and ending of the "release" relative to `dur` which will be the absolute duration of the envelope.

6.1.5 Summary

We have seen a number of useful Nyquist programming techniques. To make sure durations match, either normalize durations to 1 and stretch everything as a group using the stretch operator (`~`), or avoid stretching altogether and use explicit duration parameters everywhere. In general, use envelopes everywhere to achieve smooth transitions, and never let an oscillator output start or stop without a smooth envelope. Control is all important, so in spite of many simplified examples you will encounter, every parameter should be a candidate for control over time: amplitude, modulation, vibrato, filter cutoff, and even control functions themselves can be modulated or varied at multiple time scales. And speaking of multiple time scales, do not forget that musical gestures consisting of multiple notes or sound events can be sculpted using over-arching envelopes or smooth control changes that span whole phrases.

6.2 Granular Synthesis

We know from our discussion of the Fourier transform that that complex sounds can be created by adding together a number of sine waves. Granular synthesis uses a similar idea, except that instead of a set of sine waves whose frequencies and amplitudes change over time, we use many thousands of very short (usually less than 100 milliseconds) overlapping sound bursts or grains (76). The waveforms of these grains are often sinusoidal, although any waveform can be used. (One alternative to sinusoidal waveforms is to use grains of sampled sounds, either pre-recorded or captured live.) By manipulating the temporal placement of large numbers of grains and their frequencies, amplitude envelopes, and waveshapes, very complex and time-variant sounds can be created.

6.2.1 *Grains*

To make a grain, we simply take any sound (e.g., a sinusoid or sound from a sound file) and apply a short smoothing envelope to avoid clicks. (See Figure 6.3.) The duration is typically from around 20ms to 200ms: long enough to convey a little content and some spectral information, but short enough to avoid containing an entire note or word (from speech sounds) or anything too recognizable.

6.2.2 *Clouds of Sound*

Granular synthesis is often used to create what can be thought of as "sound clouds"—shifting regions of sound energy that seem to move around a sonic space. A number of composers, like Iannis Xenakis (99) and Barry Truax, thought of granular synthesis as a way of shaping large masses of sound by using granulation techniques. These two composers are both considered pioneers of this technique (Truax wrote some of the first special-purpose software for granular synthesis (95)). Sometimes, cloud terminology is even used to talk about ways of arranging grains into different sorts of configurations.

6.2.3 Grain Selection, Control, and Organization

In granular synthesis, we make and combine thousands of grains (sometimes thousands of grains per second), which is too much to do by hand, so we use computation to do the work, and we use high-level parameters to control things. Beyond this, granular synthesis is not a specific procedure and there is no right or wrong way to do it. It is good to be aware of the range of mechanisms by which grains are selected, processed, and organized.

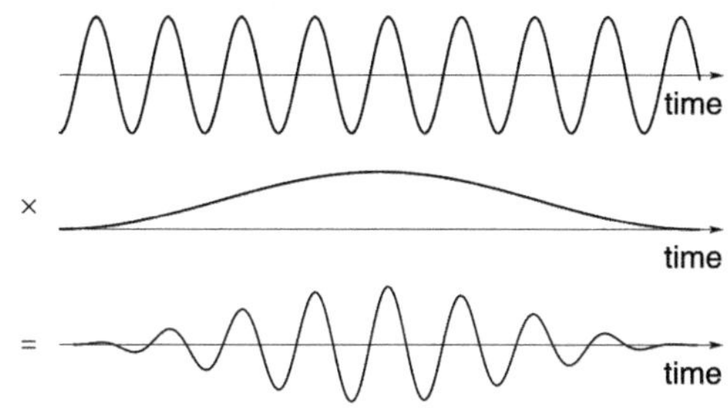

Figure 6.3: Applying a short envelope to a sound to make a grain for granular synthesis. How would a different amplitude envelope, say a square one, affect the shape of the grain? What would it do to the sound of the grain? What would happen if the sound was a recording of a natural sound instead of a sinusoid? What would be the effect of a longer or shorter envelope?

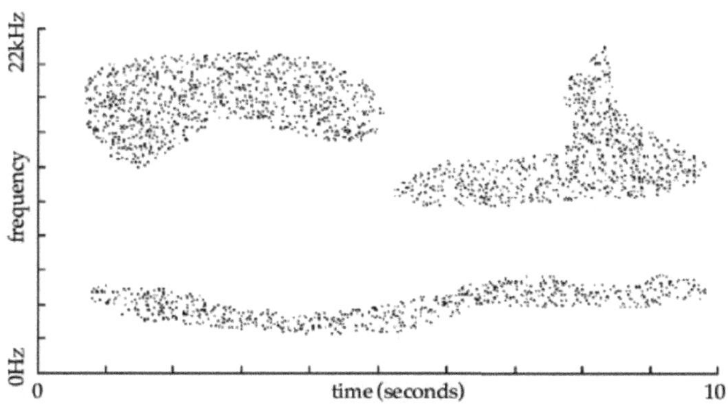

Figure 6.4: Visualization of a granular synthesis "score". Each dot represents a grain at a particular frequency and moment in time. An image such as this one can give us a good idea of how this score might sound, even though there is some important information left out (such as the grain amplitudes, waveforms, amplitude envelopes, and so on). What sorts of sounds does this image imply? If you had three vocal performers, one for each cloud, how would you go about performing this piece? Try it!

One important control parameter is density. Typically granular synthesis is quite dense, with 10 or more grains overlapping at any given time. But grains can also be sparse, creating regular rhythms or isolated random sound events.

Stochastic or statistical control is common in granular synthesis. For example, we could pick grains from random locations in a file and play them at random times. An interesting technique is to scan through a source file, but rather than taking grains sequentially, we add a random offset to the source location, taking grains *in the neighborhood* of a location that progresses through the file. This produces changes over time that mirror what is in the file, but at any given time, the cloud of sound can be quite chaotic, disguising any specific audio content or sound events in the file.

It is also possible to resample the grain to produce pitch shifts. If pitch shifting is random, a single tone in the source can become a multi-pitch cluster or cloud in the output. If you resample grains, you can shift the pitch by octaves or harmonics, which might tend to harmonize the output sound when there is a single pitch on the input, or you can resample by random ratios, creating an atonal or microtonal effect. When you synthesize grains, you can use regular spacing, e.g., play a grain every 10 ms, which will tend to create a continuous sounding texture, or you can play grains with randomized inter-onset intervals, creating a more chaotic or bubbly sound.

Some interesting things to do with granular synthesis include vocal mumblings using grains to chop up speech and make speech-sounding nonsense, especially using grains with approximately the duration of phonemes so that whole words are obliterated. Granular synthesis can also be used for time stretching: By moving through a file very slowly, fetching overlapping grains and outputting them with less overlap, the file is apparently stretched, as shown in Figure 6.5. There will be artifacts because grains will not add up perfectly smoothly to form a continuous sound, but this can be a feature as well as a limitation, depending on your musical goals.

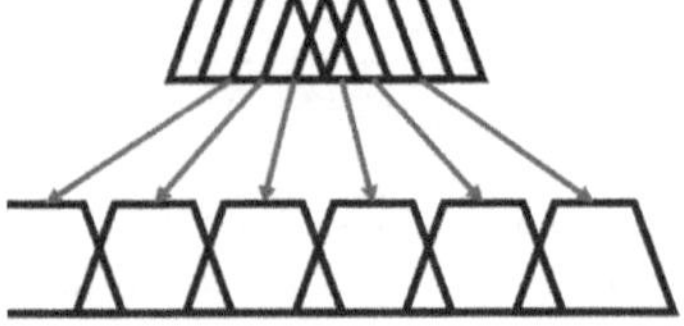

Figure 6.5: Stretching with granular synthesis.

6.2.4 Granular Synthesis in Nyquist

Nyquist does not have a "granular synthesis" function because there are so many ways to implement and control granular synthesis. However, Nyquist is almost unique in its ability to express granular synthesis using a combination of signal processing and control constructs.

6.2.4.1 Generating a Grain

Figure 6.6 illustrates Nyquist code to create an smooth envelope and read a grain's worth of audio from a file to construct a smooth grain. Note the use of duration d both to stretch the envelope and control how many samples are read from the file. Below, we consider two approaches to granular synthesis implementation. The first uses scores and the second uses seqrep.

```
function cos-pulse()
        return 0.5 * (1 + hzosc(1 / get-duration(1),
                                  *sine-table*, 270.0))
```

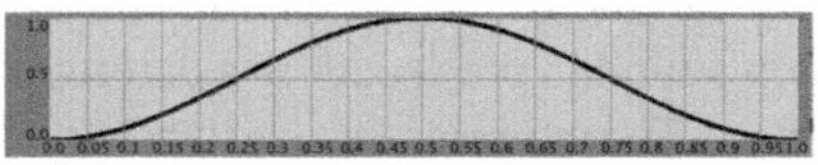

```
s-read("filename.wav", time-offset: seconds, dur: d) *
  (cos-pulse() ~ d)
```

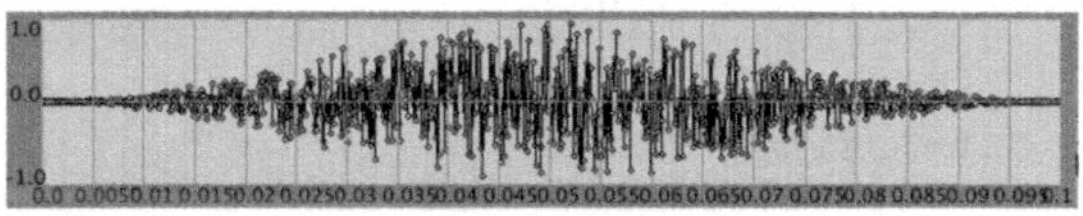

Figure 6.6: Constructing a grain in Nyquist.

6.2.5 Grains in Scores

A score for granular synthesis treats each grain as a sound event:

```
{{0 0.05 {grain offset: 2.1}}
 {0.02 0.06 {grain offset: 3.0}}
 ...}
```

The score calls upon grain, which we define below. Notice that grain durations are specified in the score and implemented through the environment, so the cos-pulse signal will be stretched by the duration, but s-read is unaffected by stretching. Therefore, we must obtain the stretch factor using get-duration(1) and pass that value to s-read as the optional dur: keyword parameter:

```
function grain(offset: 0)
  begin with dur = get-duration(1)
    return s-read("filename.wav",
                  time-offset: offset, dur: dur) *
           cos-pulse()
  end
```

Now, we can make a score with score-gen. In the following expression, we construct 2,000 grains with randomized inter-onset intervals and using pattern objects to compute the grain durations and file offsets:

```
score-gen(score-len: 2000,
          ioi: 0.05 + rrandom() * 0.01,
          dur: next(dur-pat),
          offset: next(offset-pat))
```

You could also use more randomness to compute parameters, e.g., the duration could come from a Gaussian distribution (see the Nyquist function gaussian-dist), and offset: could be computed by slowly moving through the file and adding a random jitter, e.g.,

```
max(0, sg-count * 0.01 + rrandom() * 0.2)
```

6.2.6 Grains with Seqrep

Rather than computing large scores, we can use Nyquist control constructs to create grains "on the fly". In the following example, seqrep is used to create and sum 2,000 sounds. Each sound is produced by a call to grain, which is stretched by values from dur-pat. To obtain grain overlap, we use set-logical-stop with an IOI (logical stop time) parameter of 0.05 + rrandom() * 0.01, so the grain IOI will be 50 ms $\pm$ 10 ms:

```
seqrep(i, 2000,
       set-logical-stop(
           grain(offset: next(offset-pat)) ~
               next(dur-pat),
           0.05 + rrandom() * 0.01))
```

For another example, you can install the gran extension using Nyquist's Extension Manager. The package includes a function sf-granulate that implements granular synthesis using a sound file as input.

6.2.7 Other Ideas

You might want to implement something like the tendency masks we described earlier or use a pwl function to describe how some granular synthesis parameters evolve over time. Since pwl produces a signal and you often need *numbers* to control each grain, you can use sref to evaluate the signal at a specific time, e.g., s-ref(sound, time) will evaluate sound at time.

Another interesting idea is to base granular synthesis parameters on the source sound itself. A particularly effective technique is to select grains by slowly advancing through a file, causing a time-expansion of the file content. The most interesting portions of the file are usually note onsets and places where things are changing rapidly, which you might be able to detect by measuring either amplitude or spectral centroid. If the rate at which you advanced through the file is inversely proportional to amplitude or spectral centroid, then the "interesting" material will be time-expanded, and you will pass over the "boring" steady-state portions of the signal quickly.

6.2.8 Summary

Granular synthesis creates sound by summing thousands of sound particles or grains with short durations to form clouds of sounds. Granular synthesis can construct a wide range of textures, and rich timbres can be created by taking grains from recordings of natural sounds. Granular synthesis offers many choices of details including grain duration, density, random or deterministic timing, pitch shifts, and source.

Chapter 7

Sampling and Filters

Topics Discussed: Samples, Filters, High-pass, Low-pass, Band-pass

7.1 Sampling Synthesis

Although direct synthesis of sound is an important area of computer music, it can be equally interesting (or even more so!) to take existing sounds (recorded or synthesized) and transform, mutate, deconstruct—in general, mess around with them. There are as many basic sound transformation techniques as there are synthesis techniques, and in this chapter we'll describe a few important ones. For the sake of convenience, we will separate them into time-domain and frequency-domain techniques.

7.1.1 Tape Music/Cut and Paste

The most obvious way to transform a sound is to chop it up, edit it, turn it around, and collage it. These kinds of procedures, which have been used in electronic music since the early days of tape recorders, are done in the time domain. There are a number of sophisticated software tools for manipulating sounds in this way, called *digital sound editors* or *digital audio workstations (DAWs)*. These editors allow for the most minute, sample-by-sample changes of a sound. These techniques are used in almost all fields of audio, from avant-garde music to Hollywood soundtracks, from radio station advertising spots to rap.

DOI: 10.1201/9781003782711-7

7.1.2 Time-Domain Restructuring

Composers have experimented a lot with unusual time-domain restructuring of sound. By chopping up waveforms into very small segments and radically reordering them, some noisy and unusual effects can be created. As in collage visual art, the ironic and interesting juxtaposition of very familiar materials can be used to create new works that are perhaps greater than the sum of their constituent parts.

Unique, experimental, and rather strange programs for deconstructing and reconstructing sounds in the time domain are Herbert Brün's SAWDUST (see Figure 7.1) and Argeïphontes Lyre (see Figure 7.2), written by the enigmatic Akira Rabelais. Argeïphontes Lyre provides a number of techniques for radical decomposition/recomposition of sounds—techniques that often preclude the user from making specific decisions in favor of larger, more probabilistic decisions.

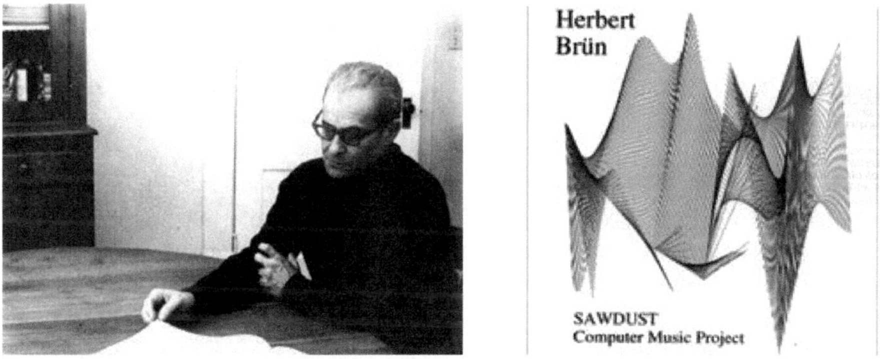

Figure 7.1: Herbert Brün said of his program SAWDUST: "The computer program which I called SAWDUST allows me to work with the smallest parts of waveforms, to link them, and to mingle or merge them with one another. Once composed, the links and mixtures are treated, by repetition, as periods, or by various degrees of continuous change, as passing moments of orientation in a process of transformations".

7.1.3 Sampling

Sampling refers to taking small bits of sound, often recognizable ones, and recontextualizing them via digital techniques. By digitally sampling, we can easily manipulate the pitch and time characteristics of ordinary sounds and use them in any number of ways (77).

We've talked a lot about samples and sampling in the preceding chapters. In popular music (especially electronic dance and beat-oriented music), the term *sampling* has acquired a specialized meaning. In this context, a sample refers to a (usually) short excerpt from some previously recorded source, such as a

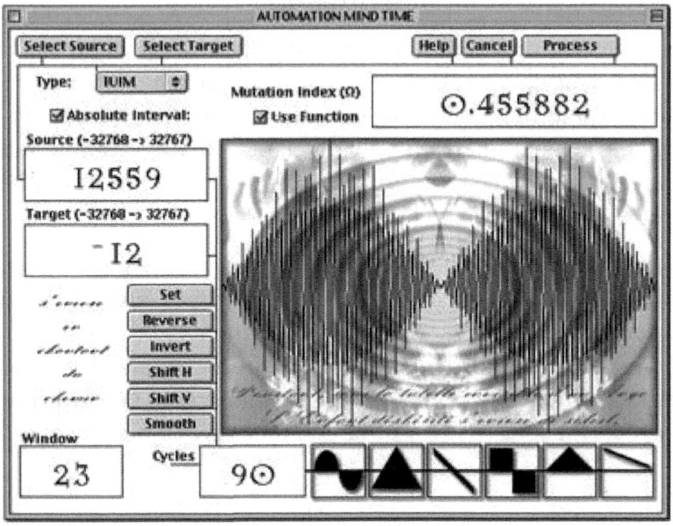

Figure 7.2: Sample GUI from Argeïphontes Lyre, for sound deconstruction. This is time domain mutation.

drum loop from a song or some dialog from a film soundtrack, that is used as an element in a new work. A *sampler* is the hardware used to record, store, manipulate, and play back samples. Originally, most samplers were stand-alone pieces of gear. Today, sampling tends to be integrated into a studio's computer-based digital audio system.

Sampling was pioneered by rap artists in the mid-1980s, and by the early 1990s it had become a standard studio technique used in virtually all types of music. Issues of copyright violation have plagued many artists working with sample-based music, notably John Oswald of "Plunderphonics" fame and the band Negativland, although the motives of the "offended" parties (generally large record companies) have tended to be more financial than artistic. One result of this is that the phrase "Contains a sample from xxx, used by permission" has become ubiquitous on CD cases and in liner notes.

Although the idea of using excerpts from various sources in a new work is not new (many composers, from Béla Bartók, who used Balkan folk songs, to Charles Ives, who used American popular music folk songs, have done so), digital technology has radically changed the possibilities.

7.1.4 Drum Machines

Drum machines and samplers are close cousins. Many drum machines are just specialized samplers—their samples just happen to be all percussion/drum-oriented. Other drum machines feature electronic or digitally synthesized drum sounds. As with sampling, drum machines started out as stand-alone pieces of hardware but now have largely been integrated into computer-based systems.

7.1.5 DAW Systems

Digital-audio workstations (DAWs) since the 1990s have had the same effect on digital sound creation as desktop publishing software had on the publishing industry in the 1980s: they've brought digital sound creation out of the highly specialized and expensive environments in which it grew up and into people's homes. A DAW usually consists of a computer with some sort of audio interface hardware for analog and digital input/output; sound recording/editing/playback/multi-track software; and a mixer, amplifier, and other sound equipment traditionally found in a home studio. Even the most modest of DAW systems can provide 16 or more tracks of CD-quality sound, making it possible for many artists to self-produce and release their work for much less than it would have cost in professional analog recording studios. This ability, in conjunction with similar marketing and publicizing possibilities opened up by the spread of the Internet, has contributed to the explosion of tiny record labels and independent releases we've seen.

In 1989, Digidesign came out with Sound Tools, the first professional tape–less recording system. With the popularization of personal computers, numerous software and hardware manufacturers developed products for computer-based digital audio production. Becoming affordable and practical in the 1990s, personal computer-based production systems have allowed individuals and institutions to make the highest-quality recordings. DAW systems have also revolutionized the professional music, broadcast, multimedia, and film industries with audio systems that are more flexible, more accessible, and more creatively oriented than ever before.

Today, DAWs come in all shapes and sizes on hardware ranging from mobile phones to desktop computers. Most DAWs can take advantage of an *audio interface*—a piece of hardware that provides two to 16 or more channels of digital and analog audio I/O (inputs and outputs). Many DAW systems also have *control surfaces*—pieces of hardware that look like a standard mixer but are really controllers for parameters in the digital audio system.

7.1.6 Sampling as a Synthesis Technique

Sampling is often used to produce musical tones or notes, and some think of sampling as the opposite of synthesis. In this view, *sampling* is based on recordings while *synthesis* produces sound by mathematical calculation. However, sample-based tone production involves considerable calculation and allows for parametric control, so we will describe it as yet another synthesis technique or algorithm.

The main attraction of sampling is that recordings of actual acoustic instruments generally sound realistic. (You might think samples by definition must *always* sound realistic, but this is an overstatement we will discuss later.) There are three basic problems with samples:

1. Samples of musical tones have definite pitches. You could collect samples for every pitch, but this requires a lot of storage, so most samplers need the capability of changing the pitch of samples through calculation.
2. Samples of musical tones have definite durations. In practice, we need to control the duration of tones, and capturing *every* possible duration is impractical, so we need the capability of changing the duration of samples.
3. Samples have a definite loudness. In practice, we need to produce sounds from soft to loud.

7.1.6.1 Pitch Control

The standard approach to pitch control over samples (here, *sample* means a short recording of a musical tone) is to change the sample rate using interpolation. If we *upsample*, or increase the sample rate, but play at the normal sample rate, the effect will be to slow down and drop the pitch of the original recording. Similarly, if we *downsample*, or lower the sample rate, but play at the normal rate, the effect will be to speed up and raise the pitch of the original recording.

To change sample rates, we interpolate existing samples at new time points. Often, "interpolation" means *linear* interpolation, but with signals, linear interpolation does not result in the desired smooth band-limited signal, which is another way of saying that linear interpolation will distort the signal; it may be a rough approximation to proper reconstruction, but it is not good enough for high-quality audio. Instead, good audio sample interpolation requires a weighted sum taken over a number of samples. The weights follow an interesting curve as shown in Figure 7.3. More samples lead to better quality, but also more computation. In early samplers, where even specialized hardware had limited performance, interpolation with less than 10 points was probably typical, but details are proprietary. Modern processors are fast enough to achieve high-quality interpolation with many more points (50 to 200 does not seem to be unusual). The specific case of transposing samples *down* and other assumptions can lead to more relaxed requirements.

Another problem with resampling is that when pitch is shifted by a lot, the quality of sound is significantly changed. For example, voices shifted to higher pitches begin to sound like cartoon voices or people breathing helium. This is unaccept-

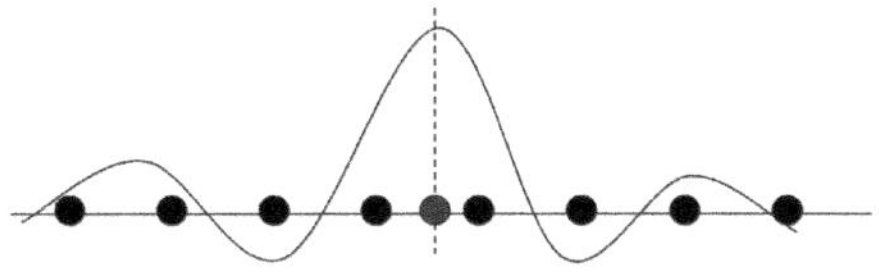

Figure 7.3: To resample a signal, we need to interpolate between existing samples in order to *reconstruct* the signal at a new time. A sequence of these new samples at a narrower or wider spacing creates a representation of the signal at a new sample rate. For each of these new samples (in this figure, the new sample will be at the dotted line), we form a weighted sum of existing samples. The weights are given by the so-called sinc function shown here (the thin wavy line). This weighted sum is essentially a low-pass filter that does in the digital domain what the reconstruction filter does in the analog domain when converting a digital signal to analog.

able, so usually, there are many samples for a given instrument. For example, one might use four different pitches for each octave. Then, pitch shifts are limited to the range of 1/8 octave, eliminating the need for extreme pitch shifts.

7.1.6.2 Duration Control

A simple way to control duration is simply to multiply samples by an envelope to end them as early as needed. However, this could require a considerable amount of memory to store long raw samples in case long notes are required. To save memory, samplers can *loop* or repeat portions of samples to sustain the sound. Usually, there is an initial *attack* portion of the sample at the beginning, and when the sample settles down to a periodic waveform, the sampler can repeat that portion of the sample. To loop samples, one must be very careful to find points where the end of the loop flows smoothly into the beginning of the loop to avoid discontinuities that impart a buzzy sound to the loop. Looping is a painstaking manual process, which is another reason to simply use longer samples as long as the added memory requirements are acceptable.

7.1.6.3 Loudness Control

A simple way to produce soft and loud versions of samples is to just multiply the sample by a scale factor. There is a difference, however, between amplitude and *loudness* in that many instruments change their sound when they play louder. Imagine a whisper in your ear vs. a person shouting from 100 yards away. Which is louder? Which has higher amplitude?

To produce variations in perceptual loudness, we can use filters to alter the spectrum of the sound. E.g., for a softer sound, we might filter out higher frequencies as well as reduce the amplitude by scaling. Another option is to record samples for different amplitudes and select samples according to the desired loudness level. Amplitude changes can be used to introduce finer adjustments.

7.1.6.4 Sampling in Nyquist

In Nyquist, the `sampler` function can be used to implement sampling synthesis. The signature of the function is:

`sampler(`*pitch*`,` *modulation*`,` *sample*`)`

The *pitch* parameter gives the desired output pitch, and *modulation* is a frequency deviation function you can use to implement vibrato or other modulation. The output duration is controlled by *modulation*, so if you want zero modulation and a duration of *dur*, use `const(0, dur)` for *modulation*. The *sample* parameter is a list of the form: (*sound pitch loop-start*), where *sound* is the sample (audio), *pitch* is the natural pitch of the sound, and *loop-start* is the time at which the loop starts. Resampling is performed to convert the natural pitch of the sample to the desired pitch computed from the *pitch* parameter and *modulation*. The `sampler` function returns a sound constructed by reading the audio sample from beginning to end and then splicing on copies of the same sound from the loop point (given by *loop-start*) to the end. Currently, only 2-point (linear) interpolation is implemented, so the quality is not high. However, you can use `resample` to upsample your *sound* to a higher sample rate, e.g., 4x and this will improve the resulting sound quality. Note also that the loop point may be fractional, which may help to make clean loops.

7.1.6.5 Summary

Sampling synthesis combines pre-recorded sounds with signal processing to adjust pitch, duration, and loudness. For creating music that sounds like acoustic instruments, sampling is the currently dominant approach. One of the limitations of sampling is the synthesis of lyrical musical phrases. While samples are great for reproducing single notes, acoustic instruments perform connected phrases, and the transitions between notes in phrases are very difficult to implement with sampling. Lyrical playing by wind instruments and bowed strings is particularly difficult to synthesize simply by combining 1-note samples. Some sample libraries even contain transitions to address this problem, but the idea of sampling all combinations of articulations, pitches, durations, and loudness levels and their transitions does not seem feasible.

7.2 Filters

The most common way to think about filters is as functions that take in a signal and give back some sort of transformed signal. Usually, what comes out is less than what goes in. That's why the use of filters is sometimes referred to as *subtractive synthesis*.

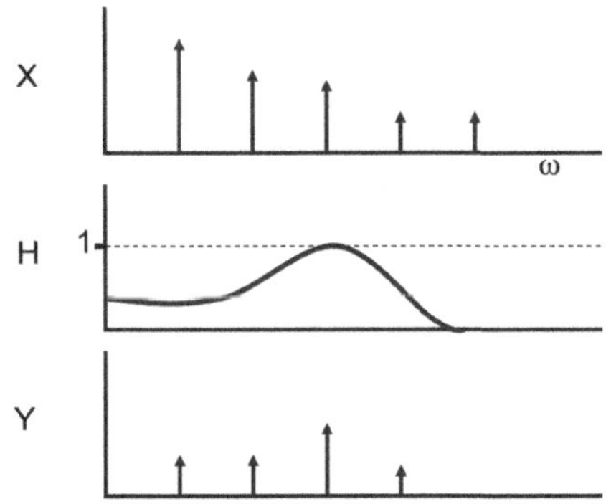

Figure 7.4: Filtering in the frequency domain. The input signal with spectrum X is multiplied by the frequency response of the filter H to obtain the output spectrum Y. The result of filtering is to reduce the amplitude of some frequencies and boost the amplitudes of others. In addition to amplitude changes, filters usually cause phase shifts that are also frequency dependent. Since we are so insensitive to phase, we usually ignore the *phase response* of filters.

It probably won't surprise you to learn that *subtractive synthesis* is in many ways the opposite of additive synthesis. In additive synthesis, we start with simple sounds and add them together to form more complex ones. In subtractive synthesis, we start with a complex sound (such as noise or a rich harmonic spectrum) and subtract, or filter out, parts of it. Subtractive synthesis can be thought of as sound sculpting—you start out with a thick chunk of sound containing many possibilities (frequencies), and then you carve out (filter) parts of it. Filters are one of the sound sculptor's most versatile and valued tools.

The action of filters is best explained in the frequency domain. Figure 7.4 explains the action of a filter on the spectrum of a signal. In terms of the magnitude spectrum, filtering is a *multiplication* operation. Essentially, the filter *scales* the amplitude of each sinusoidal component by a frequency-dependent factor. The overall frequency-dependent scaling function is called the *frequency response* of the filter.

A common misconception among students is that since filtering is multiplication in the frequency domain, and since the FFT converts signals to the frequency domain (and the Inverse FFT converts back), then filtering must be performed by an FFT-multiply-IFFT sequence. *This is false!* At least simple filters operate in the time domain (details below). Filtering with FFTs is possible but problematic because it is not practical to perform FFTs on long signals.

7.2.1 Four Basic Types of Filters

Figure 7.5 illustrates four basic types of filters: low-pass, high-pass, band-pass, and band-reject. Low-pass and high-pass filters should already be familiar to

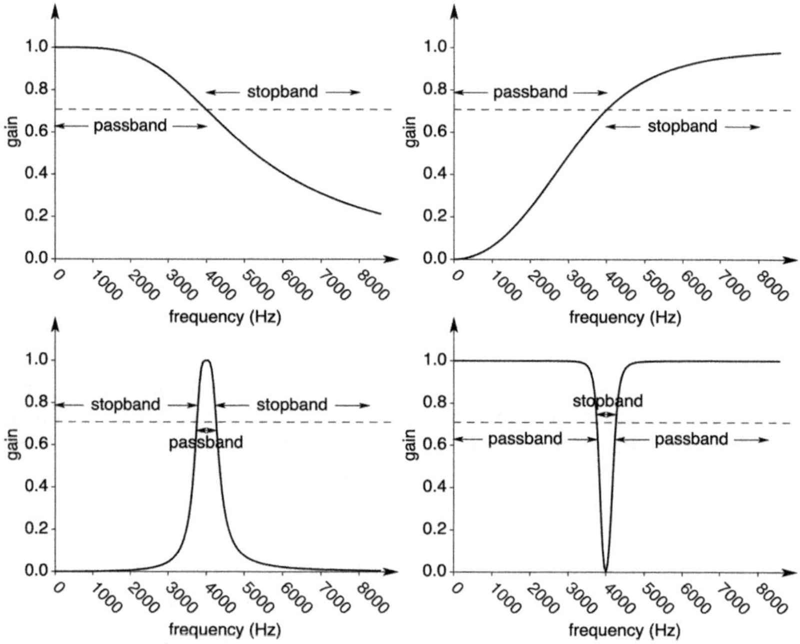

Figure 7.5: Four common filter types (clockwise from upper left): low-pass, high-pass, band-pass, band-reject. All are 2nd-order filters with cutoff or center frequencies of 4,000 Hz.

you—they are exactly like the tone knobs on a car stereo or boombox. A low-pass (also known as high-stop) filter stops, or attenuates, high frequencies while letting through low ones, while a high-pass (low-stop) filter does just the opposite.

7.2.1.1 Band-Pass and Band-Reject Filters

Band-pass and band-reject filters are basically combinations of low-pass and high-pass filters. A *band-pass* filter lets through only frequencies above a certain point and below another, so there is a *band* of frequencies that get through. A *band-reject* filter is the opposite: it stops a band of frequencies. Band-reject filters are sometimes called *notch filters*, because of the shape of their frequency response.

7.2.1.2 Low-Pass and High-Pass Filters

Low-pass and high-pass filters have a value associated with them called the *cutoff frequency*, which is the frequency where they begin “doing their thing”. So far we have been talking about *ideal*, or perfect, filters, which cut off instantly at their cutoff frequency. However, real filters are not perfect, and they can’t just stop all frequencies at a certain point. Instead, frequencies die out according to a sort of curve around the corner of their cutoff frequency. Thus, the filters in Figure 7.5 don't have right angles at the cutoff frequencies—instead they show general, more or less realistic response curves for low-pass and high-pass filters.

7.2.2 Cutoff Frequency

The cutoff frequency of a filter is defined as the point at which the signal is attenuated to 0.707 of its maximum value (which is 1.0). No, the number 0.707 was not just picked out of a hat! It turns out that the power of a signal is determined by squaring the amplitude: $0.707^2 = 0.5$. So when the amplitude of a signal is at 0.707 of its maximum value, it is at half-power. The cutoff frequency of a filter is sometimes called its *half-power point*.

7.2.3 Transition Band

The area between where a filter "turns the corner" and where it "hits the bottom" is called the *transition band*. The steepness of the slope in the transition band is important in defining the sound of a particular filter. If the slope is very steep, the filter is said to be "sharp"; conversely, if the slope is more gradual, the filter is "soft" or "gentle".

Things really get interesting when you start combining low-pass and high-pass filters to form band-pass and band-reject filters. Band-pass and band-reject filters also have transition bands and slopes, but they have two of them: one on each side. The area in the middle, where frequencies are either passed or stopped, is called the *passband* or the *stopband*. The frequency in the middle of the band is called the *center frequency*, and the width of the band is called the filter's *bandwidth*.

You can plainly see that filters can get pretty complicated, even these simple ones. By varying all these parameters (cutoff frequencies, slopes, bandwidths, etc.), we can create an enormous variety of subtractive synthetic timbres.

7.2.4 A Little More Technical: IIR and FIR Filters

Filters are often talked about as being one of two types: finite impulse response (FIR) and infinite impulse response (IIR). This sounds complicated (and can be!), so we'll just try to give a simple explanation as to the general idea of these kinds of filters.

Finite impulse response filters are those in which delays are used along with some sort of scaling. *Delays* mean that the sound that comes out at a given time uses some of the previous samples. They've been delayed and scaled before they get used.

We've talked about these filters earlier. FIRs tend to be simpler, easy to use, and easier to design than IIRs, and they are very handy for a lot of simple situations. An averaging low-pass filter, in which some number of samples are averaged and output, is an example of an FIR. A key property of FIR filters is that the output goes to zero after the maximum delay used in the filter, so the so-called filter response is finite in length.

Infinite impulse response filters are a little more complicated, because they have an added feature: feedback. You've probably seen how a microphone and speaker can have feedback: by placing the microphone in front of a speaker, you amplify what comes out and then stick it back into the system, which is amplifying what comes in, creating a sort of infinite amplification loop. Ouch! (If you're Jimi Hendrix, you can control this and make great music out of it.)

Well, IIRs are similar. Because of the feedback path, these filters can be unstable, just like feedback through a microphone, but there are filter design techniques to insure stability, so that's not a problem in practice. The feedback allows IIR filters to have an infinite response time; their output can continue to decay long after the input signal becomes zero, depending on the design.

In general, IIR filters have fewer coefficients (delays and multiplies) meaning lower computation cost for a given task, but FIR filters make it easier to achieve an arbitrary frequency response, and FIR filters can have *linear phase*, which means that all frequencies are delayed by the same amount. This is not the case with IIR filters.

Designing filters is a difficult but key activity in the field of *digital signal processing*, a rich area of study that is well beyond the range of this book (68). It is interesting to point out that, surprisingly, even though filters change the frequency content of a signal, a lot of the mathematical work done in filter design is done in the time domain, not in the frequency domain. By using things like sample averaging, delays, and feedback, one can create an extraordinarily rich variety of digital filters.

For example, the following is a simple equation for a low-pass filter. This equation just averages the last two samples of a signal (where $x[n]$ is the current sample) to produce a new sample. This equation is said to have a *one-sample delay*. You can see easily that quickly changing (that is, high-frequency) time-domain values will be "smoothed" (removed) by this equation:

$$y[n] = (x[n] + x[n-1])/2 \tag{7.1}$$

In fact, although it may look simple, this kind of filter design can be quite difficult (although extremely important). How do you know which frequencies you're

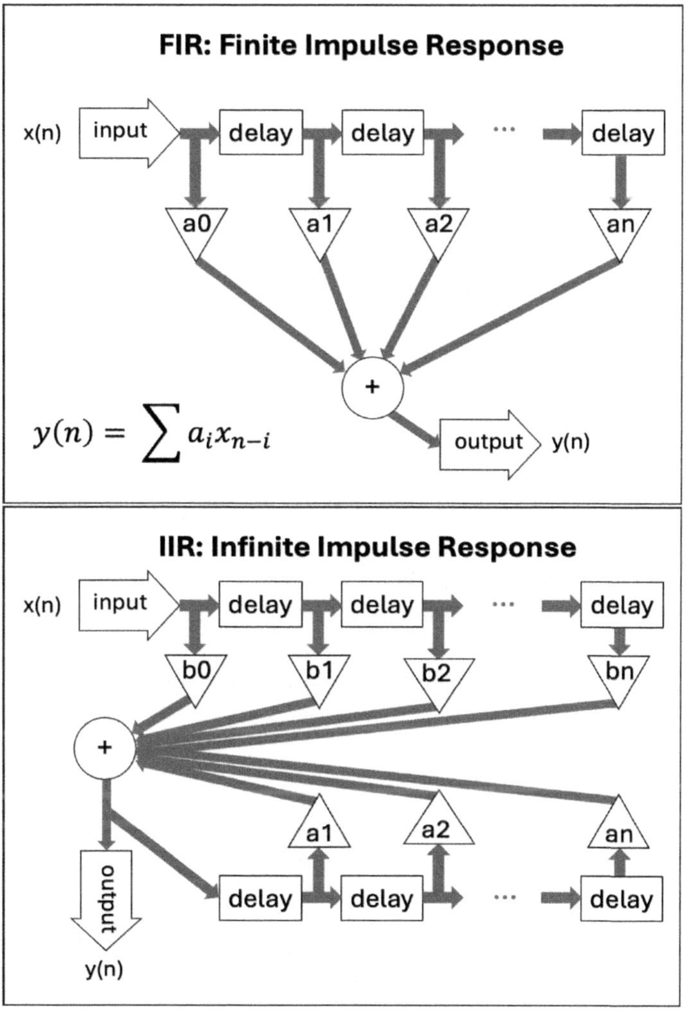

Figure 7.6: *FIR* and *IIR* filters. Filters are usually implemented in the time domain by delaying a signal and then adding weighted versions of delayed signals and the nondelayed one. These are called *finite impulse response* (FIR) filters, because what comes out uses a finite number of samples, and a sample only has a finite effect.

If you feed weighted versions of the delayed output of that process back into the signal, we create what are called *infinite impulse response* (IIR) filters. The feedback process actually allows the output to be much longer than the input.

These diagrams show typical implementations for FIR and IIR filters. Note how in the IIR diagram the output of the filter's delay is summed back into the input, causing the infinite response characteristic. That is the main difference between the two types of filters.

removing? It's not intuitive, unless you're well schooled in digital signal processing and filter theory and have some background in mathematics. The theory introduces another transform, the Laplace transform and its discrete cousin, the Z-transform, which, along with some remarkable geometry, yields a systematic approach to filter design (68).

7.2.5 Filters in Nyquist

Fortunately, you do not need to know filter design theory to use filters in Nyquist. Nyquist has an assortment of filters that will work for most purposes. The following expression applies a low-pass filter to `signal` with a cutoff frequency of `cutoff`:

```
lp(signal, cutoff)
```

Note that `cutoff` can also be a signal, allowing you to adjust the cutoff frequency over the course of the signal. Normally, `cutoff` would be a control-rate signal computed as an envelope or `pwl` function. Changing the filter cutoff frequency involves some trig functions, and Nyquist filters perform these updates at the sample rate of the control signal, so if the control signal sample rate is low (typically 1/20 of the audio sample rate), you save a lot of expensive computation. All of these built-in filters are IIR filters. For those able to design their own FIR filters, Nyquist has a convolution function to implement them.

Some other filters in Nyquist include:

- `hp` - a high-pass filter.
- `reson` - a low-pass filter with a resonance (emphasis) at the cutoff frequency and a *bandwidth* parameter to control how narrow is the resonant peak.
- `areson` - the opposite of `reson`; adding the two together recreates the original signal, so `areson` is a sort of high-pass filter with a notch at the cutoff frequency.
- `comb` - a comb filter has a set of harmonically spaced resonances and can be very interesting when applied to noisy signals.
- `eq-lowshelf`, `eq-highshelf`, and `eq-band` filters are useful for generally shaping spectra the way you would with a parametric equalizer.

- `lowpass2`, `lowpass4`, `lowpass6`, `lowpass8`, `highpass2`, `highpass4`, `highpass6`, and `highpass8` are optimized low-pass and high-pass filters with different transition slopes. The digits refer to the *order* of the filter: second order filters have a 12 dB-per-octave slope, fourth have 24 dB-per-octave slopes, etc.

All of these are described in greater detail in the *Nyquist Reference Manual.*

7.2.6 Filter Summary

Filters are essential building blocks for sound synthesis and manipulation. The effect of a filter in the frequency domain is to multiply the spectrum by a *filter response*. Most filters are actually implemented in the *time domain* using a discrete sample-by-sample process applied to a stream of samples, which eliminates the problems of dealing with finite-sized FFT frames, and is also usually faster than performing FFTs.

Chapter 8

Spectral Processing

Topics Discussed: FFT, Inverse FFT, Overlap Add, Reconstruction from Spectral Frames

8.1 FFT Analysis and Reconstruction

Previously, we have learned about the spectral domain in the context of sampling theory, filters, and the Fourier transform, in particular the fast Fourier transform, which we used to compute the spectral centroid. In this chapter, we focus on the details of converting from a time-domain representation to a frequency domain representation, operating on the frequency-domain representation, and then reconstructing the time-domain signal.

We emphasized earlier that filters are *not* typically implemented in the frequency domain, in spite of our theoretical understanding that filtering is effectively multiplication in the frequency domain. This is because we cannot compute a Fourier transform on an infinite signal or even a very long one. Therefore, our only option is to use short-time transforms as we did with computing the spectral centroid. That *could* be used for filtering, but there are problems associated with using overlapping short-time transforms. Generally, we do not use the FFT for filtering.

Nevertheless, operations on spectral representations are interesting for analysis and synthesis. In the following sections, we will review the Fourier transform, consider the problems of long-time analysis/synthesis using short-time transforms, and look at spectral processing in Nyquist. For more in-depth and technical information, see *Spectral Audio Signal Processing* Julius O. Smith III (45) and *Spectral Music Design: A Computational Approach* (51).

DOI: 10.1201/9781003782711-8

8.1.1 Review of FFT Analysis

Here again are the equations for the Fourier transform in the continuous and discrete forms:

Continuous Fourier transform
Real part:

$$R(\omega) = \int_{-\infty}^{\infty} f(t)\cos(\omega t)dt \tag{8.1}$$

Imaginary part:

$$X(\omega) = -\int_{-\infty}^{\infty} f(t)\sin(\omega t)dt \tag{8.2}$$

Discrete Fourier Transform
Real part:

$$R_k = \sum_{i=0}^{N-1} x_i \cos(2\pi ki/N) \tag{8.3}$$

Imaginary part:

$$X_k = -\sum_{i=0}^{N-1} x_i \sin(2\pi ki/N) \tag{8.4}$$

Recall from the discussion of the spectral centroid that when we take FFTs in Nyquist, the spectra appear as floating point arrays. As shown in Figure 8.1, the first element of the array (index 0) is the DC (0 Hz) component,[1] and then we have alternating cosine and sine terms all the way up to the top element of the array, which is the cosine term of the Nyquist frequency. To visualize this in a different way, in Figure 8.2, we represent the basis functions (cosine and sine functions that are multiplied by the signal), and the numbers here are the indices in the array. The second element of the array (the gray curve labeled 1), is a single period of cosine across the duration of the analysis frame. The next element in the array (the black curve labeled 2) is a single sine function over the length of the array. Proceeding from there, we have two cycles of cosine, two cycles of sine. Finally, the Nyquist frequency term has $n/2$ cycles of a cosine, forming alternating samples of +1, –1, +1, –1, +1, ... (The sine terms at frequency 0 and the Nyquist frequency $N/2$ are omitted because $\sin(2\pi ki/N) = 0$ if $k = 0$ or $k = N/2$.)

[1]This component comes from the particular case where $\omega = 0$, so $\cos \omega t = 1$, and the integral is effectively computing the average value of the signal. In the electrical world where we can describe electrical power as AC (alternating current, voltage oscillates up and down, e.g., at 60 Hz) or DC (direct current, voltage is constant, e.g., from a 12-volt car battery), the average value of the signal is the DC component or DC offset, and the rest is "AC".

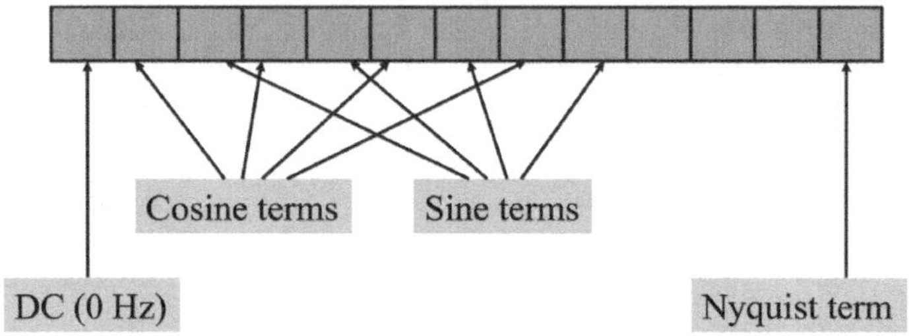

Figure 8.1: The spectrum as a floating point array in Nyquist. Note that the real and imaginary parts are interleaved, with a real/imaginary pair for each frequency bin. The first and last bin have only one number (the real part) because the imaginary part for these bins is zero.

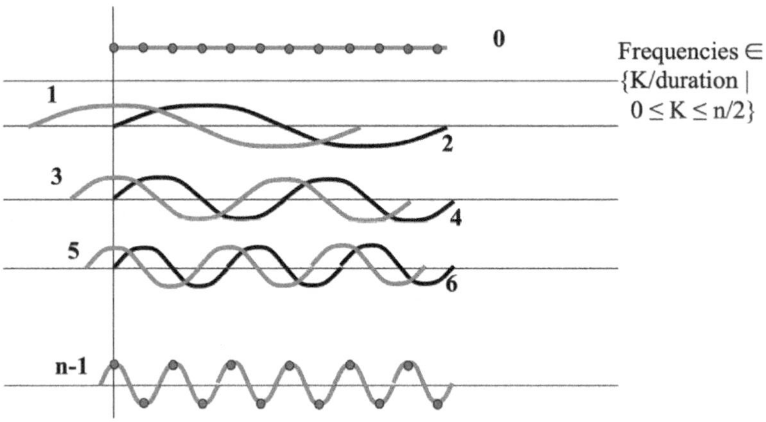

Figure 8.2: The so-called basis functions for the Fourier transform labeled with bin numbers. To compute each Fourier coefficient, form the dot product of the basis function and the signal. You can think of this as the weighted average of the signal where the basis function provides the weights. Note that all basis functions, and thus the frequencies they select from the input signal, are harmonics: multiples of a fundamental frequency that has a period equal to the size of the FFT. Thus, if the N input points represent 1/10 second of sound, the bins will represent 10 Hz, 20 Hz, 30 HZ, ..., etc. Note that we show sin functions, but the final imaginary (sin) coefficient of the FFT is negated (see Equation 8.4.)

Following the definition of the Fourier transform, these *basis functions* are multiplied by the input signal, the products are summed, and the sums are the output of the transform, the so-called Fourier *coefficients*. Each one of the basis functions can be viewed as a frequency analyzer—it picks out a particular frequency from the input signal. The frequencies selected by the basis functions are $K/duration$, where index $K \in \{0, 1, ..., n/2\}$.

Knowing the frequencies of basis functions is very important for interpreting or operating on spectra. For example, if the analysis window size is 512 samples, the sample rate is 44,100 Hz, and value at index 5 of the spectrum is large, what strong frequency does that indicate? The duration is $512/44100 = 0.01161$ s, and from Figure 8.2, we can see there are 3 periods within the analysis window, so $K = 3$, and the frequency is $3/0.01161 = 258.398$ Hz. A large value at array index 5 indicates a strong component near 258.398 Hz.

Now, you may ask, what about some near-by frequency, say, 300 Hz? The next analysis frequency would be 344.531 Hz at $K = 4$, so what happens to frequencies between 258.398 and 344.531 Hz? It turns out that each basis function is not a perfect "frequency selector" because of the finite number of samples considered. Thus, intermediate frequencies (such as 300 Hz) will have some correlation with more than one basis function, and the discrete spectrum will have more than one non-zero term. The highest magnitude coefficients will be the ones whose basis function frequencies are nearest that of the sinusoid(s) being analyzed.

8.1.2 Perfect Reconstruction

Is it possible to go from the time domain to the spectral domain and back to the time domain again without any loss or distortion? One property that works in our favor is that the FFT is information-preserving. There is a Fast Inverse short-time discrete Fourier transform, or IFFT for short, that converts Fourier coefficients back into the original signal. Thus, one way to convert to the spectral domain and back, without loss, is shown in Figure 8.3.

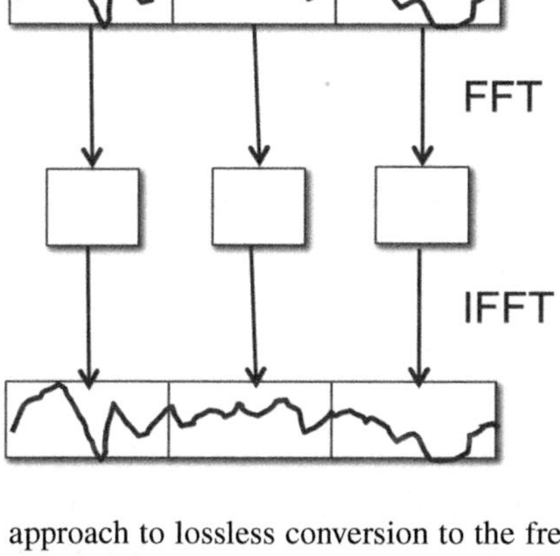

Figure 8.3: One (flawed) approach to lossless conversion to the frequency domain and back to the time domain. This works fine unless you do any manipulation in the frequency domain, in which case discontinuities will create horrible artifacts.

In general, each short-time spectrum is called a *spectral frame* or an *analysis frame*.

The problem with Figure 8.3 is that if we change any coefficients in the spectrum, it is likely that the reconstructed signal will have discontinuities at the boundaries between one analysis frame and the next. You may recall from our early discussion on splicing that cross-fades are important to avoid clicks due to discontinuities. In fact, if there are periodic discontinuities (every analysis frame), a distinct buzz will likely be heard.

Just as we used envelopes and cross-fades to eliminate clicks in other situations, we can use envelopes to smooth each analysis frame before taking the FFT, and we can apply the smoothing envelope again after the IFFT to ensure there are no discontinuities in the signal. These analysis frames are usually called *windows* and the envelope is called a *windowing function*.

Figure 8.4 illustrates how overlapping windows are used to obtain groups of samples for analysis. From the figure, you would (correctly) expect that ideal window functions would be smooth and sum to 1. One period of the cosine function raised by 1 (so the range is from 0 to 2) is a good example of such a function. Raised cosine windows (also called Hann or Hanning windows, see Figure 8.5) sum to one, if they overlap by 50%.

The technique of adding smoothed overlapped intervals of sound is related to granular synthesis. When the goal is to produce a continuous sound (as opposed to a turbulent granular texture), this approach is called *overlap-add*.

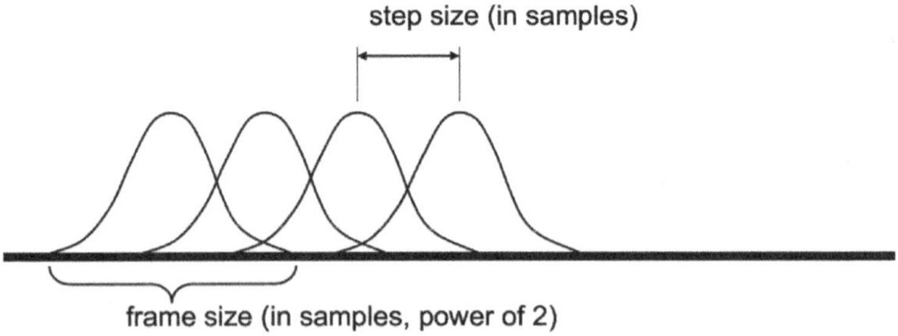

Figure 8.4: Multiple overlapping Windows. The distance between windows is the step size.

But windows are applied twice: Once *before* FFT analysis because smoothing the signal eliminates some undesirable artifacts from the computed spectrum, and once *after* the IFFT to eliminate discontinuities. If we window twice, do the

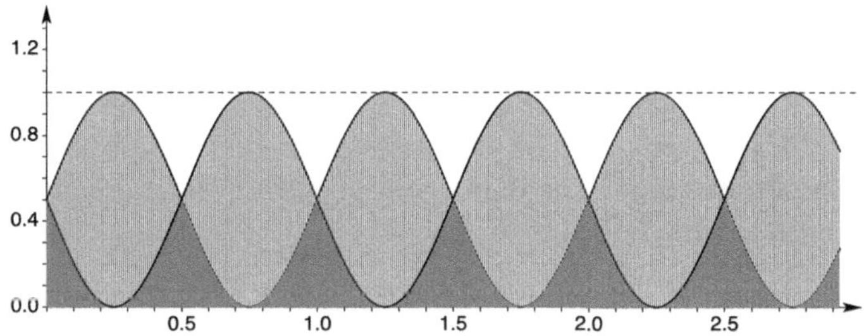

Figure 8.5: The raised cosine, Hann, or Hanning window, is named after the mathematician von Hann. This figure shows multiple Hann windows with 50% overlap, which sum to 1. But that's not enough! In practice, we multiply by a smoothing window twice: once before the FFT and once after the IFFT. See the text on how to resolve this problem.

envelopes still sum to one? Well, no, but if we change the overlap to 75% (i.e., each window steps by 1/4 window length), then the sum of the windows is one![2]

With windowing, we can now alter spectra more-or-less arbitrarily, then reconstruct the time-domain signal, and the result will be smooth and pretty well behaved.

For example, a simple noise reduction technique begins by converting a signal to the frequency domain. Since noise has a broad spectrum, we expect the contribution of noise to the FFT to be a small magnitude at every frequency. Any magnitude that is below some threshold is likely to be "pure noise", so we set it to zero. Any magnitude above threshold is likely to be, at least in part, a signal we want to keep, and we can hope the signal is strong enough to mask any noise near the same frequency. We then simply convert these altered spectra back into the time domain. Most of the noise will be removed and most of the desired signal will be retained.

8.2 Spectral Processing

In this section, we describe how to use Nyquist to process spectra.

8.2.1 *From Sound to Spectra*

Nyquist has a built-in type for sound together with complex and rich interfaces, however, there is nothing like that in Nyquist for spectra, which are represented simply as arrays of floats representing *spectral frames*. Thus, we have to design

[2]The proof is straightforward using trigonometric identities, in particular $\sin^2(t) + \cos^2(t) = 1$. If you struggled to learn trig identities for high-school math class but never had any use for them, this proof will give you a great feeling of fulfillment.

an architecture for processing spectra in Nyquist (Figure 8.6). In this figure, data flows right-to-left. We first take input sounds, extract overlapping windows, and apply the FFT to these windows to get spectral frames. We then turn those spectral frames back into time-domain frames and samples, and overlap add them to produce an output sound. The data chain goes from time domain to spectral domain and back to time domain.

In terms of control flow, everything is done in a lazy or demand-driven manner, which means we start with the output on the left. When we need some sound samples, we generate a request to the object providing samples. It generates a request for a spectral frame, which it needs to do an IFFT. The request goes to the FFT iterator, which pulls samples from the source sound, performs the FFT, and returns the spectrum to SND-IFFT.

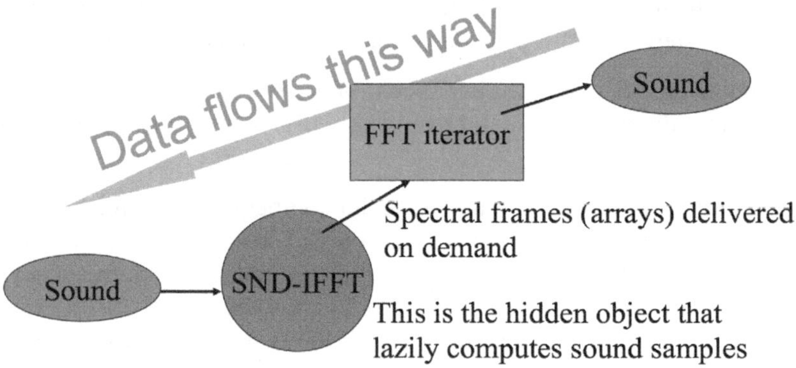

Figure 8.6: Spectral processing in Nyquist. Dependencies of sounds, unit generators, and objects are indicated by arrows. Computation is demand driven, and demand flows left-to-right following pointers to signal sources. Signal data flows right-to-left from signal sources to output signals after processing.

Given this simple architecture, we can insert a spectral processing object between SND-IFFT and FFT iterator to alter the spectra before converting them back to the time domain. We could even chain multiple spectral processors in sequence. Nyquist represents the FFT iterator in Figure 8.6 as an object, but SAL does not support object-oriented programming, so Nyquist provides a procedural interface for SAL programmers.

The following is a simple template for spectral processing in SAL. You can find more extensive commented code in the "fftsal" extension of Nyquist (use the menu in the NyquistIDE to open the extension manager to find and install it). In particular, see comments in the files `lib/fftsal/spectral-process.lsp` and in `runtime/spectral-analysis.lsp`.

To get started, we use the `sa-init` function to return an object that will generate a sequence of FFT frames by analyzing an input audio file:

```
set sa = sa-init(input: "./rpd-cello.wav",
                 fft-dur: 4096 / 44100.0,
                 skip-period: 512 / 44100.0,
                 window: :hann)
```

Next, we create a spectral processing object that pulls frames as needed from `sa`, applies the function `processing-fn` to each spectrum, and returns the resulting spectrum. The two zeros passed to `sp-init` are additional state we have added here just for example. The `processing-fn` must take at least two parameters: the spectral analysis object `sa`, and the spectrum (array of floats) to be modified. You can have additional parameters for state that is preserved from one frame to the next. In this case, `processing-fn` will have `p1` and `p2`, corresponding in number to the two zeros passed to `sp-init`.

```
set sp = sp-init(sa, quote(processing-fn), 0, 0)
```

Since SAL does not have objects, but one might want object-like behaviors, the spectral processing system is carefully implemented with "stateful" object-oriented processing in mind. The idea is that we pass state variables into the processing function and the function returns the final values of the state variables so that they can be passed back to the function on its next invocation. The definition of `processing-fn` looks like this:

```
function processing-fn(sa, frame, p1, p2)
  begin
    ... Process frame here ...
    set frame[0] = 0.0  ; simple example: remove DC
    return list(frame, p1 + 1, p2 + length(frame))
  end
```

In this case, note that `processing-fn` works with state represented by `p1` and `p2`. This state is passed into the function each time it is called. The function returns a *list* consisting of the altered spectral frame and the state values, which are saved and passed back on the next call. Here, we update `p1` to maintain a count of frames, and `p2` to maintain a count of samples processed so far. These values are not used here. A more realistic example using state variables is you might want to compute the spectral difference between each frame and the next. In that case, you could initialize `p1` to an array of zeros and in `processing-fn`, copy the elements of `frame` to `p1`. Then, `processing-fn` will be called with the current frame in `frame` as well as the previous frame in `p1`.

Getting back to our example, to run the spectral processing, you write the following:

```
play sp-to-sound(sp)
```

The `sp-to-sound` function takes a spectral processing object created by `sp-init`, calls it to produce a sequence of frames, converts the frames back to the time domain, applies a windowing function, and performs an overlap add, resulting in a sound.

Chapter 9

Vocal and Spectral Models

Topics Discussed: Source Filter Models, Linear Predictive Coding, Vocoder, VOSIM, FOF Synthesis, Phase Vocoder, MacAulay-Quatieri (MQ) Synthesis, Spectral Modeling Synthesis (SMS)

9.1 Introduction: Source-Filter Models

This chapter is about creating sounds of the human voice. You have undoubtedly heard speech synthesizers, sometimes called text-to-speech systems. Musicians have adopted speech synthesis algorithms to music and created some new algorithms used exclusively for music (13).

Why speech and singing? Vocal sounds are very important in daily life, and we are very sensitive to the sound of the human voice. Singing synthesis and vocal sounds are often used in computer music because they grab our attention. The tension formed when a sound is recognizably both human and not human at the same time makes for interesting listening. We are going to learn about how voice sounds are made, what are their characteristics and also a number of different algorithms for achieving those kinds of results.

We will begin this story of human voice and singing synthesis with the introduction to *source-filter models*.

DOI: 10.1201/9781003782711-9

9.1.1 How The Voice Works

Figure 9.1 is a diagram of a human head, taken at a cross-section so that we can see the air passageways and how the voice works. At the bottom of the diagram are the vocal folds (commonly called *vocal cords*), which is the structure that vibrates when you push air through the larynx. The waveform at the vocal fold is a series of pulses formed as the air passage opens and closes. The right side of Figure 9.1 shows roughly what the waveform looks like. Pulses from the vocal folds are rounded, and we have some control over both the shape and frequency of the pulses by using our muscles.

These pulses go into a resonant chamber that is formed by the oral cavity (the mouth) and the nasal cavity. The shape of the oral cavity can be manipulated extensively by the tongue and lips. Although you are usually unaware of your tongue and lips while speaking, you can easily attend to them as you produce different vocal sounds to get some idea of their function in speech production and singing.

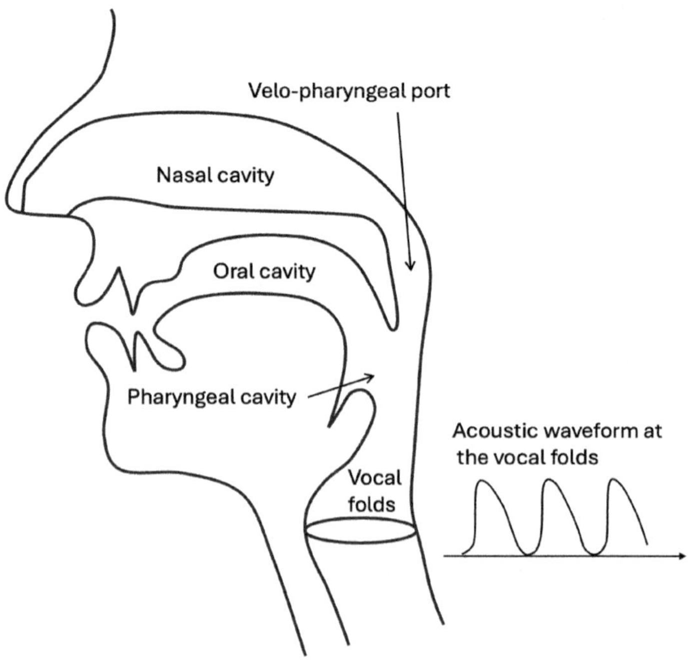

Figure 9.1: Diagram of a human head to illustrate how the voice works. The waveform at right is roughly what the "input" sound looks like coming from the vocal folds.

One of the most fundamental concepts of speech production is the vowel. Vowels are sounds we can sustain, and include "a, e, i, o, u". When speaking these vowels with same pitch and volume, what changes is the spectrum. In fact, the main characteristic of the spectral changes between different vowels are changes in *resonances*, which are narrow ranges of frequencies that are boosted. The main characteristic of a resonance is the center frequency, and the resonances with the two lowest frequencies are the most important ones in determining the vowel we hear. These two resonances are also called *formants*.

If we plot the first formant frequency versus the second formant frequency for different vowel sounds, we can get the picture shown in Figure 9.2. For example, if the first formant is a little below 500 Hz, and the second formant is around 1,500 Hz, we will get vowel sound *IR* as in "sir". On the other hand, if we increase those frequencies to around 800 Hz for the first formant and close to 2,000 Hz for the second one, we will get an *A* as in "sat", which is perceived quite differently. After plotting all of the vowels, we see that vowels form regions in the space of formant frequencies. We control those frequencies by changing the shape of our vocal tract to make vowel sounds.

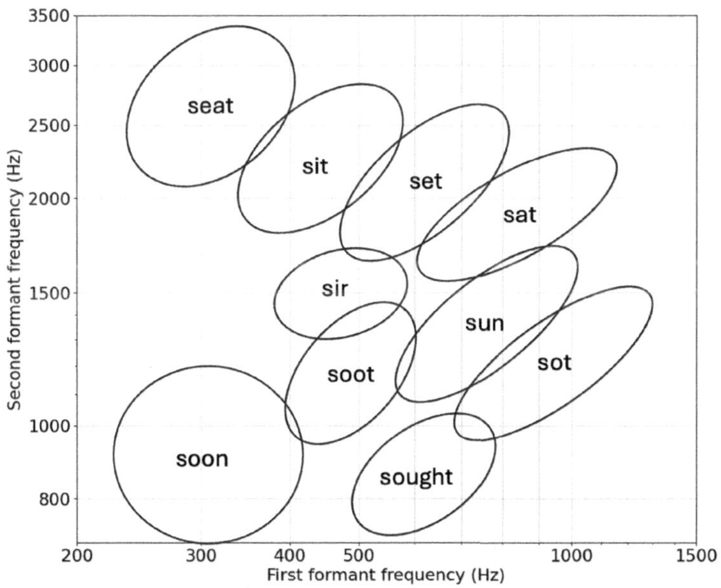

Figure 9.2: Frequency plots for vowels.

9.1.2 Source-Filter Models

The above mechanism leads to a very common and simple model which we can build for voice synthesis. It is called the *source-filter model*, which describes sound production as a *source* (e.g., the vocal folds and their production of pulses, as shown in Figure 9.1) and a *filter*, which is mainly the effect of resonances (formants) created by the vocal tract (see Figure 9.3).

The *source* in most voice synthesis systems is actually a choice of either a noise signal (whispered/unvoiced sound, where the vocal folds are not vibrating, used for sounds like "sss"), or a pulse train of periodic impulses creating *voiced* speech as is normal for vowels. The selected source input goes into the vocal tract filter, which is characterized by the resonances or formants that we saw in the previous paragraphs.

Notice that the frequency of the source (i.e., the rate of pulses) determines the pitch of the voiced sound, and this is independent of the resonant frequencies (formant frequencies). The source spectrum for voiced sounds is a harmonic series with many strong harmonics arising from the periodic pulses. The effect of filtering is to multiply the spectrum by the filter response, which boosts harmonics at or near the formant frequencies.

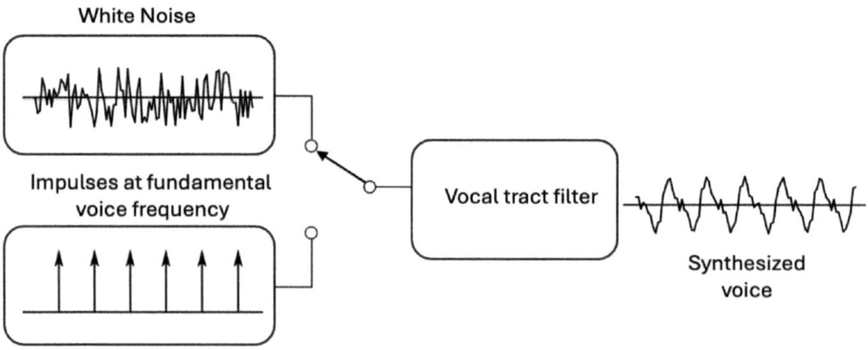

Figure 9.3: Framework of source-filter models.

9.2 Linear Predictive Coding (LPC)

In the previous section, we have learned how the source-filter model is used to model voice and produce voice sounds. Now we are going to talk about a specific speech analysis/synthesis method that can be used to construct the filter part of the source-filter model. This method is called *Linear Predictive Coding* (LPC) (29).

9.2.1 LPC Basics

The basic model of LPC is shown as the simple equation below:

$$S_n = \sum_{i=1}^{p} a_i S_{n-i}.$$

It means predicting next sample S_n as a weighted sum of past samples, where the weights are arbitrary a_i, previous samples are S_{n-i}, and p is the number of previous samples that we look at. This formulation gives rise to an *allpole* filter; in other words, the weighted sum of the samples is the filter, and the response of this filter consists of resonant peaks. We can analyze real signals to estimate the a_i. LPC analysis finds the filter that best approximates the signal spectrum. We typically choose p to be a somewhat small value, normally less than 20, so that the filter response can at best be modeled as a smooth function with a few peaks (resonances). If instead we use hundreds of coefficients, the analysis might treat each harmonic as a very sharp resonance, but we prefer not to allow this since in the source-filter model, the harmonics are produced by the source. Thus, we try to restrict the detail in the filter approximation so that it captures the fairly broad and smooth resonant formants, but not the exact wave shape or other details that come from the spectrum of the source.

9.2.2 LPC Analysis

In LPC analysis, we divide an input signal into short segments, and we estimate the a_i coefficients that minimize the overall error in predicting the S_n samples of the signal. We will skip the details of this optimization problem.

As shown in Figure 9.4, the physical analogy of LPC is a tube with varying cross-section. Think about the vocal tract: the vocal folds inject pulses into a tube, which is the throat, mouth and all the way to the mouth opening. It is not a simple tube and there is also the nasal cavity that makes a difference in the sound of your voice. (If you hold your nose and talk, you can hear the importance of the nasal cavity!) However, here we only consider a simple model: putting the sound through the tube and varying the cross-section of the tube in the same way that your tongue and mouth are varying the cross-section of your vocal tract.

Figure 9.4: The physical analogy of LPC: a tube with varying cross-section.

Figure 9.5 shows another example where the vocal tract is modeled as a tube. We start with the real vocal tract. Then, we construct a tube (on the right) by cutting layers of plastic such that the cross-section of the tube matches the cross-section of the human vocal tract. If we put a source (such as a duck call) up to this tube and listen to what comes out, the sound will be the *AH* vowel, matching the human's sound.

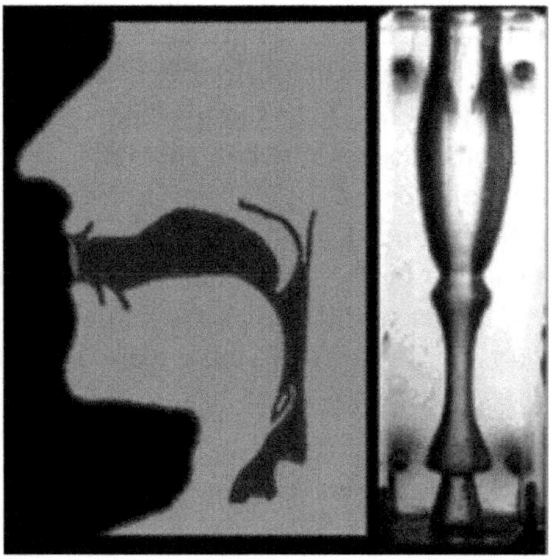

Figure 9.5: Acoustic Tube Producing "AH" (credit: www.exploratorium.edu/exhibits/vocal_vowels/vocal_vowels.html).

Another important point here is that we are not talking about a fixed shape but a shape that is rapidly changing, which makes speech possible. We are making sequences of vowel sounds and consonants by rapidly moving the tongue and mouth as well as changing the source sound. To apply LPC to speech, we analyze speech sounds in short segments (and as usual, we call short analysis segments *frames*). This is analogous to short-time windows in the STFT. At each LPC analysis frame, we re-estimate the geometry of the tube, which means we re-estimate the coefficient values that determine the filter. Frames give rise to changing coefficients, which model changes in tube geometry (or vocal tract shape).

LPC actually creates an inverse filter. Applying the inverse filter to a vocal sound yields a *residual* that sounds like the source signal. The residual may either be an estimate of glottal pulses, making the residual useful for estimating the pitch of the source, or noise-like.

Taking all this into account, an overall LPC analysis system is shown in Figure 9.6. We have an input signal and do formant analysis, which is the estimation of coefficients that can reconstruct the filter part of the source-filter model. After applying the result filter of the formant analysis to the input signal, we can get the residual and then do further analysis to detect the pitch. We can also do analysis to see if the input is periodic or not so that it gives us a decision of whether the input is voiced or unvoiced. Finally, we can compute the RMS amplitude of the signal. So, for each frame of LPC analysis, we get not only the filter part of the source-filter model, but also estimated pitch, the amplitude, and whether the source is voiced or unvoiced.

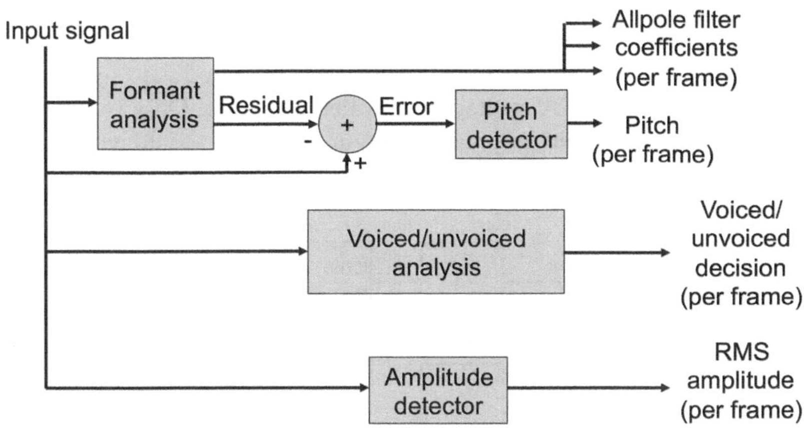

Figure 9.6: Diagram of LPC.

9.2.3 *Musical Applications*

There are many musical applications of voice sounds and source-filter models. One common application pursued by many composers is to replace the source with some other sound. For example, rather than having a pitched source or noise source based on the human voice, you can apply human sounding formants to a recording of an orchestra to make it sound like speech. This idea of taking elements from two different sounds and putting them together is sometimes called "cross-synthesis". You can also "warp" the filter frequencies to get human-like but not really human filters. Also, you can modify the source and LPC coefficients to perform time stretching, slowing speech down, or speeding up.

9.3 Vocoder

The Vocoder is related to LPC in that it makes a low-dimensional (i.e., smooth, very approximate) estimation of the spectral shape. Thus, formants can be captured and modeled. The main idea of the vocoder is that the input signal is divided into frequency "channels" and bandpass filters are used to isolate each channel and measure the amplitude in that channel. An FFT can be used since it acts as a bank of bandpass filters, but vocoders are also implemented in analog hardware with electronic filters, or you could use a bank of digital bandpass filters instead of the FFT (41, 15).

Vocoders are often used for cross-synthesis where the formants are estimated using one sound source (the "modulator") and then applied to a second sound source (the "carrier"). For example, one could analyze a voice to extract formants and apply them to chords played on a keyboard. Figure 9.7 illustrates a vocoder in this cross-synthesis application. The "Env Follow" box takes a filtered signal and extracts an amplitude "envelope" that is used to modulate the amplitude of the carrier using a "VCA"-voltage-controlled amplifier. Only two frequency bands are shown, but a typical vocoder (even in hardware) would have 8 or more channels.

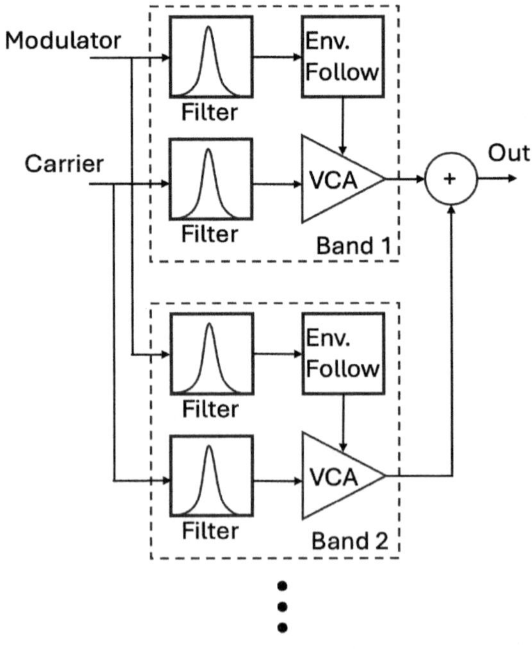

Figure 9.7: Vocoder.

9.4 VOSIM

VOSIM is a simple and fun synthesis method inspired by the voice. VOSIM is also fast and efficient. It was developed in the 70s by Kaegi and Tempelaars (46). The basic idea of VOSIM is to think about what happens in the *time domain* when a glottal pulse (pulse coming through the vocal folds) hits a resonance (a formant resonance in the vocal tract). The answer is that you get an exponentially damped sinusoid. In speech production, we have multiple formants. When a pulse enters a complex filter with multiple resonances, we get the superposition of many damped sinusoids, one for each resonance. The exact details are influenced by the shape of the pulse. VOSIM is the first of several time-domain models for speech synthesis that we will consider.

9.4.1 VOSIM Parameters

VOSIM uses a pulse train of sin^2 pulses (that is not a footnote, it means we *square* the sinusoid. Doing so doubles the pulse frequency and makes the signal non-negative.) The pulses diminish in amplitude. Figure 9.8 shows one period of VOSIM. The parameters of VOSIM are: an initial amplitude A, a period T, a decay factor b (not a continuous decay but each pulse is the previous one multiplied by a factor b), the number of pulses N, and a duration of M silence that follows the pulses. As you can see in Figure 9.8, the result is at least *somewhat* like a decaying sinusoid, and this gives an approximation of a pulse filtered by a single resonance. The fundamental frequency (establishing the pitch) is determined by the entire period, which is $NT+M$ and the resonant frequency is $1/T$, so we expect the harmonics near $1/T$ to be stronger.

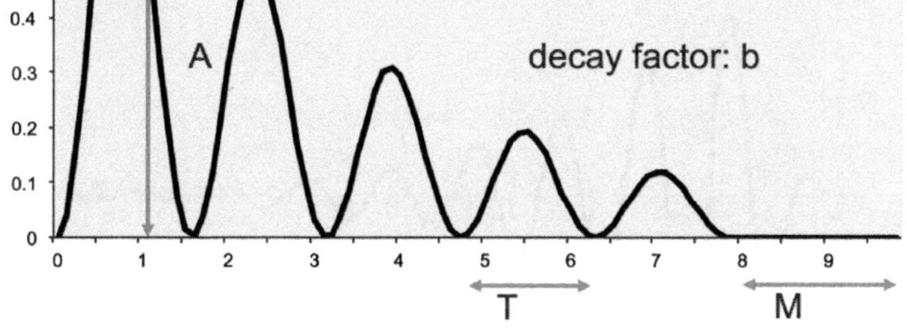

Figure 9.8: Diagram of VOSIM.

9.4.2 VOSIM Application

In the original VOSIM paper, Tempelaars used various "delta" or "increment" parameters so that the continuous parameters T, M, and b could change over time. This was probably just a simplification over using more general envelopes to control change over time. The `vosim` extension in Nyquist (open the Extension Manager in the NyquistIDE) contains some code and examples.

9.5 FOF Synthesis

FOF is a French acronym for "Formant Wave Function" (Synthesis). Like VOSIM, FOF is a time-domain approach to creating formants and speech-like sounds (79). Compared to VOSIM, FOF can be seen as a more sophisticated and more accurate model of a pulse train filtered by a resonant filter. Instead of the sine-squared pulses of VOSIM, FOF uses a sinusoid with an exponential decay (see Figure 9.9), and instead of just N pulses of the decaying resonant frequency, FOF allows the sinusoid to decay to a very small amplitude. This might result in overlapping decaying sinusoids (recall that in VOSIM, N decaying pulses are followed by M seconds of silence before the next pulse, so pulses do not overlap). This makes the implementation of FOF more difficult, and we will describe the implementation below.

One final detail about FOF is that the decaying sinusoid has an initial smooth rise time. The rise time gives some additional control over the resulting spectrum, as shown in Figure 9.10.

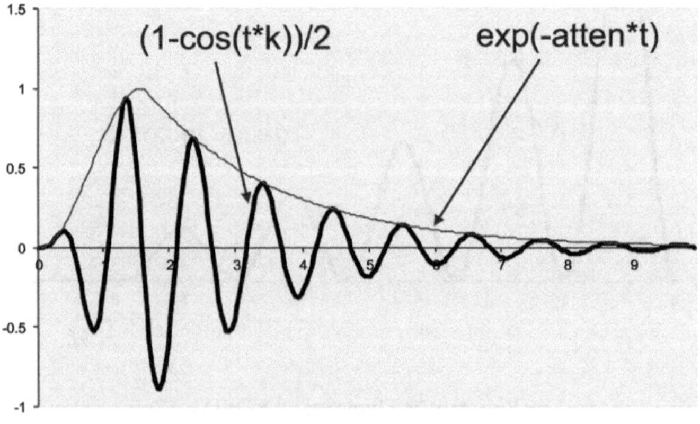

Figure 9.9: FOF.

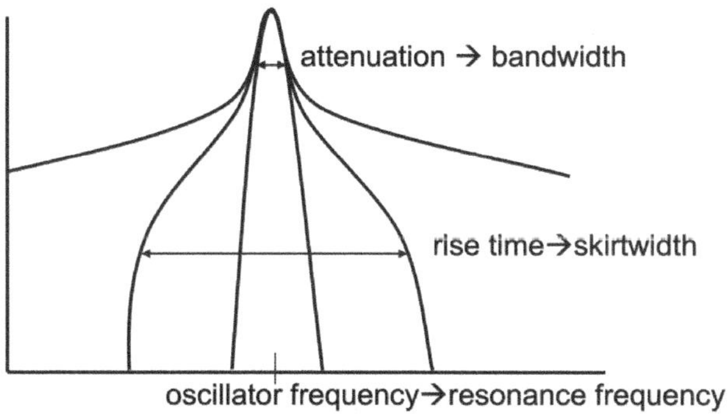

Figure 9.10: FOF in the frequency domain.

9.5.1 *FOF Analysis*

One of the advantages of FOF synthesis is that FOF parameters can be obtained automatically. The basic approach is to analyze the spectrum of a sound with an FFT. Then, analyse the shape of the FFT to detect formants. Use a FOF generator for each formant. If the spectrum indicates many harmonics, the first harmonic or the spacing between harmonics can be used as the fundamental period.

Since analysis can be performed using any spectrum, FOF is not limited to voice synthesis, but has been used for a wide range of sounds.

9.5.2 *FOF Synthesis*

Consider the FOF signal shown in Figure 9.9. This represents the response of a single formant to a single impulse—essentially a grain. Let's assume we have an *FOF generator* that can create this grain, probably using an envelope generator for the onset, a sine oscillator for the main signal, an exponential decay generator, and multipliers to combine them.

To model a periodic pulse, we need a pool of these FOF generators. We allocate one for each formant at every pulse period and release the generators back to the pool when their output decays to a negligible value. The size of the pool depends on the amount of overlap (longer decays and higher fundamental frequencies mean more overlap), so the implementation may need to make the pool size dynamically expandable or simply allocate every FOF generator from the general memory heap.

Figure 9.11 illustrates a collection of FOF "grains": at each pulse period (the fundamental frequency), there is one grain for each formant. The overlapping grains from FOF generators are summed to form a single output signal.

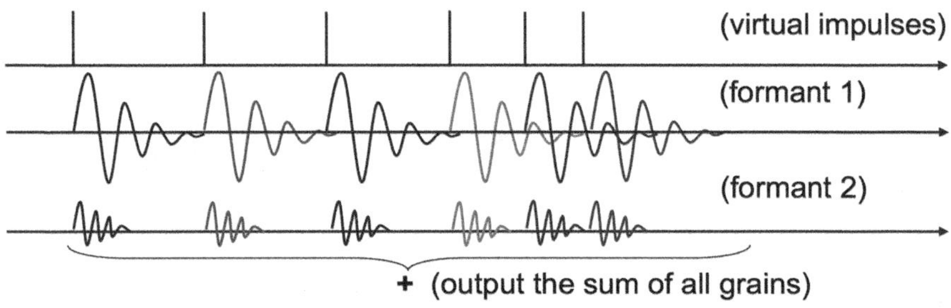

Example: Jean-Baptiste Barriere, *Chreode I*,
`https://www.youtube.com/watch?v=5AEFhybYrPg#t=128`

Figure 9.11: FOF synthesis.

9.6 Phase Vocoder

The Phase Vocoder is not really a speech synthesis method but it is often used to manipulate speech signals. The main assumption of the phase vocoder is that input sounds consist of fairly steady sinusoidal partials, there are relatively few partials and they are well-separated in frequency. If that is the case, then we can use the FFT to separate the partials into different bins (different coefficients) of the discrete spectrum. Each frequency bin is assigned an amplitude and phase. A signal is reconstructed using the Inverse FFT (IFFT) (30, 50, 71).

The main attraction of the phase vocoder is that by changing the spacing of analysis frames, the reconstructed signal can be made to play faster or slower, but without pitch changes because the partial frequencies stay the same. Time stretching without pitch change also permits pitch change without time stretching! This may seem contradictory, but the technique is simple: play the sound faster or slower (by resampling to a new sample rate) to make the pitch go up or down. This changes the speed as well, so use a phase vocoder to change the altered speed back to the original speed. Now you have pitch change without speed change, and of course you can have any combination or even time-variable pitch and speed.

When successive FFT frames are used to reconstruct signals, there is the potential that partials in one frame will be out of phase with partials in the next frame and some cancellation will occur where the frames overlap. This should not be a problem if the signal is simply analyzed and reconstructed with no manipulation, but if we want to achieve a speed-up or slow-down of the reconstructed signal, then the partials can become out of phase.

In the phase vocoder, we use phase measurements to shift the phase of partials in each frame to match the phase in the previous frame so that cancellation does not occur. This tends to be more pleasing because it avoids the somewhat buzzy sound of partials being amplitude-modulated at the FFT frame rate. In return for eliminating the frame-rate discontinuities, the phase vocoder often smears out transients (by shifting phases more-or-less randomly), resulting in a sort of fuzzy or smeared quality, especially if frames are long. As we often see (and hear), there is a time-frequency uncertainty principle at play: shorter frames give better transient (time) behavior, and longer frames give better reproduction of sustained timbres due to better frequency resolution.

9.7 McAulay-Quatieri (MQ) Synthesis

McAulay and Quatieri developed a speech compression technique where the signal is decomposed into *time-varying* as well as amplitude-varying sinusoids (58). This differs from the phase vocoder mainly in that with the phase vocoder, we assume all sinusoids are fixed in frequency and match the FFT bin frequencies.[1] In contrast, MQ analysis tracks peaks from analysis frame to analysis frame and creates a description in which sinusoids can change frequency dramatically. The analysis for MQ is quite different from phase vocoder analysis. Reconstruction is also different and relies upon a bank of sinusoid oscillators with frequency and amplitude controls. This is just additive synthesis using sinusoids.

With MQ's additive-synthesis representation, time stretching and frequency shifting are easily accomplished just by scaling the amplitude and frequency control functions. The reconstruction does not involve the IFFT or overlapping windows, so there are no problems with frames or phase discontinuities, i.e., no "buzz" at the frame rate.

Some limitations of MQ are that it takes large numbers of sinusoids to model noise sounds. Also, resonances are not modeled (similar to phase vocoder), so one cannot easily treat resonance details as control parameters. Because it uses additive synthesis, MQ is not particularly efficient or flexible. With source-filter models, we saw how one could replace the source to create a "cross-synthesis" model, but there is no obvious way to achieve cross-synthesis with MQ.

9.8 Spectral Modeling Synthesis (SMS)

Spectral Modeling Synthesis (SMS) was developed by Xavier Serra in his Ph.D. thesis work and continued in the Music Technology Group, Audiovisual Institute, Pompeu Fabra University, Barcelona. SMS extends MQ analysis/synthesis with

[1]This is a bit of over-simplification. In fact, the phase change from frame to frame in the phase vocoder indicates small deviations from the center frequency of each bin, so the phase vocoder, when properly implemented, is modeling frequencies accurately, but the model is still one where partial frequencies are modeled as fixed frequencies.

an explicit model for noise Xavier Serra and Julius O. Smith III (85). The model is shown in Figure 9.12.

You can see the box labeled "additive synthesis" and this essentially outputs a resynthesis of the input signal using MQ analysis/synthesis. Rather than stopping there, SMS subtracts this resynthesis from the input signal to obtain a *residual* signal. Assuming that most of the spectral peaks representing sinusoidal partials have been modeled, the subtraction removes them and the residual should contain mostly noise. The "spectral fitting" stage constructs a low-dimensional (i.e., few coefficients) description of the spectrum of this residual. SMS considers the sinusoidal tracks to be the "deterministic" part of the signal, and the residual noise spectrum to be the "stochastic" part of the signal.

Resynthesis is accomplished by additive synthesis of the sinusoidal tracks (as in MQ synthesis) *and* adding filtered noise, using the "stochastic" coefficients to control the noise filter. As with many synthesis techniques, one can time stretch and manipulate all the control parameters. The noise modeling in SMS allows for more accurate reconstruction as well as control over how much of the noise in the signal should be retained (or for that matter emphasized) in synthesis.

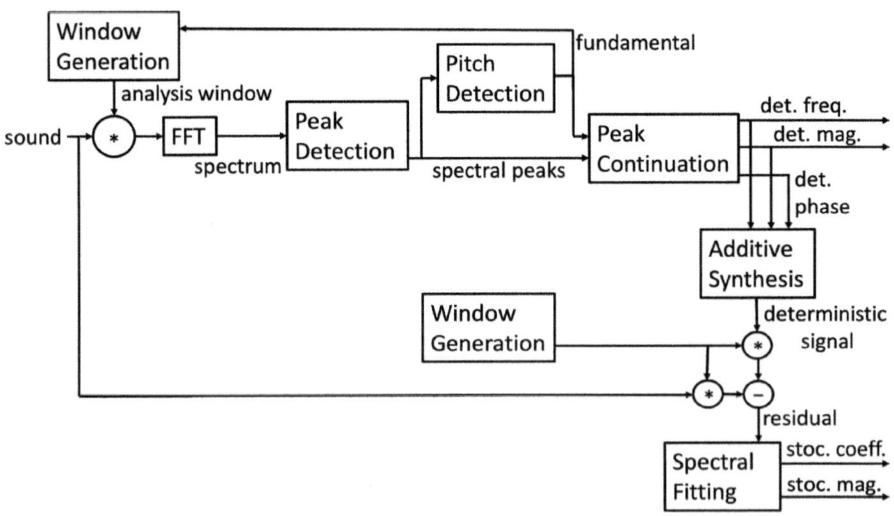

Figure 9.12: Spectral Modeling Synthesis (SMS).

9.9 Deep Network Approaches

The latest speech synthesis uses deep neural networks (DNNs) in place of manually designed models (2). The ability of DNNs to produce good articulatory control signals directly from text has dramatically improved text-to-speech synthesis quality to the point of enabling "deep fakes" that convincingly imitate recognizable speakers. It is hard to say why speech synthesis has seemingly outpaced music synthesis. There is certainly more time and effort spent on speech due to the commercial value of speech communication. Furthermore, speech seems to be acceptable with higher noise and lower bandwidth than music. Why is this? Breath noises and frequency jitter in speech production probably hide noise artifacts, and we seem more attuned to literal and emotional content than sheer sonic beauty when listening to speech. Normal speech is modulated to form words about as rapidly as possible while preserving intelligibility, so it is normal for speech sounds to have rapid fluctuations. In contrast, musical instruments often use highly resonant strings and air columns to produce highly stable oscillations where noise and frequency jitter are immediately apparent. Finally, only about 3 kHz of bandwidth is needed for very intelligible speech, and there is little frequency content in speech above 8 kHz. This is less than half the bandwidth we now consider acceptable for music. Lower sample rates definitely make learning easier.

9.10 Summary

We have considered many approaches to voice modeling and synthesis. The number of methods is some indication of the broad attraction of the human voice in computer music, or perhaps in all music, considering the prevalence of vocals in popular music. The source-filter model is a good way to think about sound production in the voice: a source signal establishes the pitch, amplitude and harmonicity or noisiness of the voice, and more-or-less independently, formant filters modify the source spectrum to impose resonances that we can perceive as vowel sounds.

LPC and the Vocoder are examples of models that actually use resonant filters to modify a source sound. These methods are open to interesting cross-synthesis applications where the source sound of some original vocal sound is replaced by another, perhaps non-human, sound.

Resonances can also be modeled in the time domain as decaying sinusoids. VOSIM and FOF synthesis are the main examples. Both can be seen as related to granular synthesis, where each source pulse creates new grains in the form of decaying sinusoids, one to model each resonance.

In the spectral domain, the phase vocoder is a powerful method that is especially useful for high-quality time-stretching without pitch change. Time-stretching also allows us to "undo" time stretch due to resampling, so we can use the phase vocoder to achieve pitch shifting without stretching. MQ analysis and synthesis models sounds as sinusoidal tracks that can vary in amplitude and frequency, and it uses addition of sinusoidal partials for synthesis. Spectral Modeling Synthesis

(SMS) extends MQ analysis/synthesis by modeling noise separately from partials, leading to a more compact representation and offering more possibilities for sound manipulation.

Although we have focused on basic sound production, the voice is complex, and singing involves vibrato, phrasing, actual speech production beyond vowel sounds, and many other details. Deep neural networks have become the state of the art for high-quality speech synthesis, especially for text-to-speech systems. Undoubtedly, there is room for more research and for applying recent developments in speech modeling to musical applications. At the same time, one might hope that the speech community could become aware of interactive control and modeling techniques as well as the need for very high quality signals arising in the computer music community.

Chapter 10

Acoustics, Perception, Effects

Topics Discussed: Pitch vs. Frequency, Loudness vs. Amplitude, Localization, Linearity, Reverberation, Echo, Equalization, Chorus, Panning, Dynamics Compression, Sample-Rate Conversion, Convolution Reverberation

10.1 Introduction

Acoustics and perception are very different subjects: acoustics being about the physics of sound and perception being about our sense and cognitive processing of sound. Though these are very different, both are very important for computer sound and music generation. In sound generation, we generally strive to create sounds that are similar to those in the real world, sometimes using models of how sound is produced by acoustic instruments. Alternatively, we may try to create sound that will cause a certain aural impression. Sometimes, an understanding of physics and perception can inspire sounds that have no basis in reality. For more information, see *Fundamentals of Musical Acoustics* (3), *The Physics of Musical Instruments* (34), and *The Psychology of Music: From Sound to Significance* (92).

Sound is vibration or air pressure fluctuations (see Figure 10.1). We can hear small pressure variations, e.g., 0.001 psi (lbs/in^2) for loud sound. (We are purposefully using English units of pounds and inches because if you inflate a bicycle tire or check tires on an automobile – at least in the U.S. – you might have some idea of what that means.) One psi $\approx$ 6895 Pascal (Pa), so 0.001 psi is about 7 Pascal. At sea level, air pressure is 14.7 pounds per square inch, while the cabin pressure in an airplane is about 11.5 psi, so 0.001 (and remember that is

DOI: 10.1201/9781003782711-10

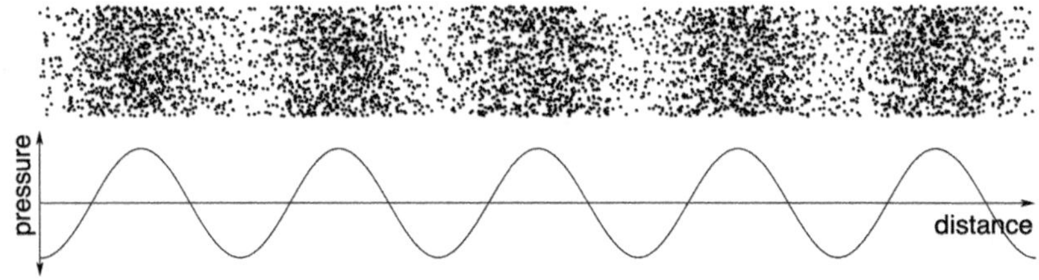

Figure 10.1: Sound is vibration or air pressure fluctuations. The top illustrates a snapshot of air molecules as a sinusoidal sound wave passes from left to right. The pressure is shown in the graph below (the "zero" axis represents local air pressure). In reality, air molecules are much more dense, and the density variation is much too small to see even if you could see air molecules!

a *loud* sound) is a tiny tiny fraction of the nominal constant pressure around us. Changes in air pressure deflect our ear drum. The amplitude of deflection of ear drum is about diameter of hydrogen atom for the softest sounds. So, we indeed have extremely sensitive ears!

What can we hear? The frequencies that we hear range over three orders of magnitude from about 20 to 20 kHz. As we grow older and we are exposed to loud sounds, our high frequency hearing is impaired, and so the actual range is typically less.

Our range of hearing, in terms of loudness, is about 120 dB, a power ratio of 10^{12}, measured from threshold of hearing to threshold of pain (discomfort from loud sounds). In practical terms, our dynamic range is actually limited and often determined by background noise. Listen to your surroundings right now and listen to what you can hear. Anything you hear is likely to *mask* even softer sounds, limiting your ability to hear them and reducing the effective dynamic range of sounds you can hear.

We are very sensitive to the amplitude spectrum. Figure 10.2 shows a spectral view that covers our range of frequency, range of amplitude, and suggests that the shape of the spectrum is something to which we are sensitive.

Real-world sounds are richly complicated and full of information and detail. We have seen many synthesis algorithms that produce very clean, simple, specific spectra, and waveforms. These *can* be musically interesting, but they are not characteristic of sounds in the "real world". This is important; *if you want to synthesize musical sounds that are pleasing to the ear*, it is important to know that, for example, real-world sounds are not simple sinusoids, they do not have constant amplitude, and so on.

Let's consider some "real-world" sounds. First, noisy sounds, such as the sound of "shhhh", tend to be broadband, meaning they contain energy at almost all fre-

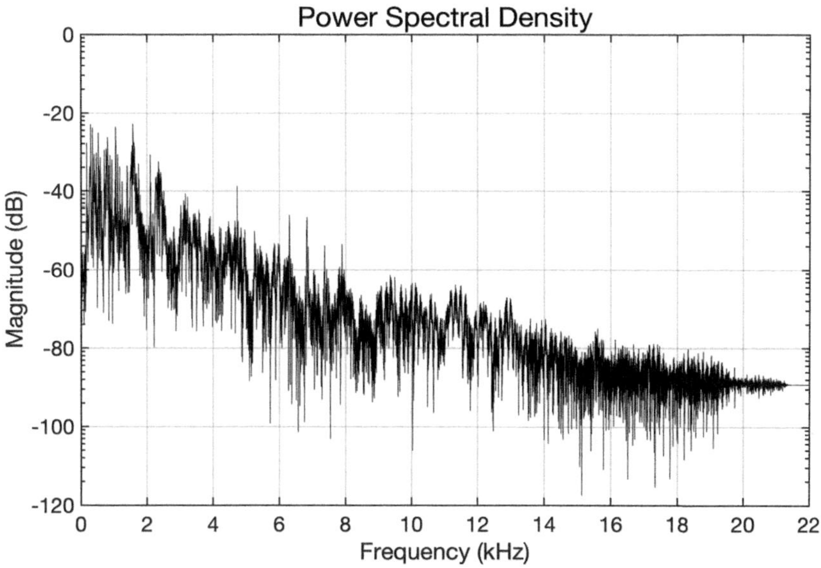

Figure 10.2: The actual spectrum shown here is not important, but the graph covers the range of audible frequencies (about 20KHz) and our range of amplitudes (about 120 dB). We are very sensitive to the shape of the spectrum.

quencies, and the amount of energy in any particular frequency, or the amplitude at any particular time, is random. The overall spectrum of noisy sounds looks like the top spectrum in Figure 10.3.

Percussion sounds on the other hand, such as a thump, bell clang, ping, or knock, tend to have resonances, so the energy is more concentrated around certain frequencies. The middle picture of Figure 10.3 gives the general spectral appearance of such sounds. Here, you see resonances at different frequencies. Each resonance produces an exponentially decaying sinusoid. The decay causes the spectral peak to be wider than that of a steady sinusoid. In general, the faster the decay, the wider the peak. It should also be noted that, depending on the material, there can be non-linear coupling between modes. In that case, the simple model of independent sinusoids with exponential decay is not exact or complete (but even then, this can be a good approximation.)

Figure 10.4 shows some modes of vibration in a guitar body. This is the top of an acoustic guitar, and each picture illustrates how the guitar top plate flexes in each mode (75, 34). At the higher frequencies (e.g., lower right in Figure 10.4), you can see patches of the guitar plate move up while neighboring patches move down. If you tap a guitar body, you will "excite" these different modes and get a collection of decaying sinusoids. The spectrum might look something like the middle of Figure 10.3. (When you play a guitar, of course, you are strumming

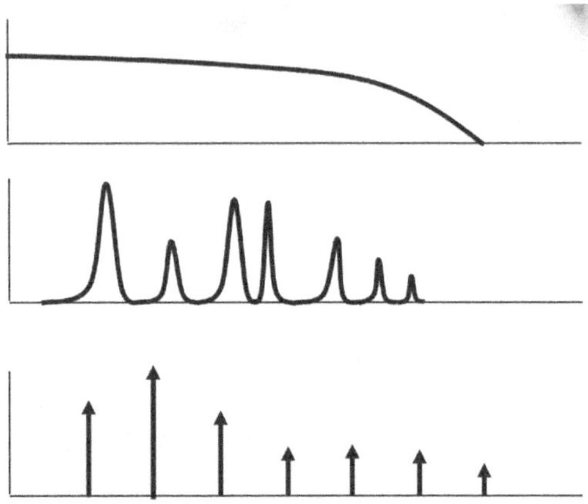

Figure 10.3: Some characteristic spectra. Can you identify them? Horizontal axis is frequency. Vertical axis is magnitude (amplitude). The top represents noise, with energy at all frequencies. The middle spectrum represents a percussion sound with resonant or "characteristic" frequencies. This might be a bell sound. The bottom spectrum represents a musical tone, which has many harmonics that are multiples of the first harmonic, or *fundamental.*

strings that have a different set of modes of vibration that give sharper peaks and a clearer sense of pitch.)

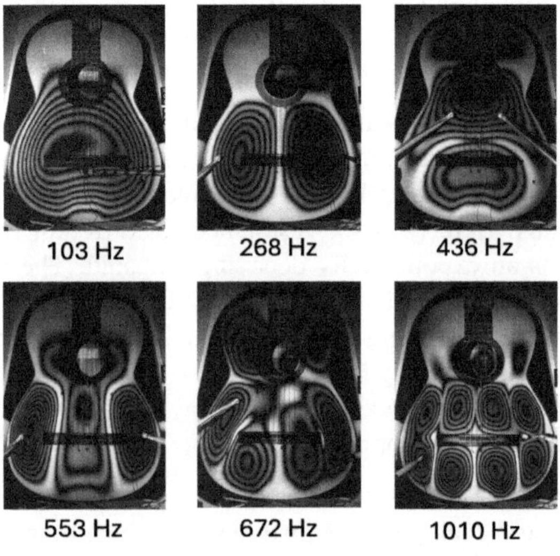

Figure 10.4: Some modes of vibration in an acoustic guitar body.
Photos by Bernard Richardson, Cardiff University.

Pitched sounds are often called *tones* and tend to have harmonically related sinusoids. For example, an "ideal" string has characteristic frequencies that form a harmonic series, as illustrated in Figure 10.5. This can be seen as a special case of vibrating objects in general, such as the guitar body (Figure 10.4.) The vibrating string just happens to have harmonically related mode frequencies.

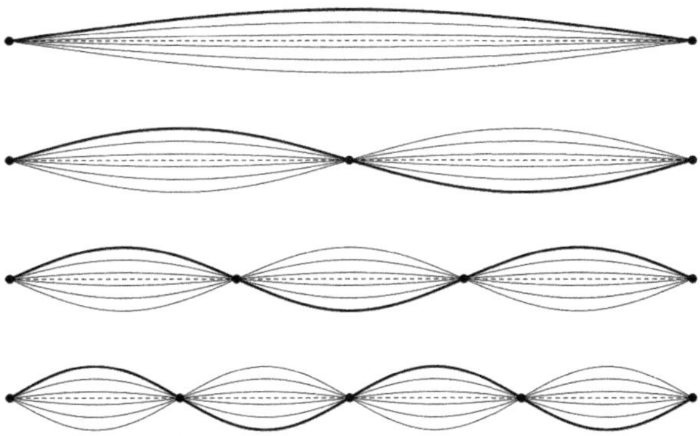

Figure 10.5: Modes of vibration in a stretched string. In an "ideal" string, the characteristic frequencies are multiples of the frequency of the first mode. The modes of vibration are independent, so the "sound" of the string is formed by the superposition of all the vibrating modes, resulting in a harmonic spectrum.

We know from previous discussions that if the signal is purely periodic, then it has harmonically related sinusoids. In other words, any periodic signal can be decomposed into a sum of sinusoids that are all multiples of some fundamental frequency. *In physical systems, periodicity is characteristic of some kind of mechanical oscillator that is driven by an outside energy source* (3). If you bow a string, sing a tone, or blow into a clarinet, you drive an oscillator with a constant source of energy, and almost invariably you end up with a stable periodic oscillation.

In summary, there are two ways to obtain harmonic or near-harmonic partials that are found in musical tones: One is to strike or pluck an object that has modes of vibration that just happen to resonate at harmonic frequencies. An example is a piano string or chime. The other is to drive oscillation with a steady input of energy, as in a bowed string or wind instrument, giving rise to a periodic signal. In addition to these sounds called "tones", we have inharmonic spectra and noisy spectra.

10.2 Perception: Pitch, Loudness, Localization

Having focused mainly on physical properties of sound and sound sources, we now turn our attention to our *perception* of sound. It is important to keep in mind that our perception does not directly correspond to the underlying physical properties of sound. For example, two sounds with the same perceived loudness might have very different amplitudes, and two pitch intervals perceived to be the same musically could not be at all the same in terms of frequency differences.

10.2.1 Pitch Perception

Pitch is fundamental to most music. Where does it come from? How sensitive are ears to pitch? Our sense of pitch is strongly related to frequency. Higher frequencies mean higher pitch. Our sense of pitch is enhanced by harmonic partials. In fact, the connection is so strong that we are unable to hear individual partials. In most cases, we collect all of these partials into a single tone that we perceive as a single pitch, that of the lowest partial.

Pitch perception is approximately logarithmic, meaning that when pitch doubles, you hear the pitch interval of one octave. When it doubles again, you hear the same interval even though now the frequency is four times as high. If we divide the octave (factor of 2 in frequency) into 12 log-spaced intervals, we get what are called musical semitones or half-steps. This arrangement of 12 equal ratios per octave (each one $\sqrt[12]{2}$) is the basis for most Western music, as shown in the keyboard (Figure 10.6).

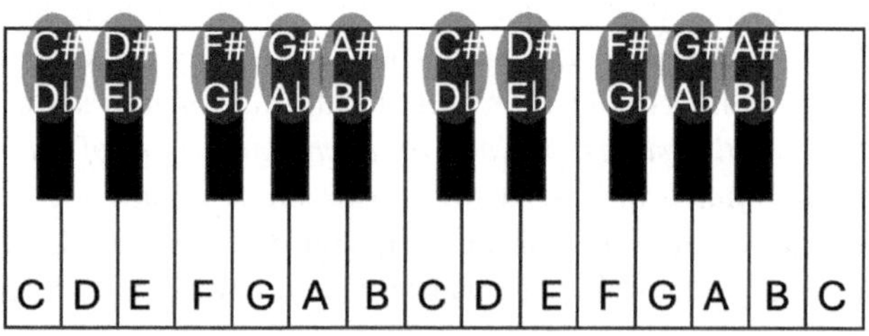

Figure 10.6: A piano keyboard. The ratio between frequencies of adjacent keys is $\sqrt[12]{2}$. Pianos are commonly tuned with a slightly larger ratio, related to the slight inharmonicity of strings, which in turn is due to the stiffness of metal strings. Synthesizer and organ keyboards commonly use $\sqrt[12]{2}$, however.

We can divide a semitone ($\sqrt[12]{2}$) into 100 log-spaced frequency intervals called cents. Often cents are used in studies of tuning and intonation. We are sensitive to about 5 cents, which is a ratio of about 0.3%. No wonder it is so hard for musicians to play in tune!

10.2.2 Amplitude

The term *pitch* refers to *perception* while *frequency* refers to *objective* or *physical* repetition rates. In a similar way, *loudness* is the perception of *intensity* or *ampli-*

tude of sound. Here, we introduce some terminology and units of measurement for amplitude. Below, we will return to the topic of loudness.

There are multiple ways of defining amplitude. One definition is: "a measure of a periodic function's change over a single period". Figure 10.7 illustrates the three different ways amplitude may be measured:

1. The peak amplitude
2. The peak-to-peak amplitude
3. The root mean square (RMS) amplitude.

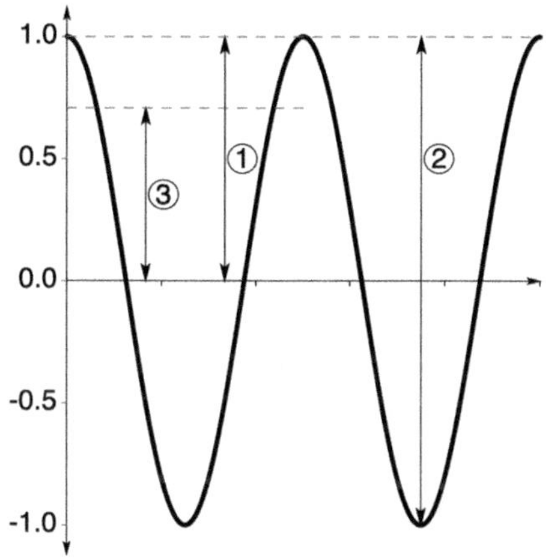

Figure 10.7: Three different ways of measuring amplitude.

In specifying amplitude in code, we are mostly using the peak amplitude of a signal. Thus, the amplitude of a sine wave, $y = \sin(t)$, is 1, and the amplitude of $y = 2\cos(t)$ is 2. When we multiply an oscillator in Nyquist by an envelope, we're varying the amplitude of that oscillator over time.

10.2.2.1 Volume

There is no one formal definition for what the volume of sound means. Generally, volume is used as a synonym for loudness. In music production, adjusting the volume of a sound usually means to move a volume fader on, e.g., a mixer. Faders can be either linear or logarithmic, so again, it is not exactly clear what volume means (i.e., is it the fader position, or the perceived loudness?).

10.2.2.2 Power

Power is the amount of work done per unit of time; e.g., how much energy is transferred by an audio signal. Hence, the average power $\bar{P}$ is the ratio of energy

E to time t: $\bar{P} = E/t$. Power is usually measured in watts (W); which are joules (J) per second: $J/s = W$. The power of a sound signal is proportional to the squared amplitude of that signal. Note that in terms of relative power or amplitude, it does not really matter whether we think of amplitude as the instantaneous amplitude (i.e., the amplitude at a specific point in time), or the peak, the peak-to-peak, or the root mean square amplitude over a single period. It makes no significant difference to ratios.

10.2.2.3 Pressure

In general, the pressure p is the amount of force F applied perpendicularly (normal) to a surface area divided by the size a of that area: $p = F/a$. Pressure is normally measured in pascal (Pa), which is newtons (N) per square meter. Thus, $Pa = N/m^2$.

10.2.2.4 Intensity

Intensity I is the energy E flowing across a unit surface area per unit of time t: $I = \frac{E}{a}\frac{1}{t}$. For instance, the energy from a sound wave flowing to an ear. As the average power $\bar{P} = E/t$, we can express the intensity as $I = \bar{P}/a$, meaning the power flowing across a surface of area a. The standard unit area is one square meter, and therefore we measure intensity in W/m^2; i.e., watts per square meter.

10.2.2.5 Range of Human Hearing

Just as the frequency range of the human ear is limited, so is the range of intensity. For a very sensitive listener, and a 1 kHz frequency:

- The threshold of hearing $t_h = 10^{-12} W/m^2$
- The limit of hearing (due to pain and injury caused by sound) is $l_h = 1W/m^2$ (the threshold of pain).

The perceptual range of intensity for a 1 kHz frequency is an impressive $l_h/t_h = 1/10^{-12} = 10^{12}$, or a trillion to one.

10.2.2.6 The Bel Scale

The bel, abbreviated B (note capitalizations), is a sound intensity scale named in honor of the renowned Alexander Graham Bell (1847–1922). Given the enormous range of human hearing, one bel is defined as a factor of 10 in intensity or power as follows:

$$bels = \log_{10} \frac{I}{I_0}$$

where I is intensity or power and I_0 is a reference. In other words, bel is the log ratio of intensity or power. Measuring the range of intensity for human hearing

H in bels, we get:

$$H \text{ bel} = \log_{10} \frac{l_h}{t_h} = 12$$

For sound, we measure intensity, but in other situations, such as an electrical signal, we measure total *power*, e.g., as watts, since there is no area to divide by. Since bel (B) is a ratio, the units cancel out, so we can use the bel for both intensity and power.

10.2.2.7 The Decibel Scale (dB)

Using just a range $H = 12$ to express the entire range of hearing is inconvenient, so it is customary to use decibels, abbreviated dB, instead. One bel is 10 dB. The intensity range of human hearing is therefore 120 dB.

10.2.2.8 Decibels for Comparing Sound Intensity Levels

Decibels are most commonly used to compare the intensity levels of two sounds. As shown in the definition of *bels* above, we take the intensity I of some sound and compare it to a reference intensity I_0. This reference is arbitrary. For example, instead of using t_h as the reference intensity, we could use the limit of hearing l_h, and thus measure down from pain instead of measuring up from silence. With this reference, the threshold of hearing becomes –120 dB.

10.2.2.9 Decibels for Comparing Amplitude Levels

A common confusion arises when working with intensity and amplitudes. We just saw that given an intensity ratio r, we can express the ratio in decibels using $10\log_{10} r$. This also works for a ratio of power because power and intensity are proportional. However, when we are working with amplitudes, this formula does not apply. Why? Because the decibel is a measure of power or intensity ratio. Since power is proportional to the square of amplitude, a different formula must be used for amplitudes. For two amplitudes A and B, we can use the power formula if we square them. Then we can simplify the expression:

$$dB = 10\log_{10} \frac{A^2}{B^2} = 10\log_{10}(\frac{A}{B})^2 = 20\log_{10} \frac{A}{B}$$

Main idea: for power or intensity we use $10\log_{10} ratio$, but for amplitudes, we must use $20\log_{10} ratio$.

10.2.2.10 Other dB Variants

You see the abbreviation dB in many contexts.

- **dBa** uses the so-called A-weighting to account for the relative loudness perceived by the human ear; based on equal-loudness contours.
- **dBb** and **dBc** are similar to **dBa**, but apply different weighting schemes.
- **dBm** (or *dBmW*) is the power ratio in dB of a measured power referenced to one milliwatt (mW); used e.g., in radio, microwave, and fiber optic networks as a measure of absolute power.
- **dB SPL** – see below.

10.2.2.11 Amplitude and Gain in Recording Equipment

In a music studio, we usually want to measure down from the limit of the loudest sound that can be recorded without introducing distortion from the recording equipment. This is why it is standard, e.g., in mixing consoles and music software to use volume faders and meters that show negative dB. In this context, 0 dB is the upper limit for recording without distortion; let's call it the limit of recording $= l_r$. Hence, the loudest sound we may record without any distortion has intensity $I = l_r$, and the corresponding dB is $10\log_{10}\frac{l_r}{l_r} = 0$ dB. Note that it is customary for producers of recording gear to leave some amount of head room at the top of this scale to safeguard against distortion, which is why you'll see some positive dB values above 0 dB on meters and faders.

10.2.2.12 Sound Pressure

Measuring the intensity of a sound signal is usually not practical (or possible); i.e., measuring the energy flow over an area is tricky. Fortunately, we can measure the average variation in pressure. Pressure is the force applied normal to a surface area, so if we sample a sufficiently large area we'll get a decent approximation; this is exactly what a microphone does!

It is worth noting that we can relate sound pressure to intensity by the following ratio:

$$\frac{\Delta p^2}{V\delta}$$

where Δp is the variation in pressure, V is the velocity of sound in air, and δ is the density of air. What this tells us is that intensity is proportional to the square of the variation in pressure. This applies to plane waves in air.

10.2.2.13 dB SPL (Sound Pressure Level)

Sound pressure level is defined as the average pressure variation per unit area. The dB SPL is defined as $20\log_{10}\frac{P}{P_0}$, where the reference pressure, P_0, is 0.00002 Pa, which is approximately the threshold of hearing at 1 kHz.

10.2.2.14 The Microphone: Measuring Sound Pressure

Most microphones use electromagnetic induction to transform the sound pressure applied to a diaphragm into an electrical signal; as shown in Figure 10.8.

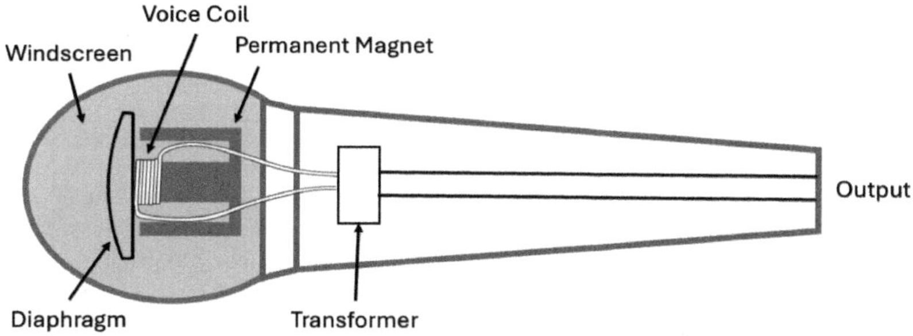

Figure 10.8: In a so-called dynamic microphone, a diaphragm vibrates a coil in a magnetic field, producing an electrical signal that passes through a transformer to raise its impedance and voltage and provide isolation. Modern microphones may use a small amplifier instead of the transformer. Condenser and ribbon microphones use other mechanisms to convert sounds to electrical signals.

For more information on loudness, dB, intensity, pressure, etc., see *Musimathics* Vol. 1 (55).

10.2.3 Loudness

Loudness is a perceptual concept. Equal loudness does necessarily result from equal amplitude because the human ear's sensitivity to sound varies with frequency. This sensitivity, the loudness, is depicted in equal-loudness contours for the human ear; often referred to as the Fletcher-Munson curves. Fletcher and Munson's data were revised to create an ISO standard. The ISO 2003 revision is illustrated in Figure 10.9 below. (An even newer revision, 2023, introduces some very minor changes.) Each curve traces changes in amplitude required to maintain equal loudness as the frequency of a sine tone varies. In other words, each curve depicts amplitude as a function of frequency at a constant loudness level.

Loudness is commonly measured in phons.

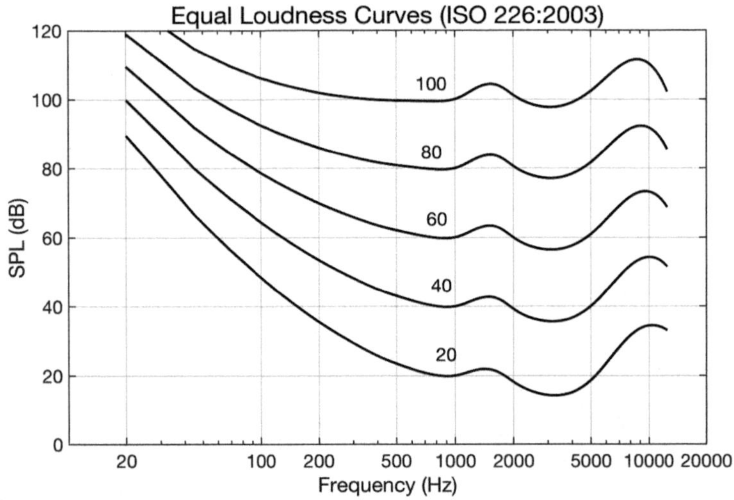

Figure 10.9: Equal-loudness contours from ISO 226:2003 revision. Each curve shows the sound pressure level (SPL) measured in dB required at each frequency to produce a particular perceptual loudness, measured in Phons. Curves show levels for 20, 40, 60, 80, and 100 Phons.

10.2.3.1 Phon

Phon expresses the loudness of a sound in terms of a reference loudness. That is, the phon level of a sound, A, is the dB SPL (defined earlier) of a reference sound—of frequency 1 kHz—that has the same (perceived) loudness as A. Zero phon is the limit of audibility of the human ear; inaudible sounds have negative phon levels.

10.2.3.2 Rules of Thumb

Loudness is mainly dependent on amplitude, and this relationship is approximately logarithmic, which means equal ratios of amplitude are more-or-less perceived as equal increments of loudness. We are very sensitive to small ratios of frequency, but we are not very sensitive to small ratios of amplitude. To double loudness you need about a 10-fold increase in intensity or about 10 dB. We are sensitive to about 1 dB of amplitude ratio with careful listening. 1 dB is a change of about 12%.

The fact that we are not so sensitive to amplitude changes is important to keep in mind when adjusting amplitude. If you synthesize a sound and it is too soft, try scaling it by a factor of 2 (about 6 dB). People are often tempted to make small changes, e.g., multiply by 1.1 to make something louder, but in most cases, a 10% change is not even audible (less than 1 dB).

Loudness also depends on frequency because we are not so sensitive to very high and very low frequencies. The Fletcher-Munson Curve contours shown above are lowest around 4 kHz where we are most sensitive. The curve is low here because a low amplitude at 4 kHz sounds as loud as higher amplitudes at other frequencies. If you sweep a sinusoid from low frequency to high frequency at equal amplitude, you will hear that the sound appears to get louder until you hit around 4 kHz, and then the sound begins to get quieter. Depending on how loud it is, you might stop hearing it at some point before you hit 20 kHz, even if you can hear loud sounds at 20 kHz.

It should be noted that these curves are based on sinusoids. In most music, low pitches actually consist of a mixture of harmonics, some of which can have rather high frequencies. So even if you cannot hear the fundamental because it is too low or too quiet, you might hear the pitch, which is implied by the upper partials (to which you are more sensitive). This is also why, on your laptop, you can hear a piano tone at the pitch C_2 (below the bass clef, with a fundamental frequency of about 65 Hz), even though your laptop speaker is barely able to produce any output at 65 Hz. You might try this SAL command, which plays a piano tone followed by a sine tone:

```
play seq(note(pitch: c2), osc(c2))
```

It is instructive to listen to this *using a quiet volume setting* with good headphones. You should hear the two tones at the same pitch. Then, listen to the same sounds on your built-in laptop speaker. You will probably not hear the second tone, indicating that your computer cannot produce frequencies that low. And yet, the pitch of the first tone, even with *no fundamental frequency present* retains the same pitch!

10.2.4 Localization

Localization is the ability to perceive direction of the source of a sound and perhaps the distance of that sound. We have multiple cues for localization, including relative amplitude, phase or timing, and spectral effects of the pinnae (outer ears). Starting with amplitude, if we hear something louder in our right ear than our left ear, then we will perceive that the sound must be coming from the right, all other things be equal.

We also use relative phase or timing for localization: if we hear something arrive earlier in our right ear than our left ear, then we will perceive that sound as coming from the right.

The third cue is produced by our pinnae or outer ears. Sound reflects off the pinnae, which are very irregularly shaped. These reflections cause some cancellation or reinforcement at particular wavelengths, depending on the direction of the sound source and the orientation of our head. Even though we do not know the exact spectrum of the source sound, our amazing brain is able to disentangle all this information and compute something about localization. This is especially important for the perception of elevation, i.e., is the sound coming from ahead or above? In either case, the distance to our ears is the same, so whether the source is ahead or above, there should be no difference in amplitude or timing. The only difference is in spectral changes due to our outer ears and reflections from our shoulders.

All of these effects or cues can be described in terms of filters. Taken together, these effects are sometimes called the HRTF, or *Head-Related Transfer Function*. (A "transfer function" describes the change in the spectrum from source to destination.) You might have seen some artificial localization systems, including video games and virtual reality application systems based on HRTF. The idea is, for each source to be placed in a virtual 3D space, compute an appropriate HRTF and apply that to the source sound. There is a different HRTF for the left ear and right ear, and typically the resulting stereo signal is presented through headphones. Ideally, the headphones are tracked so that the HRTFs can be recomputed as the head turns and the angles to virtual sources change.

Environmental cues are also important for localization. If sounds reflect off walls, then you get a sense of being in a closed space, how far away the walls are, and what the walls are made of. Reverberation and ratio of reverberation to direct sound are important for distance estimation, especially for computer music if you want to create the effect of a sound source fading off into the distance. Instead of just turning down the amplitude of the sound, the direct or dry sound should diminish faster than the reverberation sound to give the impression of greater distance.

Finally, knowledge of the sound source, including vision, recognition, etc. is very important to localization. For example, merely placing a silent loudspeaker in front of a listener wearing headphones can cause experimental subjects to localize sound at the loudspeaker, ignoring whatever cues are present in the actual sound!

10.2.5 More Acoustics

The speed of sound is about 1 ft/ms. Sound travels at different speeds at different altitudes, different temperatures and different humidities, so it is probably more useful to have a rough idea of the speed of sound than to memorize a precise number. (But for the record, the speed of sound is 343 m/s in dry air at 20° C.) Compared to the speed of light, sound is painfully slow. For example, if you stand in front of a wall and clap, you can hear that the sound reflects from the wall surfaces, and you can perceive the time for the clap to travel to the wall and reflect back. Our auditory system merges multiple reflections when they are close in time (usually up to about 40 ms), so you do not perceive echoes until you stand back 20 feet or so from the reflecting wall.

In most listening environments, we do not get just one reflection, called an echo. Instead, we get a diffuse superposition of millions of echos as sound scatters and bounces between many surfaces in a room. We call this *reverberation*. In addition to reflection, sound refracts (bends around objects). Wavelengths vary from 50 feet to a fraction of an inch, and diffraction is more pronounced at lower frequencies, allowing sound to bend around objects.

Linearity is a very important concept for understanding acoustics. Let's think about the transmission of sounds from the source of sound to the listener. We can think of the whole process as a function F shown in the equations below, where $y = F(x)$ means that source x is transformed by the room into y at the ear of the listener. *Linearity* means that if we increase the sound at the source, we will get a proportional increase at the listening side of channel F. Thus, $F(ax) = aF(x)$. The other property, sometimes called the *superposition*, is that if we have two sources: pressure signals x_1 and x_2, and play them at the same time, then the effect on the listener will be the sum of individual effect from x_1 and x_2:

$$F(ax) = aF(x), \quad F(x_1 + x_2) = F(x_1) + F(x_2)$$

Why does linearity matter? First, air, rooms, performance spaces are very linear. Also, many of processes we used on sounds such as filters are designed to be linear. Linearity means that if there are two sound sources playing at the same time, then the signal at the listening end is equivalent to what you get from one sound plus what you get from the other sound. Another interesting thing about linearity is that we can decompose a sound into sinusoids or components (i.e., compute the Fourier transform). If we know what a linear system does to each one of those component frequencies, then by the superposition principle, we know what the system does to any sound, because we can: break it up into component frequencies, compute the transfer function at each of the frequencies and sum the results together. That is one way of looking at what a filter does. A filter associates different scale factors with each frequency, and because filters are linear, they weight or delay frequencies differently but independently. If we add two sounds and put them through the filter, the result is equivalent to putting the two sounds through the filter independently and summing the results.

10.2.6 Summary: Acoustics and Perception

Now we summarize this discussion of acoustics and perception. Acoustics refers to the physics of sound, while perception concerns our sense of sound. As summarized in Figure 10.10, pitch is the perception of (mainly) frequency, and loudness is the perception (mainly) of amplitude or intensity. Our perception of pitch and loudness is roughly logarithmic with frequency and amplitude. This relationship is not exact, and we saw in the Fletcher-Munson Curve that we are more sensitive to some frequencies than others. Generally, everything else we perceive

Perception	Acoustic Phenomenon
Pitch	Frequency (20-20 kHz range)
Loudness	Intensity (120 dB range)
Timbre	Spectrum (and other)

Figure 10.10: A comparison of concepts and terms from perception (left column) to acoustics (right column).

is referred to as timbre, and you can think of timbre as (mainly) the perception of spectral shape. In addition to these properties, we can localize sound in space using various cues that give us a sense of direction and distance.

Struck objects typically exhibit characteristic frequencies with exponential decay rates (each mode of vibration has its own frequency and decay). In contrast, driven oscillators typically exhibit almost exactly periodic signals and hence harmonic spectra.

Our discussion also covered the speed of sound (roughly 1 ft/ms), transmission of sound as equivalent to filtering and the superposition principle.

10.3 Effects and Reverberation in Nyquist

There are a lot of effects and processes that you can apply to sound with Nyquist. Some are described here, and you can find more in the *Nyquist Reference Manual.* There are also many sound processing functions you can install with the Nyquist Extension Manager (in the NyquistIDE). For more on audio effects in general, a good starting point is *DAFX: Digital Audio Effects* Udo Zölzer (100).

10.3.1 Delay or Echo

In Nyquist, we do not need any special unit generator to implement delay. We can directly create delay simply by adding sounds using an offset. Recall that Nyquist sounds have a built-in starting time and duration which are both immutable, so applying a shift operator to a sound does not do anything. However, the cue behavior takes a sound as parameter and returns a new sound that has been shifted according to the environment. So, we usually combine cue with the shift operator @, and a delay expression has the form:

`cue(`*sound*`) @ `*delay*

10.3.2 Feedback Delay

An interesting effect is to not only produce an echo, but to add an attenuated copy of the output back into the input of the effect, producing a series of echoes that die away exponentially. There is a special unit generator in Nyquist called `feedback-delay` with three parameters: `feedback-delay(`*sound*`,` *delay*`,` *feedback*`)`. Figure 10.11 shows the echo algorithm: The input comes in and is stored in memory in a first-in-first-out (FIFO) queue; samples at the end of the buffer are recycled by adding them to the incoming sound. This is an efficient way to produce many copies of the sound that fade away. The *delay* parameter must be a number (in seconds). It is rounded to the nearest sample to determine the length of the delay buffer. The amount of *feedback* should be less than one to avoid an exponential increase in amplitude.

Figure 10.11: Echo algorithm in Nyquist.

Note that the duration of the output of this unit generator is equal to the duration of the input, so if the input is supposed to come to an end and then be followed by multiple echos, we need to append silence to the input source to avoid a sudden ending. The example below uses `s-rest()` to construct 10 seconds of silence, which follows the *sound*.

```
feedback-delay(seq(sound, s-rest(10)), delay, feedback)
```

In principle, the exponential decay of the `feedback-delay` effect never ends, so it might be prudent to use an envelope to smoothly bring the end of the signal to zero:

```
feedback-delay(seq(sound, s-rest(10)), delay, feedback)  *
pwlv(1, d + 9, 1, d + 10, 0)
```

where *d* is the duration of *sound*. The sound is extended with 10 seconds of silence, so the envelope remains at 1 for the sound duration plus 9 seconds, then linearly falls to zero at sound duration + 10.

10.3.3 Comb Filter

Consider a feedback delay with a 10 ms delay. If the input is a sinusoid with 10 ms period (100 Hz), the echoes superimpose on one another and boost the amplitude of the input. The same happens with 200 Hz, 300 Hz, 400 Hz, etc. sinusoids because they all repeat after 10 ms. Other frequencies will produce echoes that do not add constructively and are not boosted much. Thus, this feedback delay will act like a filter with resonances at multiples of a fundamental frequency, which is the reciprocal of the delay time. The frequency response of a comb filter looks like Figure 10.12. Longer decay times gives the comb filter sharper peaks, which means the output has a more definite pitch and longer "ring".

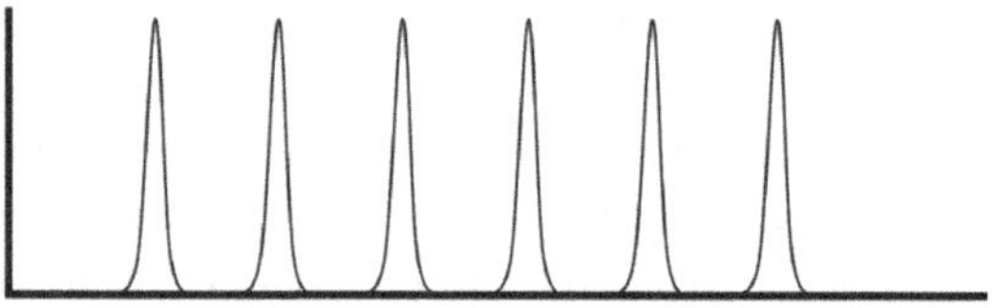

Figure 10.12: Filter response of a comb filter. The horizontal axis is frequency and the vertical axis is amplitude. The comb filter has resonances at multiples of some fundamental frequency.

The code below shows how to apply a comb filter to *sound* in Nyquist. A comb filter emphasizes (resonates at) frequencies that are multiples of the *hz* parameter. The decay time of the resonance is given by *decay*. The *decay* may be a sound or a number. In either case, it must also be positive. The resulting sound will have the start time, sample rate, etc. of *sound*. One limitation of `comb` is that the actual delay will be the closest integer number of sample periods to 1/*hz*, so the resonance frequency spacing will one that divides the sample rate evenly.

`comb(`*sound*`,` *decay*`,` *hz*`)`

10.3.4 Equalization

Equalization is generally used to adjust spectral balance. For example, we might want to boost the bass, or boost the high frequencies, or cut some objectionable frequencies in the middle range. The function `nband(`*input, gains*`)` takes an array of gains, one for each band, where the bands are evenly divided across the 20–20kHz range. An interesting possibility is using computed control functions to make the equalization change over time.

The Equalizer Editor in Nyquist provides a graphical equalizer interface for creating and adjusting equalizers. It has a number of sliders for different frequency bands, and you can slide them up and down and see graphically what the frequency response looks like. You can use this interface to create functions to be used in your code. Equalizers are named `eq-0`, `eq-1`, etc., and you select the equalizer to edit using a pull-down menu. The "Set" button should be used to record changes.

The following expression in Nyquist is a fixed- or variable-parameter, second-order midrange equalization (EQ) filter:

`eq-band(`*signal*`,` *hz*`,` *gain*`,` *width*`)`

The *hz* parameter is the center frequency, *gain* is the boost (or cut) in dB, and width is the half-gain width in octaves. Alternatively, *hz*, *gain*, and *width* may be sounds, but they must all have the same sample rate, e.g., they should all run at the control rate or at the sample rate.

You can look up filters in the Nyquist manual for many more filters and options.

10.3.5 Chorus

The chorus effect is a very useful way to enrich a simple and dry sound. Essentially, the "chorus" effect is a very short, time-varying delay that is added to the original sound. Its implementation is shown in Figure 10.13. The original sound passes through the top line, while a copy of the sound with some attenuation is added to the sound after a varying delay, which is indicated by the diagonal arrow.

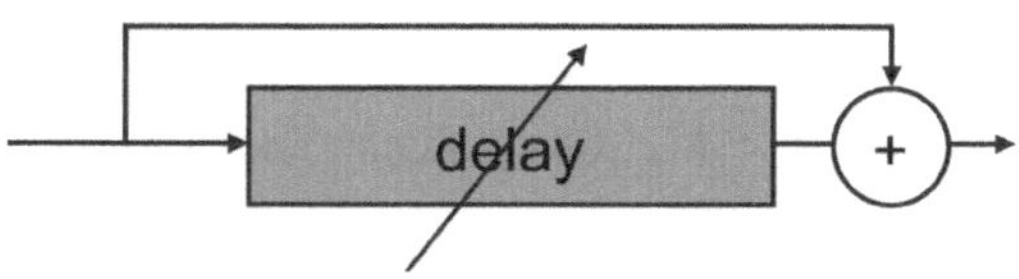

Figure 10.13: Chorus effect algorithm. A signal is mixed with a delayed copy of itself. The delay varies, typically by a small amount and rather slowly.

To implement chorus in Nyquist, you need to first load library `time-delay-fns`[1] and then call the `chorus` function as shown below:

`chorus(`*sound*`, delay:` *delay*`, depth:` *depth*`, rate:` *rate*`,`
`saturation:` *saturation*`, phase:` *phase*`)`

Here, a chorus effect is applied to *sound.* All parameters may be arrays as usual. The chorus is implemented as a variable delay modulated by a sinusoid shifted by *phase* degrees oscillating at *rate* Hz. The sinusoid is scaled by *depth.* The delayed signal is mixed with the original, and *saturation* gives the fraction of the delayed signal (from 0 to 1) in the mix. Default values are *delay* = 0.03, *depth* = 0.003, `rate` = 0.3, *saturation* = 1.0, and *phase* = 0.0 (degrees).

See also the *Nyquist Reference Manual* for the functions `stereo-chorus` and `stkchorus`.

[1] In the future, `time-delay-fns` will be an extension installed with the Extension Manager.

10.3.6 Panning

Panning refers to the simulation of location by splitting a signal between left and right (and sometimes more) speakers. When panning a mono source from left to right in a stereo output, you are basically adjusting the volume of that source in the left and right channels. Simple enough. However, there are multiple reasonable ways of making those adjustments. In the following, we shall cover the three most common ones.

A typical two-speaker stereo setup is depicted in Figure 10.14; the speakers are placed symmetrically at ±45-degree angles, and equidistant to the listener, who is located at the so-called "sweet-spot", while facing the speakers.

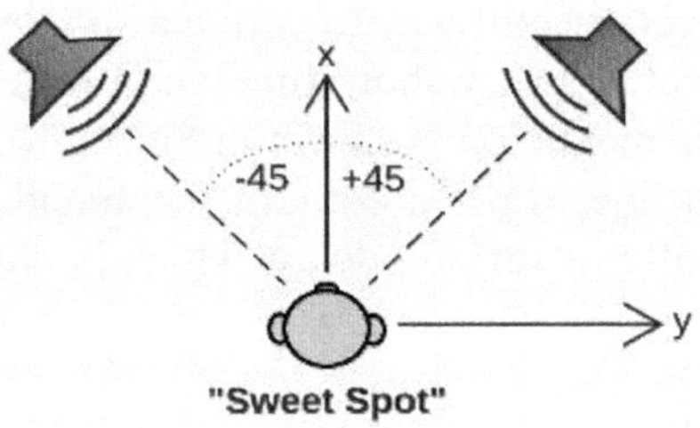

Figure 10.14: Speaker positioning and sweet spot.

Note that the range of panning (for stereo) is thus 90 degrees. However, it is practical to use radians instead of degrees. By convention, the left speaker is at 0 radians and the right speaker is at $\pi/2$ radians, giving us a panning range of $\theta \in [0; \pi/2]$, with the center position at $\theta = \pi/4$.

10.3.6.1 Linear Panning

The simplest panning strategy is to adjust the channel gains (volumes) linearly with inverse correlation.

> **Main idea**: For a stereo signal with gain 1, the gains of the left and right channels should sum to 1; i.e., $L(\theta) + R(\theta) = 1$.

With the panning angle $\theta \in [0; \pi/2]$, we thus get the gain functions:

$$L(\theta) = (\frac{\pi}{2} - \theta)\frac{1}{\frac{\pi}{2}} = (1 - \theta\frac{2}{\pi})$$

and

$$R(\theta) = \theta\frac{1}{\frac{\pi}{2}} = \theta\frac{2}{\pi}$$

as plotted in Figure 10.15.

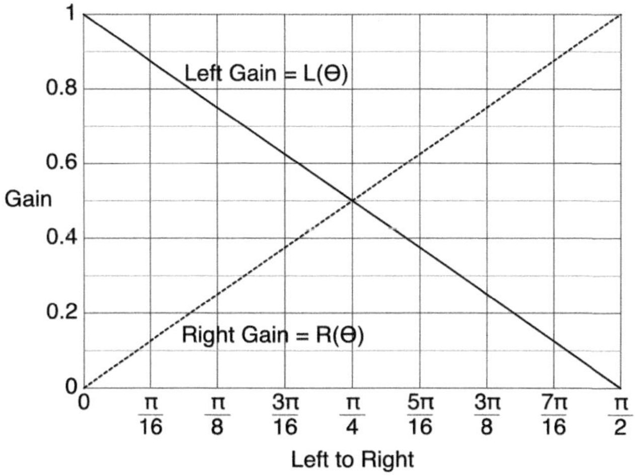

Figure 10.15: Linear panning.

A drawback of implementing panning in this way is that, even though the gains $L(\theta)$ and $R(\theta)$ always sum to 1, the loudness of the signal is still affected. Linear panning creates a "hole-in-the-middle" effect, such that the signal is softer at the middle than at the side-positions. At the center position, where $\theta = \pi/4$, we have $L(\pi/4) + R(\pi/4) = 1$. However, when a signal is panned to the center, the amplitudes coming from two speakers will typically not sum (unless they are perfectly in phase). In general, due to reflections and phase differences, the power is additive.[2] If we add power (proportional to the squared amplitude) we get $L^2(\pi/4) + R^2(\pi/4) = 0.5^2 + 0.5^2 = 0.5$. Expressed in dB, measuring down from the maximum gain (amplitude) of 1 (0 dB), we get $10\log_{10}(0.5)$ dB = -3 dB. Thus, when a signal is panned to the middle, it sounds 3 dB quieter than when panned fully left or right!

10.3.6.2 Constant Power Panning

One way of dealing with the "hole-in-the-middle" effect is to use *constant power panning*. Basically, we change the linear functions for $L(\theta)$ and $R(\theta)$ to the sine and cosine functions, letting $L(\theta) = \cos(\theta)$ and $R(\theta) = \sin(\theta)$.

> **Main idea**: power is proportional to the squared amplitude, and $\cos^2 + \sin^2 = 1$.

Thus, $L(\theta) = \cos(\theta)$ and $R(\theta) = \sin(\theta)$ yields constant power panning.

As seen in the Figure 10.16, this boosts the center, giving us a gain of $cos(\pi/4) = \sin(\pi/4) = 0.71$ as opposed to the 0.5 center gain we saw with linear panning.

[2] This also relates to the law of conservation of energy.

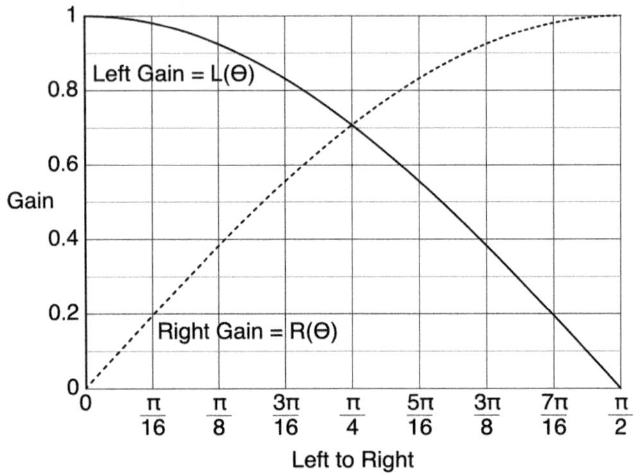

Figure 10.16: Constant power panning.

Now, the power of the signal at the center is $L^2(\pi/4)+R^2(\pi/4) = \cos^2(\pi/4)+\sin^2(\pi/4) = 1$, which is $10\log_{10}(\frac{1}{1})$ dB = 0 dB. The per-channel attenuation is $20\log_{10}(0.71) = -3$ dB. Thus, the center pan position is boosted by 3 dB[3] compared to linear panning, and the total power at every pan position is 0 dB.

10.3.6.3 -4.5 dB Pan Law (the compromise)

What if our statement that power is additive is wrong? If amplitudes add, then the center pan position will get a 3 dB boost. This can happen if you convert stereo to mono by adding the left and right channels (so anything panned to the center is now added perfectly in phase), or if you sit in exactly the right spot for left and right channels to add in phase.[4] The idea behind the –4.5 dB law is to split the difference between constant power and linear panning—a kind of compromise between the two. This is achieved by simply taking the square root of the product of the two laws, thus we have $L(\theta) = \sqrt{(\frac{\pi}{2}-\theta)\frac{2}{\pi}\cos(\theta)}$, and $R(\theta) = \sqrt{\theta\frac{2}{\pi}\sin(\theta)}$; as plotted in Figure 10.17.

As we can see on the plot, the center gain is now at 0.59, and hence the per-channel attenuation is $10\log_{10}(\frac{.59^2}{1^2})$ dB = -4.5 dB, which is exactly in between that for the previous two laws. The power of the signal at the center is now

[3] In fact, the exact number is not 0.71 but $\sqrt{2}$, which in dB is approximately 3.0103. This is so close to 3 that even formal texts refer to this number as "3 dB", and a linear factor of 2 is often called "6 dB" instead of 6.0206. This is similar to calling 1,024 bytes "one kilobyte". If you ever wonder how a factor of 2 got to be exactly 6 dB, well, it didn't!

[4] This still does not violate the law of conservation of energy. In a room, even mono signals cannot stay in phase everywhere, so the total power is conserved even if there are some "hot spots".

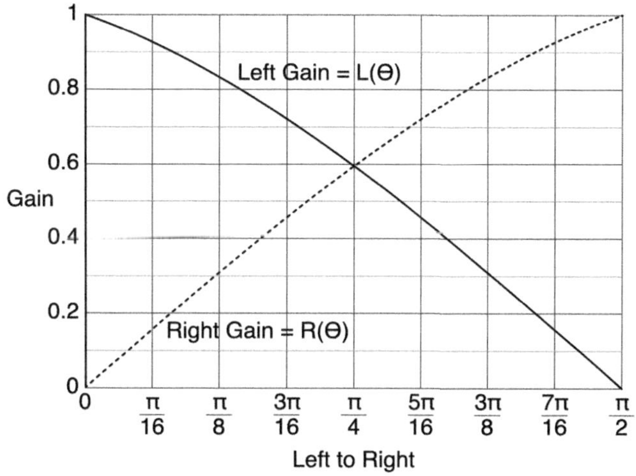

Figure 10.17: The –4.5 dB pan law.

$L^2(\pi/4)+R^2(\pi/4) = .59^2+.59^2 = 0.71$, corresponding to $10\log_{10}(\frac{.59^2+.59^2}{1^2})$ dB $= -1.5$ dB. If amplitudes are additive when stereo is converted to mono, the center pan signal is boosted by 1.5 dB. When signals are panned to the center and not heard in phase, the center pan signal is attenuated by 1.5 dB.

10.3.6.4 Which Pan Law to Use When?

According to a number of sources (and as an interesting historic aside), back in the 1930's, the Disney corporation tested different pan laws on human subjects, and found that constant power panning was preferred by the listeners. Then, in the 1950's, the BBC conducted a similar experiment and concluded that the –4.5 dB compromise was the better pan law. Now, we know next to nothing about the details of those experiments, but their results might make sense if we assume that Disney's focus was on movie theaters and the BBC's was on TV audiences. Let's elaborate on that. It all depends on the listening situation. That is, how are the speakers placed, what is the size of the room, where is the listener placed, and can we expect the listener to stay in the same place? If the speakers are placed close to each other in a small room (with very little reverb) or if the listener is in the sweet spot, then one can reasonably expect that the phases of the signals from the two speakers will add up constructively (at least at lower frequencies, acting pretty much as one single speaker (at least at lower frequencies); as depicted in Figure 10.18.

In such a case where signals are in phase so that the left and right amplitudes sum, the sounds that are panned to the center will experience up to 3 dB of boost with constant power panning but a maximum of only 1.5 dB boost using the –4.5 dB compromise. Thus, the –4.5 dB rule might give more equal loudness panning.

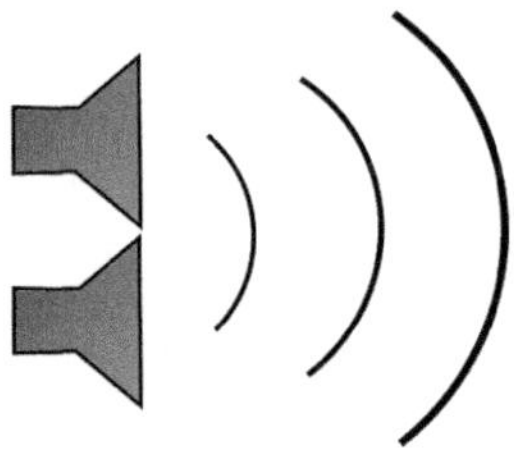

Figure 10.18: Two speakers in phase acting as one.

It could also be that the BBC considered mono TV sets where the left and right channels are added perfectly in phase. In this case, the –4.5 dB compromise gives a 1.5 dB boost to center-panned signals vs. a 3 dB boost with constant power panning. (Recall that linear panning is ideal for mono reproduction because the center-panned signals are not boosted at all. However, linear panning results in the "hole-in-the-middle" problem for stereo.)

On the other hand, if the speakers are placed far from each other in a big room, then the phases will not add up constructively; as seen in Figure 10.19.

Figure 10.19: Two speakers out of phase; phases do not add constructively.

Furthermore, in this case, the listeners are probably not always placed at the sweet spot—there are probably multiple listeners placed at different distances and angles to the speakers (as in a movie theater). One would expect constant power panning to produce more uniform loudness at all panning positions in this situation.

Given the variables of listener position, speaker placement, and possible stereo-to-mono conversion, there is no universal solution that optimizes panning. Both constant power panning and the –4.5 dB compromise are widely used, and both are preferred over linear panning.

10.3.6.5 Panning and Room Simulation

A more sophisticated approach to panning is to consider that in stereo recording, a left-facing microphone signal is very different from that of a right-facing microphone. Signal differences have to do with room reflections and the source location. A sound source at stage left will undergo different modifications getting to each microphone, and similarly for the source at stage right. Thus there are *four* different paths from sources to microphones, and that is considering only two source locations! Some panning systems take these paths into consideration or even integrate panning with reverberation simulation.

10.3.6.6 Panning in Nyquist

In Nyquist, panning splits a monophonic signal (single channel) into stereo outputs (two channels; recall that multiple channel signals are represented using arrays of sounds), and the degree of left or right of that signal can be controlled by either a fixed parameter or a variable control envelope:

`pan(`*sound*`,` *where*`)`

The pan function pans *sound* (a behavior) according to *where* (another behavior or a number). *Sound* must be monophonic. The *where* parameter should range from 0 to 1, where 0 means pan completely left, and 1 means pan completely right. For intermediate values, the sound is scaled *linearly* between left and right.

10.3.7 Compression/Limiting

A Compression/Limiting effect refers to automatic gain control, which reduces the dynamic range of a signal. Do not confuse dynamics compression with data compression such as producing an MP3 file. When you have a signal that ranges from very soft to very loud, you might like to boost the soft part. Alternatively, when you have a narrow dynamic range, you can expand it to make soft sounds much quieter and louder sounds even louder.

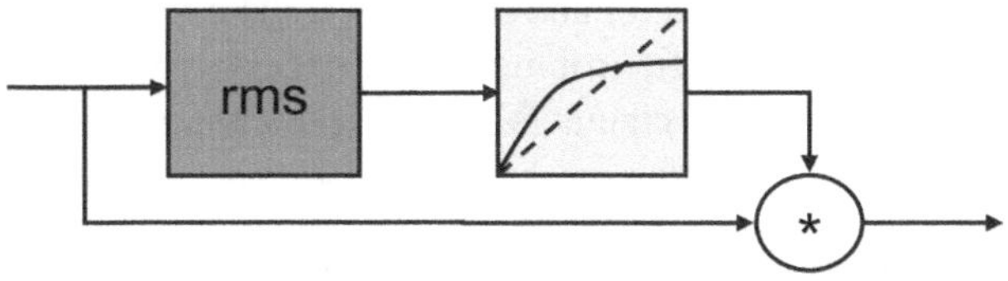

Figure 10.20: Compression/Limiting effect. The input signal is analyzed to obtain the RMS (average) amplitude. The amplitude is mapped to obtain a gain, and the signal is multiplied by the gain. The solid line shown in the mapping (at right) is typical, indicating that soft sounds are boosted, but as the input becomes increasingly loud, the gain is less, reducing the overall dynamic range (i.e., the variation in amplitude is compressed.)

The basic algorithm for compression is shown in Figure 10.20. The compressor detects the signal level with a Root Mean Square (RMS) detector[5] and uses table lookup to determine how much gain to place on the original signal at that point. The implementation in Nyquist is provided by the Nyquist Extension named `compress`, and there are two useful functions in the extension. The first one is `compress`, which compresses *input* using *map*, a compression curve probably generated by `compress-map`.[6] Adjustments in gain have the given *rise-time* and *fall-time*. *lookahead* tells how far ahead to look at the signal, and is *rise-time* by default. Another function is `agc`, an automatic gain control applied to *input*. The maximum gain in dB is *range*. Peaks are attenuated to 1.0, and gain is controlled with the given *rise-time* and *fall-time*. The look-ahead time default is *rise-time*.

`compress(`*input*`,` *map*`,` *rise-time*`,` *fall-time*`,` *lookahead*`)`

`agc(`*input*`,` *range*`,` *rise-time*`,` *fall-time*`,` *lookahead*`)`

10.3.8 Reverse

Reverse is simply playing a sound backwards. In Nyquist, the reverse functions can either reverse a sound or a file, and both are part of the Nyquist extension named `reverse`. If you reverse a file, Nyquist reads blocks of samples from the file and reverses them, one-at-a-time. Using this method, Nyquist can reverse very long sounds without using much memory. See `s-read-reverse` in the *Nyquist Reference Manual* for details.

To reverse a sound, Nyquist must evaluate the whole sound in memory, which requires 4 bytes per sample plus some overhead. The function `s-reverse(`*sound*`)` reverses *sound*, which must be shorter than `*max-reverse-samples*` (currently initialized to 25 million samples). This function does sample-by-sample processing without an efficiently compiled unit generator, so do not be surprised if it calls the garbage collector a lot and runs slowly. The result starts at the starting time given by the current environment (not necessarily the starting time of *sound*). If *sound* has multiple channels, a multiple channel, reversed sound is returned.

[5]The RMS analysis consists of squaring the signal, which converts each sample from positive or negative amplitude to a positive measure of power, then taking the mean of a set of consecutive power samples perhaps 10 to 50 ms in duration, and finally taking the square root of this "mean power" to get an amplitude.

[6]`compress-map(`*compress-ratio*`,` *compress-threshold*`,` *expand-ratio*`,` *expand-threshold*`,` *limit*`,` *transition*`,` *verbose*`)` constructs a map for the compress function. The map consists of two parts: a compression part and an expansion part. The intended use is to compress everything above compress-threshold by *compress-ratio*, and to downward expand everything below *expand-threshold* by *expand-ratio*. Thresholds are in dB and ratios are dB-per-dB. 0 dB corresponds to a peak amplitude of 1.0 or RMS amplitude of 0.7. If the input goes above 0 dB, the output can optionally be limited by setting `limit:` (a keyword parameter) to `T`. This effectively changes the compression ratio to infinity at 0 dB. If `limit:` is `nil` (the default), then the *compression-ratio* continues to apply above 0 dB.

10.3.9 Sample-Rate Conversion

Nyquist has high-quality interpolation to alter sample rates. There are a lot of sample rate conversions going on in Nyquist behind the scenes: Nyquist implicitly changes the sample rate of control functions such as produced by `env` and `lfo` from their default sample rate which is 1/20 of the audio sample rate. When you multiply an envelope by an audio rate signal, Nyquist *linearly* interpolates the control function. This is reasonable with most control functions because, if they are changing slowly, linear interpolation will be a good approximation of higher-quality signal reconstruction, and linear interpolation is fast. However, if you want to change the sample rate of audio, for example if you read a file with a 48 kHz sample rate and you want the rate to be 44.1 kHz, then you should use high-quality sample-rate conversion to avoid distortion and aliasing that can arise from linear interpolation.

The algorithm for high-quality sample-rate conversion in Nyquist is a digital low pass filter followed by digital reconstruction using *sinc* interpolation. There are two useful conversion functions:

`force-srate(`*srate*`,` *sound*`)`

returns a sound which is up- or down-sampled to *srate*. Interpolation is linear, and no pre-filtering is applied in the down-sample case, so aliasing may occur:

`resample(`*snd*`,` *rate*`)`

Performs high-quality interpolation to reconstruct the signal at the new sample rate. The result is scaled by 0.95 to reduce problems with clipping. (Why? Interestingly, an interpolated signal can reconstruct peaks that exceed the amplitude of the original samples.)

Nyquist also has a variable sample-rate function:

`sound-warp(`*warp-fn*`,` *signal*`,` *wrate*`)`

applies a warp function *warp-fn* to *signal* using function composition. If the optional parameter *wrate* is omitted or NIL, linear interpolation is used. Otherwise, high-quality sample interpolation is used, and the result is scaled by 0.95 to reduce problems with clipping. Here, *warp-fn* is a mapping from score (logical) time to real time, and *signal* is a function from score time to real values. The result is a function from real time to real values at a sample rate of `*sound-srate*`. See the *Nyquist Reference Manual* for details about *wrate*.

To perform high-quality stretching by a fixed ratio, as opposed to a variable ratio allowed in `sound-warp`, use `scale-srate` to stretch or shrink the sound, and then `resample` to restore the original sample rate.

10.3.10 Sample Size Conversion (Quantization)

Nyquist allows you to simulate different sample sizes using the unit generator `quantize`:

quantize(*sound*, *steps*)

This unit generator quantizes *sound* as follows: *sound* is multiplied by *steps* and rounded to the nearest integer. The result is then divided by *steps*. For example, if *steps* is 127, then a signal that ranges from –1 to +1 will be quantized to 255 levels (127 less than zero, 127 greater than zero, and zero itself). This would match the quantization Nyquist performs when writing a signal to an 8-bit audio file. The *sound* may be multi-channel.

10.3.11 Reverberation

A reverberation effect simulates playing a sound in a room or concert hall. Typical enclosed spaces produce many reflections from walls, floor, ceiling, chairs, balconies, etc. The number of reflections increases exponentially with time due to secondary, tertiary, and additional reflections, and also because sound is following paths in all directions.

Typically, reverberation is modeled in two parts:

- Early reflections, e.g., sounds bouncing off one wall before reaching the listener, are modeled by discrete delays.
- Late reflections become very dense and diffuse and are modeled using a network of all-pass and feedback-delay filters.

Reverberation often uses a low-pass filter in the late reflection model because high frequencies are absorbed by air and room surfaces.

Reverberation has a roughly exponential decay, which implies a fixed ratio (commonly measured in dB) in power or amplitude over a fixed period of time. Therefore, the rate of decay of reverberation is conventionally described by RT60, the time to decay to –60 dB relative to the peak amplitude. (–60 dB is about 1/1000 in amplitude.) Typical values of RT60 are around 1.5 to 3 s, but much longer times are easy to create digitally and can be very interesting.

In Nyquist, the `reverb` function provides a simple reverberator. You will probably want to mix the reverberated signal with some "dry" original signal, so you might like this function:

```
function reverb-mix(s, rt, wet)
  return s * (1 - wet) + reverb(s, rt) * wet
```

Nyquist also has some reverberators from the Synthesis Tool Kit: `nrev` (similar to Nyquist's reverb), `jcrev` (ported from an implementation by John Chowning), and `prcrev` (created by Perry Cook). See the *Nyquist Reference Manual* for details. All of these reverberator designs stem from the seminal paper by Manfred Schroeder (82).

10.3.11.1 Convolution-based Reverberators

Reverberators can be seen as very big filters with long irregular impulse responses. Many modern reverberators measure the impulse response of a real room or concert hall and apply the impulse response to an input signal using convolution (recall that filtering is equivalent to multiplication in the frequency domain, and that is what convolution does).

With stereo signals, a traditional approach is to mix stereo to mono, compute reverberation, then add the mono reverberation signal to both left and right channels. In more modern reverberation implementations, convolution-based reverberators use 4 impulse responses because the input and output are stereo. There is an impulse response representing how the stage-left (left input) signal reaches the left channel or left ear (left output), the stage-left signal to the right channel or right ear, stage-right to the left channel, and stage-right to the right channel.

Nyquist has a `convolve` function to convolve two sounds. There is no Nyquist library of impulse responses for reverberation, but see `www.openairlib.net/`, `oramics.github.io/sampled/IR/Voxengo/` and other sources. Convolution with different sounds (even if they are not room responses) is an interesting effect for creating new sounds.

10.3.12 Summary

Many audio effects are available in Nyquist. Audio effects are crucial in modern music production and offer a range of creative possibilities. Synthesized sounds can be greatly enhanced through audio effects including filters, chorus, and delay. Effects can be modulated to add additional interest.

Panning algorithms are surprisingly non-obvious, largely due to the "hole-in-the-middle" effect and the desire to minimize the problem. The –4.5 dB panning law seems to be a reasonable choice unless you know more about the listening conditions.

Reverberation is the effect of millions of "echoes" caused by reflections off of walls and other surfaces when sound is created in a room or reflective space. Reverberation echos generally become denser with greater delay, and the sound of reverberation generally has an approximately exponential decay.

Chapter 11

Physical Modeling

Topics Discussed: Mass-Spring Models, Karplus-Strong, Waveguide Models, Guitar Models

11.1 Introduction

One promising way to create sounds is to simulate or model an acoustic instrument. If the model is accurate, then the details of control and vibration can in principle lead to realistic sounds with all the control possibilities of physical instruments. This approach might be called physics-based modeling, but the common terminology is simply *physical models* (4). Physical models can be contrasted with *abstract synthesis* or the use of mathematical functions (such as FM synthesis and Additive synthesis), *sampling*, and *source-filter models*. None of these alternative approaches really capture the complexities of physical systems. When aspects of physical systems defy analysis, we can resort to simulation to compute and predict the behavior of those systems. However, even simulation is selective and incomplete. The key is to model the interesting aspects while keeping the overall simulation and its computation tractable.

Like all of the synthesis methods we have covered, physical modeling is not one specific technique, but rather a variety of related techniques. Behind them all, however, is the basic idea that by understanding how sound, vibration, air, and strings behave in some physical system (an instrument), we can model that system in a computer and thereby generate realistic sounds through computation.

DOI: 10.1201/9781003782711-11

11.2 Mass-Spring Model

A simple example of a physical model is the Mass-Spring model consisting of a string and a set of masses attached to the string (shown in Figure 11.1) (7). This is a discrete approximation of a continuous string where mass is distributed uniformly throughout the length of the string. By "lumping" the mass at a finite set of points, we can use digital simulation to model the string. In the model, we consider the string between masses to be massless springs that pull on the masses with a force that is proportional to the stretch of the spring.

To analyze all the forces here: the springs are pulling on the objects in opposite directions, the masses at the ends are assumed fixed. Because the springs are pulling in both directions, there is little/no longitudinal force on the objects, but there is a vertical restoring force. So when the string is bent up with the concave side facing down, some of the forces on the masses are downward, as shown by "Restoring Force" in Figure 11.1. Conversely, when the string is down with the concave side facing up, the net force is pulling up. These forces will accelerate the objects. If we put the string in this configuration and release it, then the left half will accelerate downward and right half would go upward. As the masses are pulled to zero displacement, or to a straight line between the end points, there is no more net force on the objects but the masses will keep moving and stretch the string in the opposite direction until the restoring force can slow them down and reverse the direction. This motion will repeat, causing the string to oscillate.

Figure 11.1: Mass-Spring Model of a String.

This is a computationally expensive model because you have to compute the force on each one of the masses and store the velocity and position of the masses for each time step of the simulation. But computers are fast, and discrete time simulation is mostly multiplies and adds, so you can easily run interesting models (including this one) in real time. The number of modes (partials) that you can support corresponds to the number of masses. Also, you can add stiffness and other interesting properties into the string, e.g., the string can be non-linear, it can have a driving force, there can be friction, etc.

11.3 Karplus-Strong Plucked String Algorithm

Let's take a look at a variation of the Mass-Spring model. This is a really simple but very effective physical model of a plucked string, called the *Karplus-Strong algorithm* (so named for its principal inventors, Kevin Karplus and Alex Strong) (49). One of the first musically useful physical models (dating from the early 1980s[1]), the Karplus-Strong algorithm has proven quite effective at generating a variety of plucked-string sounds (acoustic and electric guitars, banjos, and kotos) and even drum-like timbres (48). Nyquist has an improved implementation in the function `pluck`.

Here's a simplified view of what happens when we pluck a string: At first the string is highly energized and it vibrates, creating a fairly complex (meaning rich in harmonics) sound wave whose fundamental frequency is determined by the mass and tension of the string. Gradually, thanks to friction between the air and the string, as well as the dissipation of energy in the form of sound waves, the string's energy is depleted. The higher frequencies tend to lose energy the fastest, so the wave becomes less complex as it decays, resulting in a purer tone with fewer harmonics. After some amount of time all of the energy from the pluck is gone, and the string stops vibrating.

If you have access to a stringed instrument, particularly one with some very low notes, give one of the strings a good pluck and see if you can see and hear what's happening based on the description above.

11.3.1 How a Computer Models a Plucked String with the Karplus-Strong Algorithm

Now that we have a physical idea of what happens in a plucked string, how can we model it with a computer? The Karplus-Strong algorithm does it like this: first we start with a buffer full of random values—noise. (A buffer is just some computer memory (RAM) where we can store a bunch of numbers.) The numbers in this buffer represent the initial energy that is transferred to the string by the pluck. The Karplus-Strong algorithm looks like this:

$$Y_t = \frac{1}{2}(Y_{t-p} + Y_{t-p-1})$$

Here, p is the period or length of the buffer, t is the current sample count, and Y is the output of the system.

[1]When I was an undergraduate at Rice University, a graduate student was working with a PDP-11 mini-computer with a vector graphics display. There were digital-to-analog converters to drive the display, and the student had connected them to a stereo system to make a primitive digital audio system. I remember his description of the synthesis system he used, and it was exactly the Karplus-Strong algorithm, including initializing the buffer with random numbers. This was in the late 1970s, so it seems Karplus and Strong *reinvented* the algorithm, but certainly deserve credit for publishing their work.

To generate a waveform, we start reading through the buffer and using the values in it as sample values. If we were to just keep reading through the buffer over and over again, we would get a complex, periodic, pitched waveform. It would be complex because we started out with noise, but pitched because we would be repeating the same set of random numbers. (Remember that any time we repeat a set of values, we end up with a pitched sound.) The pitch we get is directly related to the size of the buffer (the number of numbers it contains) we're using, since each time through the buffer represents one complete cycle (or period) of the signal.

Now, here's the trick to the Karplus-Strong algorithm: each time we read a value from the buffer, we average it with the last value we read. It is this averaged value that we use as our output sample. (See Figure 11.2.) We then take that averaged sample and feed it back into the buffer. That way, over time, the buffer gets more and more averaged (this is a simple filter, like the averaging filter, Equation 7.1). Let's look at the effect of these two actions separately.

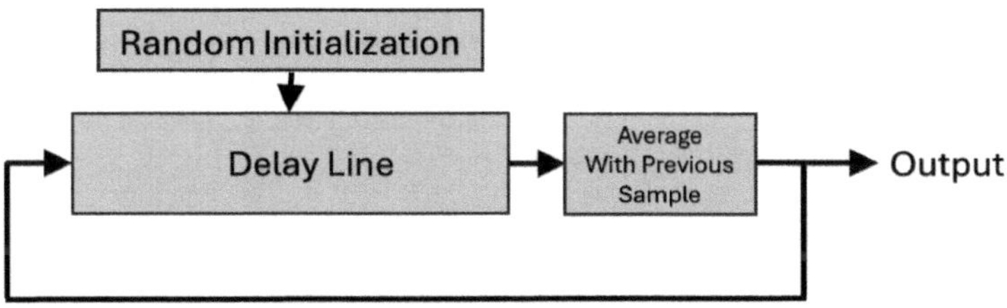

Figure 11.2: Schematic view of a computer software implementation of the basic Karplus-Strong algorithm. For each note, the computer memory buffer is filled with random values (noise). To generate a sample, values are read from the buffer and averaged. The newly calculated sample is both sent to the output stream and stored back into the buffer. When the end of the buffer is reached, we simply wrap around and continue reading at the beginning. This sort of setup is often called a circular buffer. After many iterations of this process, the buffer's contents will have been transformed from noise into a simple waveform. If you think of the random noise as a lot of energy and the averaging of the buffer as a way of lessening that energy, this digital explanation is not all that dissimilar from what happens in the real, physical case.

11.3.2 Averaging and Feedback

First, what happens when we average two values? Averaging acts as a low-pass filter on the signal. Since high frequencies have a high rate of change, averaging has a bigger effect on high frequencies than low ones. So, averaging a signal effectively reduces high frequencies.

The "over time" part is where feeding the averaged samples back into the buffer comes in. If we were to just keep averaging the values from the buffer but never actually putting the average back into the buffer, then we would be stuck with a static waveform. We would keep averaging the same set of random numbers, so we would keep getting the same results.

Instead, each time we generate a new sample, we store it back into the buffer. That way our waveform evolves as we move through it. The effect of this low-pass filtering accumulates over time, so that as the string "rings", more and more of the high frequencies are filtered out of it. Figure 11.3 illustrates how the contents of the Karplus-Strong buffer changes and decays over time. After enough times through the process, the signal has been averaged so many times that it reaches equilibrium—the waveform is a flat line and the vibration has died out.

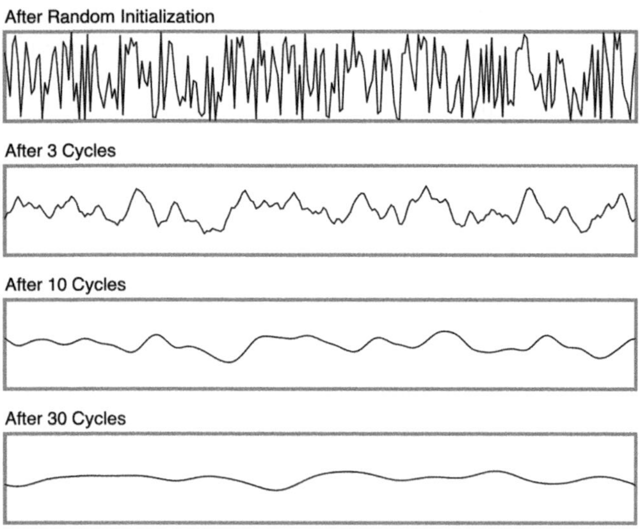

Figure 11.3: Applying the Karplus-Strong algorithm to a random waveform. After 30 passes through the filter/feedback cycle, all that's left of the wild random noise is a gently curving wave. The result is much like what we described in a plucked string: an initially complex, periodic waveform that gradually becomes less complex over time and ultimately fades away.

Physical models generally offer clear, "real world" controls that can be used to play an instrument in different ways, and the Karplus-Strong algorithm is no exception: we can relate the buffer size to pitch, the initial random numbers in the buffer to the energy given to the string by plucking it, and the low-pass buffer feedback technique to the effect of air friction on the vibrating string.

11.4 Waveguide Model

Now, we consider another model of the string, called the *waveguide model*, introduced by Julius O. Smith III (43). In a real string, waves travel down the string until they reach the end where the wave is reflected and travels back in the opposite direction. A vibrating string is actually a wave traveling up and down the string, reflecting at both ends, and the left-going and right-going waves sum through superposition to determine the displacement of the string at any given location and time.

It is easy to model wave travel in one direction: we simply delay the samples by storing incoming samples in an array (wrapping around when we reach the end), and reading out older samples. This allows a delay up to the length of the array. If we ignore friction and other losses, a string carrying a waveform can be modeled as a delay.

To model left-going *and* right-going waves, we simply use two one-way models, i.e., two delays. The output of one delay connects to the input of the other. (See Figure 11.4.) If we want the amplitude of the string at some particular point, we access *both* delays (the left-going and right-going wave models) and sum the amplitudes.

11.4.1 "Lumped" Filters

Now, what about losses? In a continuous string, there should be loss at every step of the way through the string. Since this would be computationally expensive, we use a shortcut and compute the total losses for the entire trip from one end of the string to the other. This can be expressed as a filter that we can apply to the output of the delay. This so-called "lumped" filter is efficient and can give the same effect as accumulating tiny losses at each sample of delay.

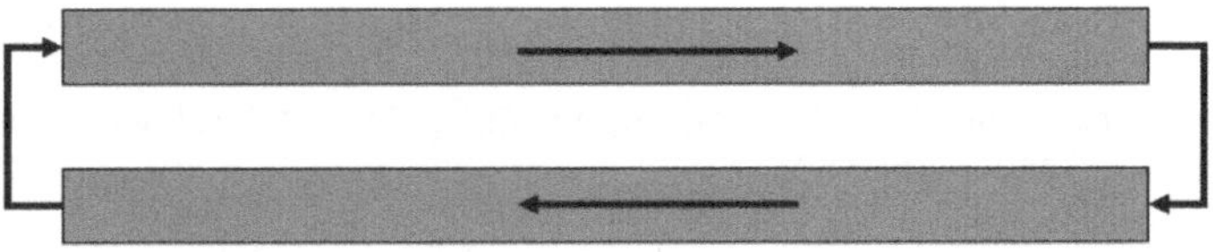

Figure 11.4: A waveguide model. The right-going and left-going wave, which are superimposed on a single string, are modeled separately as simple delays. The signal connections at the ends of the delays represent reflections. A waveguide can also model a column of air as in a flute.

11.5 Mechanical Oscillator

To make a sustained sound, we must overcome the losses in the waveguide. The case of the bowed string is probably the easiest to understand, so we will start there. Figure 11.5 illustrates the oscillation in a bowed string. The bow alternately sticks to and slips across the string. Rather than reaching a steady equilibrium where the bow pulls the string to some steady stretched configuration, the "slip" phase reduces friction on the string and allows the string to move almost as if were plucked. Interestingly, string players put rosin on the bow, which is normally sticky, but when the string begins to slip, the rosin heats up at a molecular level which lowers friction, encouraging the slipping to continue (88). Eventually, the natural vibration of the string causes the string to move in the direction of the bow and stick once again. It's amazing to think that rosin on the string and bow can heat and cool at audio rates!

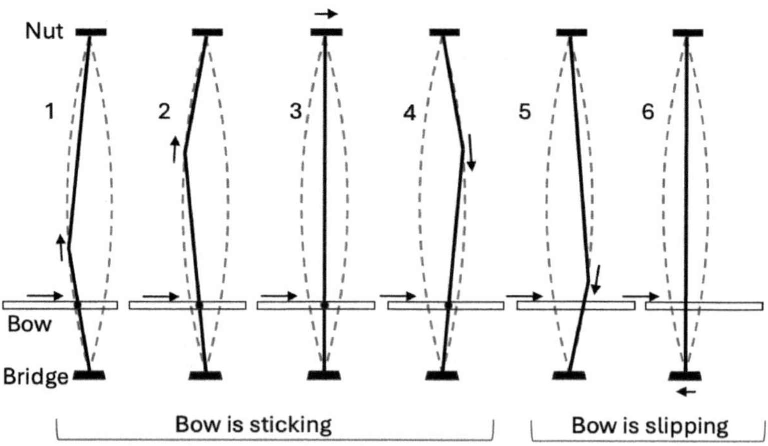

Figure 11.5: A bowed string is pulled by the bow when the bow sticks to the string (1 through 4). At some point the bow does not have enough friction to pull the string further, and the string begins to slip. The sliding reduces the friction on the string, which allows it to stretch in opposition to the bowing direction (5 and 6). Finally, the stretching slows the string and the bow sticks again, repeating the cycle.

11.5.1 McIntyre, Woodhouse (1979) + Schumacher (1983)

An important advance in physical models came from McIntyre and Woodhouse who resorted to models to help understand the nature of oscillation in acoustical instruments (60). Later, Schumacher, a physics professor at Carnegie Mellon University, visited McIntyre and Woodhouse to learn more about their work and the three physicists wrote a paper that formed the basis for a lot of work in the field of Computer Music (59).

Their model follows the basic ideas we have outlined so far. Rather than a bi-directional waveguide, they combined the two delays into one as shown in Figure 11.6, with a single low-pass filter to model losses over the entire loop. Since the model is for a woodwind rather than a bowed string, the delay is considered to represent a traveling pressure wave rather than string displacement. McIntyre, Woodhouse, and Schumacher added a non-linear element to generate oscillation.

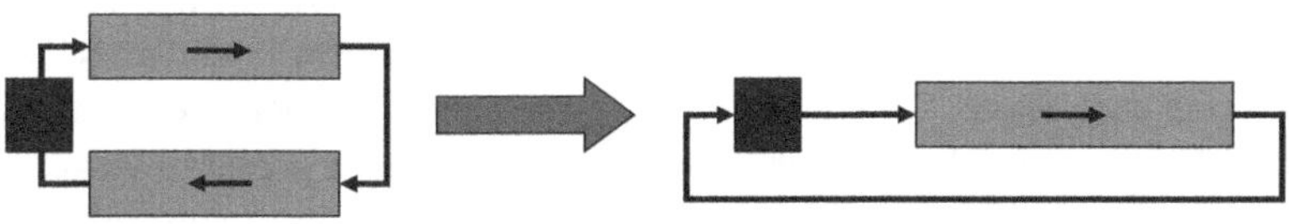

Figure 11.6: McIntyre Woodhouse model consisting of a delay representing sound traveling through the bore of a clarinet and a filter representing the losses over the round trip. The figure shows that the single delay is equivalent to a bi-directional waveguide with perfect reflection at one end.

11.5.2 Smith: Efficient Reed-Bore and Bow-String Mechanisms (ICMC 86)

Julius Smith was influenced by McIntyre, Woodhouse, and Schumacher and developed computer music instruments that model the clarinet and violin Julius O. Smith III (42).

Figure 11.7 shows Smith's clarinet model. It includes a waveguide with low-pass filter (–LP in the figure). At the left side of the figure is a model of the reed, which has non-linear behavior that enables oscillation. A clarinet *reed* is a thin, flat, flexible plate that vibrates over an opening to the clarinet's body or *bore*. The reed acts as a valve to let air in when the reed is up or open, and to block the air when the reed is down or closed.

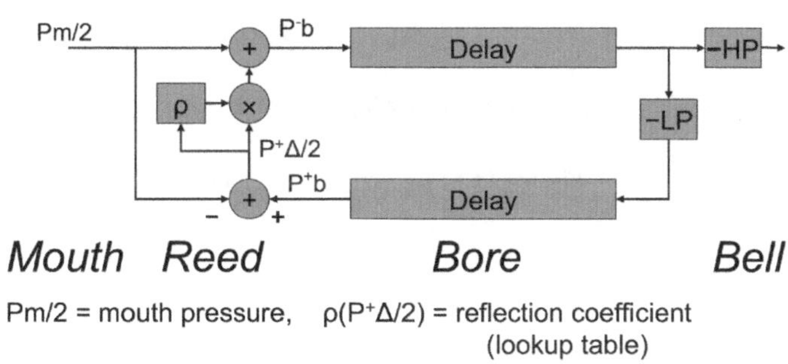

Figure 11.7: Clarinet model.

To understand oscillation in the clarinet model, we can follow the "story" of one period (3). To begin with, the reed is open and pressure from the mouth enters the clarinet. The pressure also closes the reed valve, at least to some extent. The high pressure front travels to the bell, the flare at the end of the clarinet, where the pressure is reflected. The reflection is inverted, so now the pressure front is negative. The negated pressure wave returns to the reed, where it is reflected again. This time, the reflection does not invert the wave because this end is effectively closed. The negative pressure acts to close the reed even further. The negative pressure returns to the bell, is inverted again, and reflects back to the reed as a positive pressure wave. This positive pressure tends to open the reed, allowing air through the reed valve, which reinforces the positive pressure wave, and another cycle begins. If the addition of energy or pressure compensates for losses, a sustained oscillation will result.

Figure 11.8 illustrates a bowed string model. In this model, the bow is not at the end of the string, so there is one waveguide from the bow to the bridge (where strings are anchored over the body) and one waveguide from the bow to the nut (where strings are anchored at the end of the fingerboard). The bow has a nonlinear element (ρ in the figure) that models the change in friction between the stick and slip phases.

Also, the model includes a filter between the bridge and the output. In a violin, the bridge transfers vibration from strings to the body, and the body radiates sound into the room. The body has resonances and radiates in a frequency-dependent manner, so a filter to model the transfer of sound from bridge to room is important to getting a violin-like sound.

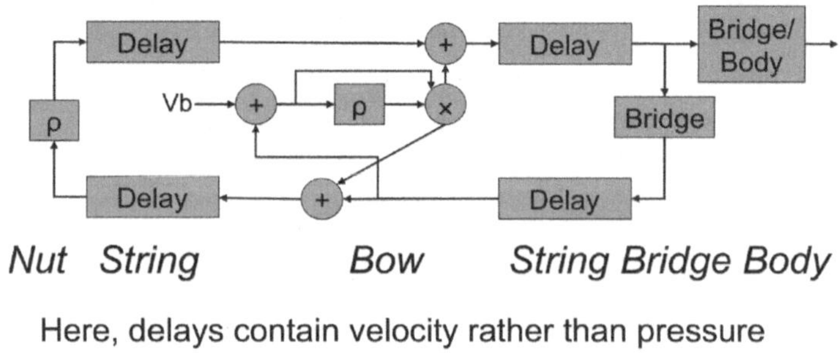

Figure 11.8: Bowed String Model.

11.6 Flute Physical Model

Figure 11.9 is a simple model for a flute, showing a single delay that models the round-trip through the flute, a low-pass filter (LP) to model the losses, and a high-pass filter (HP) to model radiation into the room.

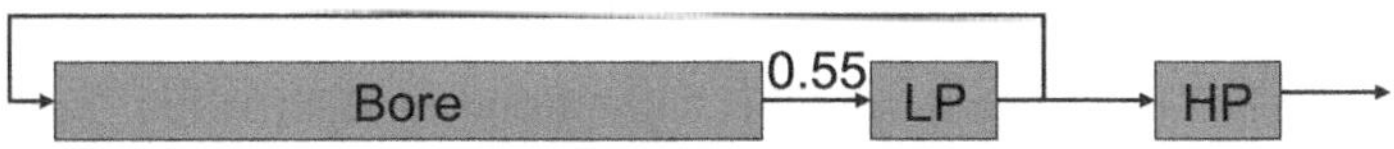

Figure 11.9: Flute Physical Model.

Figure 11.10 shows a more elaborate model by Perry R. Cook (12) that includes a mouthpiece to drive sustaining oscillation. The input to the mouthpiece is the sum of a smooth pressure envelope (the breath) and some random noise (turbulence). As with other models, there must be some non-linearity or the model will simply settle into a steady state. In this case, the non-linearity is $x - x^3$, which is simple but enough to allow oscillation to occur.

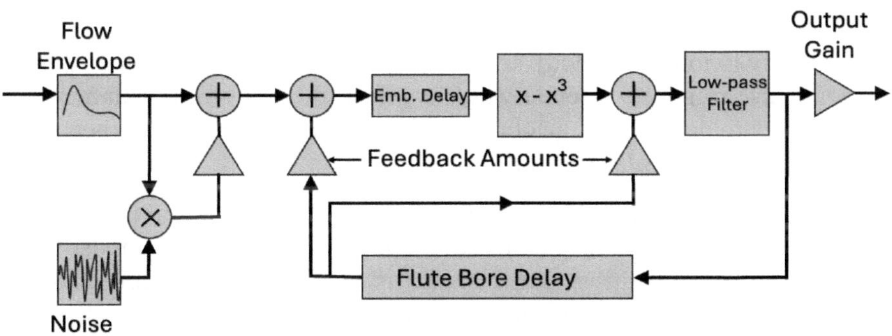

Figure 11.10: Flute Physical Model.

11.7 Physical Models in Nyquist

Nyquist has a number of built-in physical models. Many of them come from the Synthesis Tool Kit (STK) (14).

`pluck(`*pitch*`,` *dur*`,` *final-amp*`)` is an extended Karplus-Strong plucked string model. The extension inserts a filter into the loop (besides the simple averaging filter we learned about) to allow sub-sample delays needed for accurate tuning. In addition, the rate of decay can be modified by the optional parameters *dur* and *final-amp*. Increasing either or both parameters lowers the decay rate. You might want to multiply by an envelope to avoid a click at the end if the *final-amp* is high.

`clarinet(`*step*`,` *breath-env*`)` is a basic STK clarinet model. There are several variations on this model in Nyquist that allow continuous control over frequency, breath envelope, vibrato, reed-stiffness, and noise through additional parameters. See the *Nyquist Reference Manual* for details.

`sax(`*step*`,` *breath-env*`)` is a basic STK saxophone model (called "saxophony"). As with `clarinet`, there are variations with additional parameters.

Other models can be found in the *Nyquist Reference Manual.*

11.8 Commuted Synthesis

One of the problems with physical models of guitars, violins, and pianos is that vibrating strings excite a complex 3-dimensional body that is computationally hard to simulate. We can assume that the body is a kind of complex filter. We can characterize the body by tapping it at the bridge or point where the string is attached and measuring the impulse response.

Now, one way to model the body is to simply convolve the string force with the body's impulse response. In other words, we just filter the string with the body filter and we are done. But convolution is expensive, so researchers thought of another approach Julius O. Smith III (44).

Consider a piano model with a hammer model that transmits force to a string model, the string model transmits force to a bridge, and the body model filters the bridge force to obtain an output. Now, *the string and body are both just filters*! Multiplication and convolution and linear filters are all commutative (it's all more-or-less the same thing), so we can *switch the order of the string and body filters.* This makes no sense physically, but in our simulation, instead of driving the string with an impulse (as if hit by a hammer), we can drive the string with the impulse response of the body! Thus, for every note, we just have to "play" the impulse response into the string model, saving the need for a complex body filter on the output.

For strings, the commuted synthesis model is a little more complex because the bow is repeatedly pumping energy into the string. We need to run a bowed string model to detect when the bow slip occurs. Then, we treat that as the driving impulse, and every time the bow slips, we drive a *second* string model with the violin body impulse response. We take the output from this second string model.

11.9 Electric Guitar Model

Charles R. Sullivan developed an interesting guitar model (91). His work was motivated more by obtaining usable control than by being a faithful model.

The basic model is shown in Figure 11.11, and you can see that this is closely related to the Karplus-Strong model. The low-pass filter determines the decay rate of the string and can also change the effective length (and frequency) of the string by inserting additional delay. In this model, an FIR filter is used:

$$y_n = a_0 x_n + a_1 x_{n-1} + a_2 x_{n-2}$$

but this potentially has gain at zero Hz (DC).

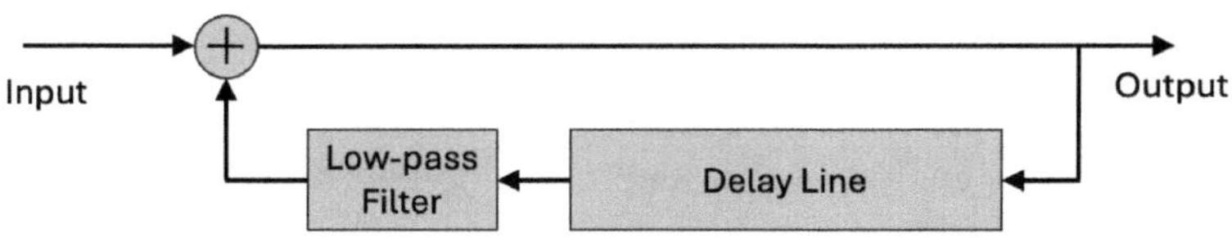

Figure 11.11: Electric Guitar Model by Charles R. Sullivan. The model is based on Karplus-Strong, but the low-pass filter is customized and the model allows continuous input through the summation node to allow for plucking while the string is still vibrating and feedback.

11.9.1 Loop Filter Design

To eliminate DC, we can add a high-pass filter:

$$y_n = a_0 x_n + a_1 x_{n-1} + b_1 y_{n-1}$$

We also want to provide continuous tuning, for which we need a sub-sample delay. Simple linear interpolation:

$$y_n = c_0 x_n + c_1 x_{n-1}$$

can be used, but this also produces attenuation (low-pass filter), so we can adjust the FIR to provide only the additional attenuation required.

After all this, the model is still not perfect and might require a compensating boost at higher frequencies, but Sullivan decided to ignore this problem: Sometimes higher frequencies will suffer, but the model is workable.

11.9.2 Tuning and Glissandi

For tuning, we can just round the desired delay length to an integer number of samples and use interpolation to add the remaining fractional length. To achieve *glissando*, where the pitch changes continuously, we slowly change c_0, c_1 in the interpolator. When one coefficient reaches 1, we can change the delay length by 1, flip c_0, c_1, and there is no glitch, but we are ready to continue the glissando.

However, changing the loop length will require a change in the loop FIR filter. It is expensive to recalculate all the filters every sample, so Sullivan updates the filters once per period. There may be small artifacts, but these will generate harmonics that are masked by the string harmonics.

11.9.3 Distortion

In electric guitars, distortion of a single note just adds harmonics, but distortion of a sum of notes is not the sum of distorted notes: distortion is not linear, so all those nice properties of linearity do not apply here.

Sullivan creates distortion using a soft clipping function so that as amplitude increases, there is a gradual introduction of non-linear distortion. The signal is x and the distorted signal is $F(x)$ in the following equation, which is plotted in Figure 11.12:

$$F(x) = \begin{cases} \frac{2}{3} & x \geq 1 \\ x - \frac{x^3}{3} & -1 < x < 1 \\ -\frac{2}{3} & x \leq -1 \end{cases}$$

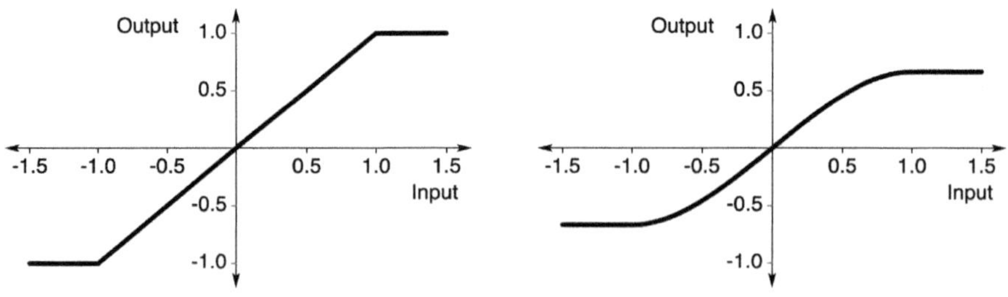

Figure 11.12: Distortion functions. At left is "hard clipping" where the signal is unaffected until it reaches limits of 1 and –1, at which points the signal is limited to those values. At right is a "soft clipping" distortion that is more like analog amplifiers with limited output range. The amplification is very linear for small amplitudes, but diminishes as the signal approaches the limits of 1 and –1.

11.9.4 Feedback

A wonderful technique available to electric guitarists is feedback, where the amplified signal is coupled back to the strings which then resonate in a sustained manner. Figure 11.13 illustrates Sullivan's configuration for feedback. There are many parameters to control gain and delay. Sullivan notes that one of the inter-

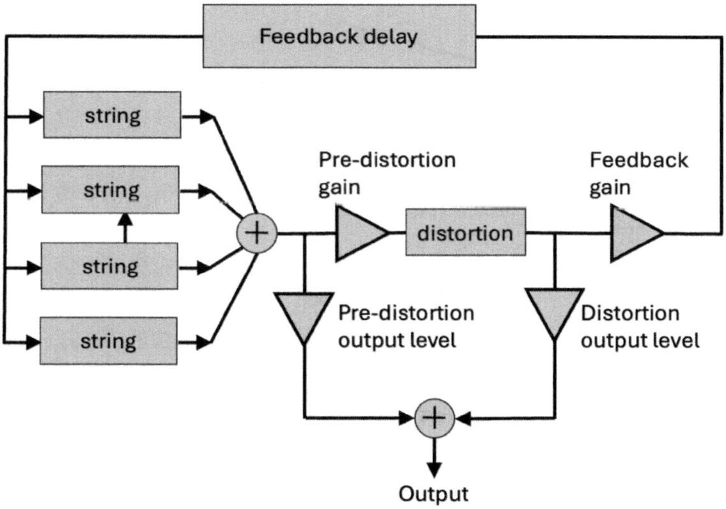

Figure 11.13: Feedback is achieved by feeding some of the output through a delay and back into each string model.

esting things about synthesizing guitar sounds with feedback is that even though it is hard to predict exactly what will happen, once you find parameter settings that work, the sounds are very reproducible. One guiding principle is that the instrument will tend to feedback at periods that are multiples of the feedback delay. This is quite different from real feedback with real guitars, where the player must interact with the amplifier and guitar, and particular sounds are hard to reproduce.

11.9.5 Initializing the String

When plucking a guitar string in this model, how should we initialize the string? In the Karplus-Strong model, strings are just initialized with random numbers, but this is not necessary, and it can be more interesting to simulate plucking as displacing the string at a particular point and releasing it. Plucking closer to the end of the string gives a brighter sound (try it if you have a guitar)! Figure 11.14 (a) shows the desired geometry of the initial string configuration. In the light of what we know about waveguides, this initial position must be split as right- and left-going waves as shown in Figure 11.14 (b). If there is a single delay (as in Karplus-Strong), we need to concatenate the right- and left-going wave configurations, resulting in an initial value as shown in Figure 11.14 (c).

11.9.6 Additional Features

Sullivan's electric guitar model is interesting because it shows how models can be extended incrementally to incorporate various features, either for study or for

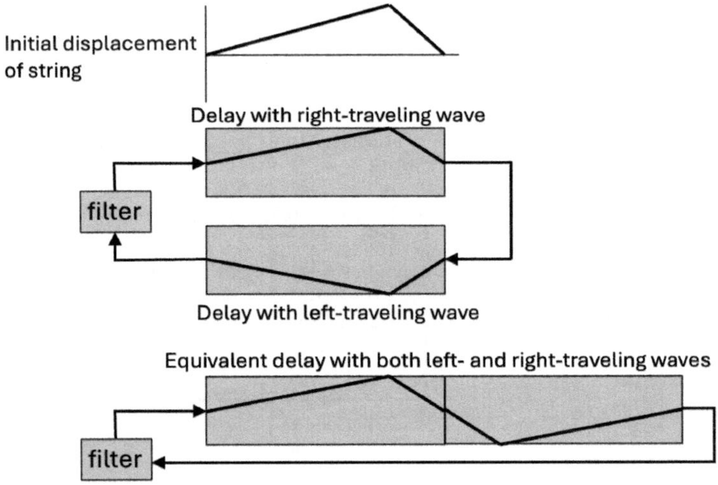

Figure 11.14: Initializing the string. The physical string shape contains both left- and right-going waves so we need to combine them to get a full round-trip initial waveform.

additional sound generation and control. There are still more things one could do with this model, including:

- Adding guitar body resonances,
- Coloration and distortion of guitar amplifiers,
- Effects processors, including:
  - Distortion,
  - Wah-wah pedals,
  - Chorus, etc.

11.10 Analysis Example

One of the challenges of physical models is that we need many parameters to make the model behave like real acoustic instruments. In some cases, parameters are obtained by trial-and-error, or else calculated, e.g., given a desired pitch, we can calculate the length of a waveguide.

However, it is interesting to estimate parameters from real sounds, and doing this enables us to check on whether the model is really capturing the behavior of the acoustic instrument. We present an example of the analysis of acoustic guitar sounds to estimate physical model parameters. This example should give some idea of how parameter estimation can be approached. The word *estimation*

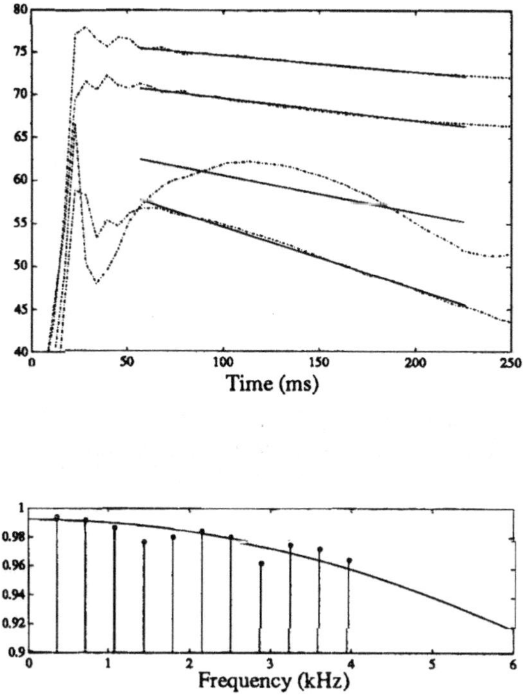

Figure 11.15: Analysis Example, from Karjalainen, Valimaki, and Janosy (47). At top, temporal envelopes of the four lowest harmonics of a guitar tone, with straight line fits. The amplitude scale is in dB. At bottom, estimated magnitude spectrum (circles) is used to fit a 1st-order IIR filter response.

should be emphasized—we rarely get the chance to measure anything exactly or directly.

In Figure 11.15, we see a plot of the amplitudes of harmonics of a plucked guitar string as they decay over time. Since decay is mainly due to losses as the wave travels up and down the string, we can fit lines to the curves and estimate the loss as a function of frequency. (Note that the decay should be exponential, so by plotting on a dB (log) scale, the decays appear as straight lines.)

After measuring the decay at different frequencies, we can fit a filter to the data, as shown in the lower half of the figure (47). If the filter is simple as shown, the fit will not be perfect, but measurement errors will tend to average out and the overall trend of the filter is likely to be well-estimated. Alternatively, one could fit a complex filter exactly to all the data points, but this would run the risk of "overfitting", or incorporating measurement errors into the model.

11.10.1 Driving Force

Another part of the model we might like to measure is the driving force on the string. After fitting a filter to the string recording, we can create an inverse filter, apply that to the recording, and end up with a "residual" that represents the input. Then, we can drive the string model with the residual to get a realistic sound.

11.11 2D Waveguide Mesh

The 1-dimensional waveguide can be extended to 2 or 3 dimensions. This adds a lot of computation, but allows us to model plates and drums in the 2D case, and resonant chambers and wind instruments in the 3D case.

Figure 11.16 shows a 2D waveguide mesh and the modeled propagation of a wave over a surface in work by Van Duyne and Smith (31).

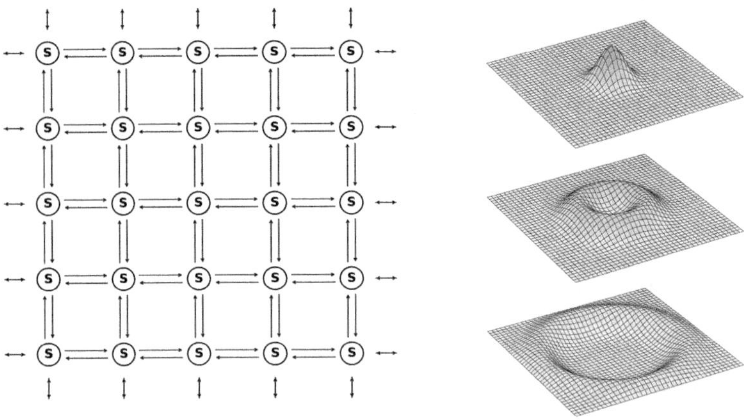

Figure 11.16: 2D Waveguide Mesh and some simulation results.

11.12 Summary

Physical models simulate physical systems to create sound digitally. A common approach is to model strings and bores (in wind instruments) with recirculating delays, and to "lump" the losses in a filter at some point in the loop. Non-linear elements are added to model how a driving force (a bow or breath) interacts with the wave in the recirculating delay to sustain an oscillation. Digital waveguides offer a simple model that separates the left- and right-going waves of the medium.

11.12.1 Advantages of Physical Modeling

One advantage of physical models is that non-linear vibrating systems have complex behaviors. Simulations can create complex and interesting behaviors that tend to arise naturally from models. In spite of potentially complex behavior, physical models tend to have a relatively small set of controls that are meaningful and intuitively connected to real-world phenomena and experience. Models also tend to be modular. It is easy to add coupling between strings, refine a loop filter, etc. to obtain better sound quality or test theories about how instruments work.

11.12.2 Disadvantages of Physical Models

On the other hand, the real 3D world resists simplifications. For example, violin bodies are very complex and perceptually important. When simplifications break down, physical model computation becomes very high. For example, there are experiments using 3D waveguide models of brass instruments that run on supercomputers much slower than real time.

Control is also difficult. Just as real instruments require great skill and practice, we should not expect simple inputs will immediately result in great sounds. It is difficult to invert recorded sounds to determine the control required to produce them. Consider all the muscles and motions involved in playing the violin or trumpet, or the fact that it takes years to become an accomplished performer on these instruments. One answer to this problem is that physical models should form the basis of new instruments that can be controlled in real time by humans. These instruments might be as difficult to play as acoustic instruments, but they might have interesting new sounds and capabilities worth the learning effort.

In short, physical models are *models* and not necessarily even realistic simulations. Therefore, the approach is sometimes called *physics-inspired* or *physics-based* modeling. In spite of limitations of this approach, the variety of ways in which sounds are created in the real world has inspired a wealth of new methods for the world of digital audio. In the next section, we consider models that take their inspiration from the perspective of the sound itself or the listener rather than the sound source.

Chapter 12

Spectral Modeling, Algorithmic Control, 3D Sound

Topics Discussed: Additive Synthesis, Table-Lookup Synthesis, Spectral Interpolation Synthesis, Algorithmic Control of Signal Processing, 3D Sound, Head-Related Transfer Functions, Multi-Speaker Playback

Previously, we considered *physical models* which simulate physical systems from which we get vibration and sound. In contrast, we can think about sound in more perceptual terms: What do we hear? And how can we create sounds that contain acoustic stimuli to create desired impressions on the listener? Your first reaction might be that our hearing is so good, the only way to create the impression of a particular sound is to actually make that exact sound. But we know, for example, that we are not very sensitive to phase. We can scramble the phase in a signal and barely notice the difference. This leads to the idea that we can recreate the *magnitude spectrum* of a desired sound, perhaps without even knowing how the sound was created or knowing much about the details of the sound in the time domain.

This approach is sometimes called *spectral modeling* and it is a powerful alternative to *physical modeling*. While *physical modeling* requires us to understand something about the sound *source*, *spectral modeling* requires us to understand the sound *content*. We can often just measure and manipulate the spectra of desired sounds, giving us an approach that is simple to implement and relatively

DOI: 10.1201/9781003782711-12

easy to control. In this section, we consider variations on spectral modeling, from additive synthesis to spectral interpolation.

One of the earliest synthesis methods drew upon the intuition that if all sounds could be represented as sums of sine waves, why not simply add sine waves to create the desired sound? This *additive synthesis* approach is not the most efficient one, and another intuition, that musical tones are mostly periodic, led to the idea of constructing just one period and repeating it to create tones.

12.1 Additive Synthesis

Additive synthesis usually means the summation of sinusoids to create complex sounds. In this approach, every partial has independent frequency and amplitude, giving unlimited freedom (according to what we know about Fourier analysis and synthesis) to create any sound. Earlier, we studied analysis/synthesis systems such as MQS and SMS showing that analysis and synthesis are possible. We also learned that parametric control is somewhat limited. For example, time-stretching is possible, but more musical control parameters such as articulation, formant frequencies, and vibrato do not map directly to any additive synthesis parameters.

12.1.1 Table-Lookup Synthesis

If we are willing to limit sinusoidal (partial) frequencies to harmonics and work with a fixed waveform shape, then we can save a lot of computation by creating a table containing one period of the periodic waveform. Usually, the table is over-sampled (the sample rate is much higher than twice that of the highest harmonic) so that inexpensive linear interpolation can be used to "read" the table at different rates. By stepping through the table by a variable increment and performing linear interpolation between neighboring samples, we can get frequency control. A simple multiplication provides amplitude control.

Here is a software implementation of a table-lookup oscillator, building on the algorithm introduced in Section 1.2.5. This code computes `BLOCK_SIZE` samples every time `osc` is called. In a real implementation, we would keep the `table` and current `phase` variables in a structure or object so that we could avoid these as global variables and have more than one oscillator instance. This code does not implement amplitude control, so the output should be multiplied by an amplitude envelope separately as given below:

```
float table[513] =  ... some waveform ... ;
double phase = 0.0;

void osc(double hz, float table[], float out[]) {
    double incr = hz * 512 / sample_rate;
```

```
        for (int i = 0; i < BLOCK_SIZE; i++) {
            int iphase = floor(phase);
            double x1 = table[iphase];
            out[i] = x1 + (phase - iphase) *
                             (table[iphase+1] - x1);
            phase += incr;
            if (phase >= 512) phase = phase - 512;
        }
    }
```

One trick in this code is that `table` should be initialized to a 512-point waveform, with the first value duplicated as the 513th entry. By duplicating the first sample at the end, we insure that the expression `table[iphase + 1]` (used to interpolate between two samples in the table) never accesses a value outside the bounds of the array, particularly when the `phase` exceeds 511 but has not "wrapped around" to zero.

Table-lookup oscillators have two basic parameters: frequency and amplitude, and otherwise they are limited to a fixed wave shape, but often table-lookup oscillators can be combined with filters or other effects for additional control and spectral variation.

12.2 Spectral Interpolation Synthesis

One simple idea to introduce spectral variation into table-lookup oscillators is to use *two* tables and interpolate between them, as shown in Figure 12.1. With no constraints, this could lead to phase cancellation and unpredictable results, but if the phases of harmonics are identical in both tables, and if the tables are accessed at the same offset (i.e., index or phase), then when we interpolate between tables, we are also interpolating between the magnitude spectra of the two tables. This is interesting! With interpolation between tables, we can create *any* smoothly varying harmonic spectrum.

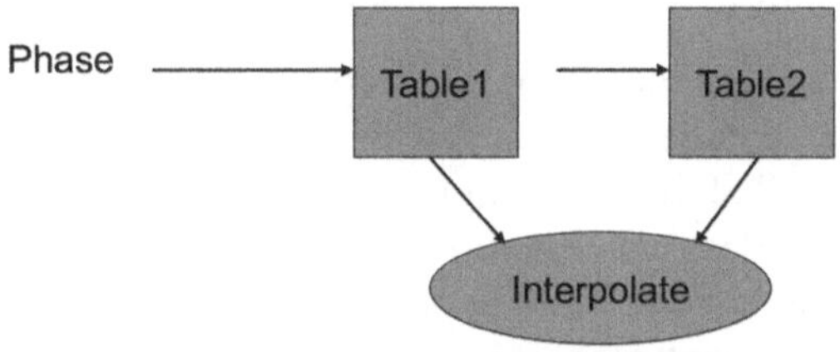

Figure 12.1: Basic Spectral Interpolation. Phase is incremented after each sample to scan through tables as in a simple table-lookup oscillator, but here, the phase is used for two table lookups, and the output is an interpolation between Table 1 and Table 2.

There are some commercial synthesizers that use a 2D joystick to control real-time interpolation between 4 spectra. This can be an interesting control strategy and is related to using filters to modify spectra—in both cases, you get a low dimensional (1D cutoff frequency or 2D interpolation) control space with which to vary the spectrum.

12.2.1 Time-Varying Spectrum

Perhaps more interesting (or is it just because I invented this?) is the idea that the spectrum can evolve arbitrarily over time (84). For example, consider a trumpet tone, which typically follows an envelope of getting louder, then softer. As the tone gets softer, it gets less bright because higher harmonics are reduced disproportionately when the amplitude decreases. If we could record a sequence of spectra, say one spectrum every 100 ms or so, then we could capture the spectral variation of the trumpet sound. The storage is low (perhaps 20 harmonic amplitudes per table, and 10 tables per second, so that is only 200 samples per second). The computation is also low: Consider that full additive synthesis would require 20 sine oscillators at the sample rate for 20 harmonics. With spectral interpolation, the cost is only 2 table lookups per sample. We also need to compute tables from stored harmonic amplitudes, but tables are small, so the cost is not high. Overall, we can expect spectral interpolation to run 5 to 10 times faster than additive synthesis, or only a few times slower than a basic table-lookup oscillator.

Of course, if we just want to reproduce recorded instrument tones, maybe sampling is a better approach because it captures inharmonic attack transients very well. While the storage cost is higher, the computational cost of sampling (mostly due to sample-rate conversion to control frequency) is in the same range as spectral interpolation synthesis. But with sampling, we are stuck with a particular recording of every tone and we have little control over it. With spectral interpolation, we have the opportunity to *compute* the evolving spectrum.

12.2.2 Use Pitch and Amplitude to Compute Spectra

One successful approach that is especially good for wind instrument simulation is to model the spectrum as a function of amplitude and frequency. We carefully record instruments playing crescendos (increasing loudness) at different pitches. Then we analyze these tones to get a matrix of spectra at different pitch and loudness levels. As shown in Figure 12.2, we input desired frequency and amplitude, do a lookup in our 2D matrix to find the appropriate next spectrum, then use spectral interpolation to smoothly change to that spectrum. As long as amplitude and frequency are slowly changing, as in vibrato and amplitude envelopes, the output will realistically change spectrum just like the real instrument. In fact, when amplitude is changing rapidly, we cannot hear the spectral changes very well. In our

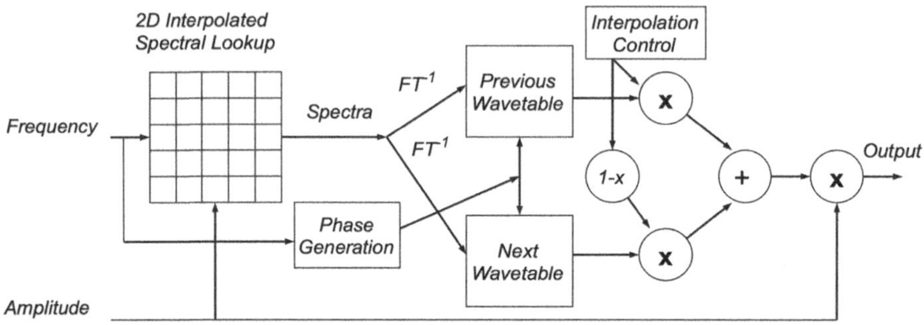

Figure 12.2: Computation for Spectral Interpolation Synthesis. Frequency and amplitude are input controls. The spectrum is varied by mapping the current frequency and amplitude to a spectrum stored in a matrix. This may be an interpolated lookup using the 4 nearest data points (spectra) to yield smooth spectral variations as a function of the continuous frequency and amplitude signals. There is also interpolation through time from one spectrum to the next, using a two-table-lookup oscillator. Since amplitude variations may need to be quite rapid, the amplitude scaling takes place at audio rates just before the output.

model (Figure 12.2), we normalize all the spectra in the 2D matrix so everything comes out of the spectral interpolation oscillator at about the same level, and we multiply that by the amplitude envelope. This captures the rapidly varying amplitude envelope faithfully, and at least approximately does the right thing with the spectrum, even though spectral changes may lag behind or be smoothed out a little.

This basic approach is used in the Dannenberg Brass software for Native Instruments Reaktor synthesizer. (`https://www.native-instruments.com/en/reaktor-community/reaktor-user-library/entry/show/13607/`). This implementation credits this author but was developed without any direct collaboration.

12.2.3 Dealing with Rapid and Inharmonic Attacks

The "pure" spectral interpolation synthesis model works well for some instruments, but others, particularly brass and saxophones,[1] have distinctive attack sounds that are too inharmonic and noisy to recreate from harmonic waveforms. The solution is to combine sampling with spectral interpolation, using short sampled attacks of about 30 ms duration. It is tricky to join the sampled attacks smoothly to table-lookup signals because a rapid cross-fade causes phase cancellation if the sample and table are not matched in phase. The solution is to make the sample long enough (and 30 ms is usually enough) that it settles into a

[1] Saxophones are also made of brass, but are considered woodwinds.

harmonic spectrum. Then, we perform analysis on the end of the attack to obtain the amplitude and phase of each partial. This becomes the first waveform, and every waveform after that has to keep the same phase relationship. With these tricks, we can achieve realistic, inharmonic or noisy attacks, and then control the evolution of the harmonic spectrum using almost arbitrary amplitude and frequency controls.

12.2.4 Where Do We Get Control Information?

This raises the question of where to get amplitude and frequency controls. In traditional synthesis research, illustrated at the left of Figure 12.3, control is considered an input to the instrument, which is characterized by some synthesis algorithm (perhaps a physical model or a vocal model, etc.). To evaluate the synthesis technique, we make sounds with the synthesizer and (often) compare to acoustic sounds. The assumption is that if the comparison is not good, we should go back and fix the synthesis algorithm.

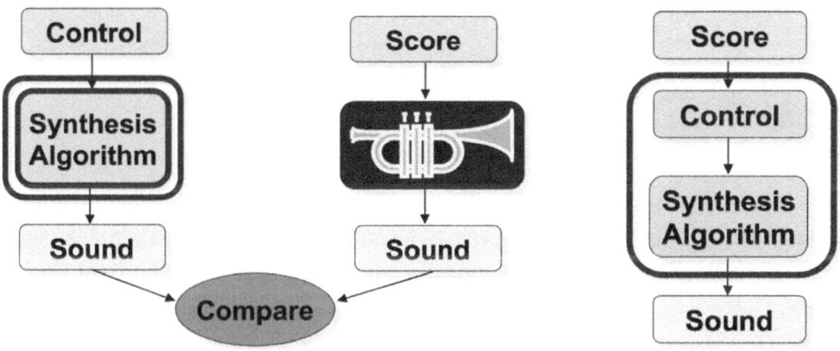

Figure 12.3: *Left:* Traditional approach to synthesis algorithm research and development. It is assumed that control functions are not critical and not part of the synthesis algorithm. *Right:* The SIS approach. Control and synthesis are considered to be related and must be developed and optimized together. Both control *and* synthesis are critical to good, realistic, and musical output.

12.2.4.1 The SIS Research Approach

In contrast, the approach of Spectral Interpolation Synthesis is that *control is an integral part of the synthesizer* (22). If you do not control a synthesis algorithm properly, it will never sound natural. This idea is illustrated on the right of Figure 12.3. Research has shown that crude ADSR envelopes, and even envelopes derived from the analysis of individual acoustic instrument tones, do not give musical results *even if the synthesis algorithm is perfect*, so it follows that decades of synthesis research are based on faulty assumptions!

12.2.4.2 Divide-and-Conquer: Performance Model vs. Synthesis Model

To develop control for spectral interpolation, we take the divide-and-conquer approach shown in Figure 12.4 of separating the control problem from the synthesis problem (but keep in mind that we need both together to get good sounds in the end). In this model, the input is a *score*—the notes we want to play, along with phrase marks, loudness indications, and perhaps other annotations. The *performance model* models how the performer interprets the score and produces controls for the instrument—in the spectral interpolation approach, this is mainly amplitude and frequency. Then, we use the synthesis model (Figure 12.2) to convert control signals into sound.

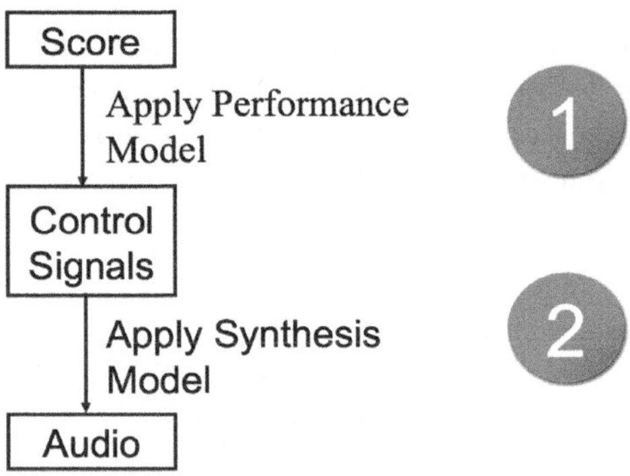

Figure 12.4: The divide-and-conquer approach. Even though control and synthesis must both be considered as part of the problem of musical sound synthesis, we can treat them as two sub-problems.

12.2.4.3 Research Model: Synthesis Refinement

Given this framework, we can develop and refine the synthesis model by extracting control signals from real audio produced by human performers and acoustic instruments. As shown in Figure 12.5, the human-produced control signals are used to drive the synthesis, or *instrument*, model, and we can listen to the results and compare them directly to the actual recording of the human. If the synthesis sounds different, we can try to refine the synthesis model. For example, dissatisfaction with the sound led us to introduce sampled attacks for brass instruments.

Note that the ability to drive the instrument model with amplitude and frequency, in other words parameters directly related to the *sound* itself, is a big advantage over physical models, where we cannot easily measure physical parameters, like bow-string friction or reed stiffness, that are critical to the behavior of the model.

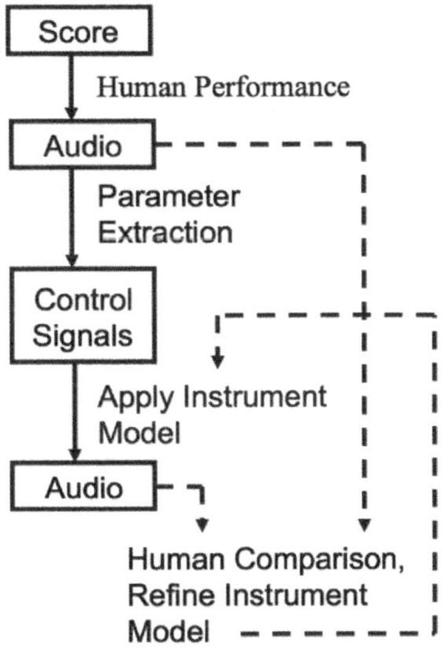

Figure 12.5: Synthesis refinement. To optimize and test the synthesis part of the SIS model, control signals can be derived from actual performances of musical phrases. This ensures that the control is "correct", so any problems with the sound must be due to the synthesis stage. The synthesis stage is refined until the output is satisfactory.

12.2.4.4 Research Model: Control Refinement

Assuming we have produced a good-sounding synthesizer, we can then turn to the control problem. The idea here is to get humans to perform scores, extract control information, drive the synthesis with controls, and produce a sound. This output from *measured* control signals represents the best we could hope to achieve since a human produced the control with a real instrument. Now, we can also translate the score to controls with a *performance model.* If we do not like the results, we can improve the model and keep iterating until we have something we like. This is shown in Figure 12.6.

12.2.5 A Study of Trumpet Envelopes

We will now discuss a particular study that followed the paradigm just described. My students and I constructed a good spectral-interpolation-based trumpet synthesizer and set out to obtain good control envelopes from scores. This discussion is not just relevant to spectral interpolation synthesis. The findings are relevant to any synthesis method and help explain some of the subtleties we find in acoustic instrument synthesis.

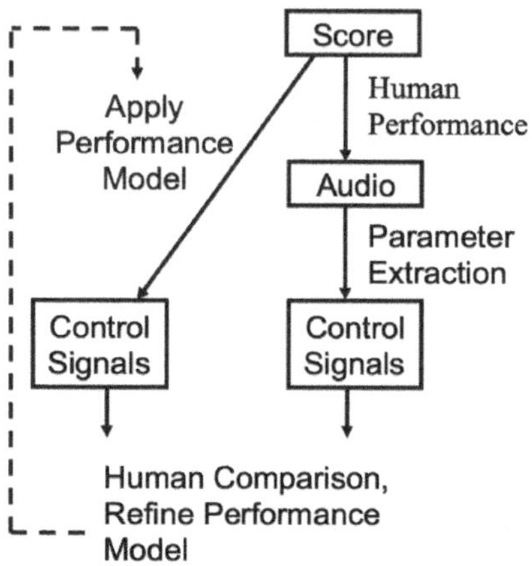

Figure 12.6: Control refinement. Having developed an adequate synthesis model (see Figure 12.5), we compare controls from a performance model to controls extracted from human performance. Both controls are synthesized by the known-to-be-good synthesis model, so any problems can be attributed to the performance model that computes controls. The model is refined until the output sounds good compared to the output based on human performance.

The main conclusion of this work is that:

- envelopes are largely determined by context;
- envelope generation techniques can improve synthesis.

In early experiments, we studied the question of how the context of notes in the score affect the center of mass of amplitude envelopes. The *center of mass* tells us, if we were to cut out the envelope shape from a piece of cardboard, where would the shape balance? If the beginning of the note is loud, the center of mass will be earlier. If the sound grows steadily, the center of mass will be later. This is one of the simplest measures of shape and a good place to start.

Figure 12.7 shows some results of this study (24). The multiple curves show great consistency from one performance to the next when the same music is played, but there is a striking difference between the envelopes on the left, from articulated tones, to the ones on the right, from slurred tones. Some results from measuring center of mass include:

- When the previous pitch is lower and the next pitch is higher (we call this an "up-up" condition), notes showed a later center of mass than other combinations;
- Large pitch intervals before and after the tone resulted in an earlier center of mass than small intervals;

- Legato articulation gave a later center of mass than others (this is clearly seen in Figure 12.7).

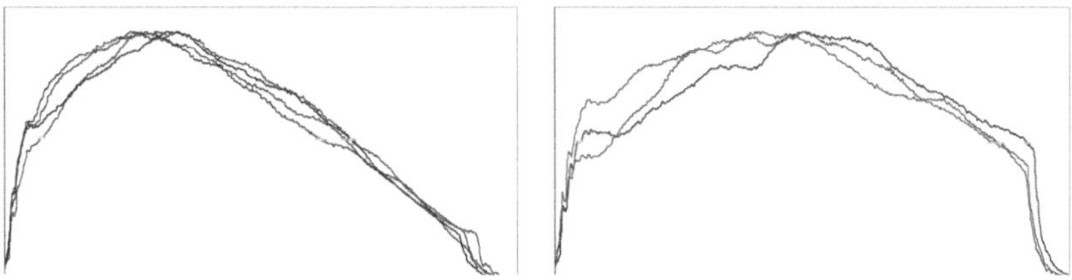

Figure 12.7: Context influences amplitude envelopes. The envelopes on the left are from the second of three articulated (tongued) notes. At right, the envelopes are from the second of three slurred notes. It is clear that articulation and context are significant factors in determining envelope shape. There is not a single "characteristic" trumpet envelope, and measuring the envelope of one tone out of context will not produce many of the features seen above.

12.2.5.1 Envelope Model

The center of mass does not offer enough detail to describe a complete trumpet envelope. A more refined model is illustrated in Figure 12.8. In this model, the envelope is basically smooth as shown by the dashed line, but this overall shape is modified at the beginning and ending, as shown inside the circles. It is believed that the smooth shape is mainly due to large muscles controlling pressure in the lungs, and the beginning and ending are modified by the tongue, which can rapidly block or release the flow of air through the lips and into the trumpet.

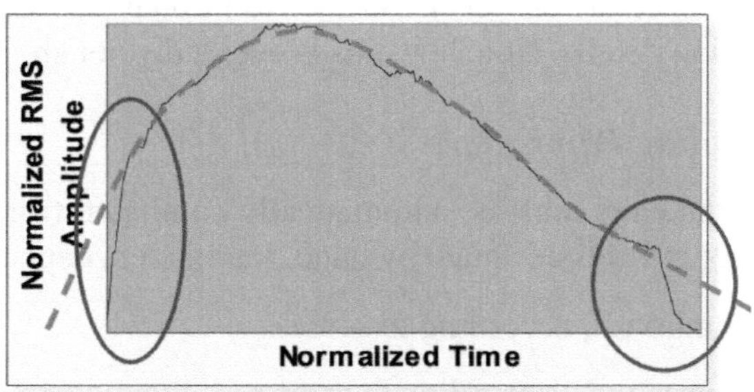

Figure 12.8: The "tongue and breath" envelope model is based on the idea that there is a smooth shape (dashed line) controlled by the diaphragm, upper body, and lungs, and this shape is modified at note transitions by the tongue and other factors. (Deviations from the smooth shape are circled.)

The next figure (Figure 12.9) shows a typical envelope from a slurred note where the tongue is not used. Here, there is less of a drop at the beginning and ending. The drop in amplitude (which in the data does not actually reach zero or silence), is probably due to the disruption of vibration when valves are pressed and the pitch is changed. Whatever is going on physically, the idea of a smooth breath envelope with some alterations at the beginning and ending seems reasonable.

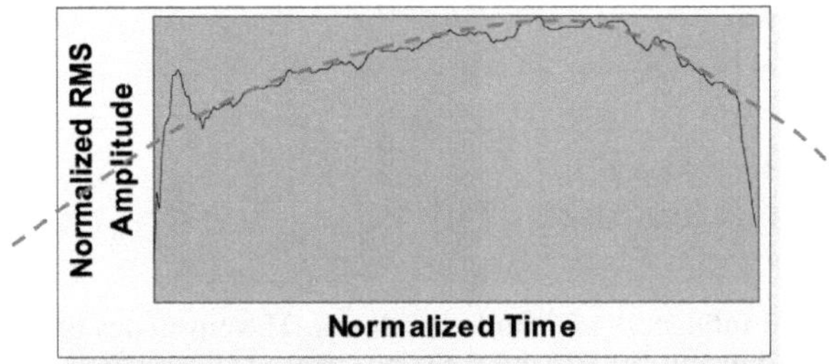

Figure 12.9: The envelope of a slurred note. This figure shows that the "tongue and breath" model also applies to the envelopes of slurred notes (shown here). The deviations at the beginning and ending of the note may be due to trumpet valves blocking the air or to the fact that oscillations are disrupted when the pitch changes.

Based on looking at many envelopes, we conclude that a "breath envelope" is useful to give the overall shape, and a specific attack and decay should be added to incorporate fine details of articulation. This envelope model is shown in detail in Figure 12.10, which shows 9 discrete parameters used to describe the continuous curve. The generic "breath envelope" shown in the upper part of the figure is an actual envelope from a long trumpet tone. By taking a range of the whole envelope, from *tf* to *tt*, we can get a more rounded shape (smaller *tf* larger *tt*) or a flatter shape (*tf* and *tt* close in time), and we can shift the center of mass earlier (later *tf* and *tt*) or later (earlier *tf* and *tt*). Additional parameters control the beginning and ending details. Note how this is decidedly not an ADSR envelope!

12.2.5.2 Computing Parameters

All 9 envelope parameters must be automatically computed from the score. Initially, we used a set of rules designed by hand. Parameters depend on:

- pitch (in semitones, according to score);
- duration (in seconds, according to score);
- begin-phrase (is this the first note in a phrase?);
- end-phrase (is this the last note in a phrase?);
- from-slur (is there a slur from preceding note?);
- to-slur (is there a slur to the next note?);
- direction-up (is this note higher than preceding note?).

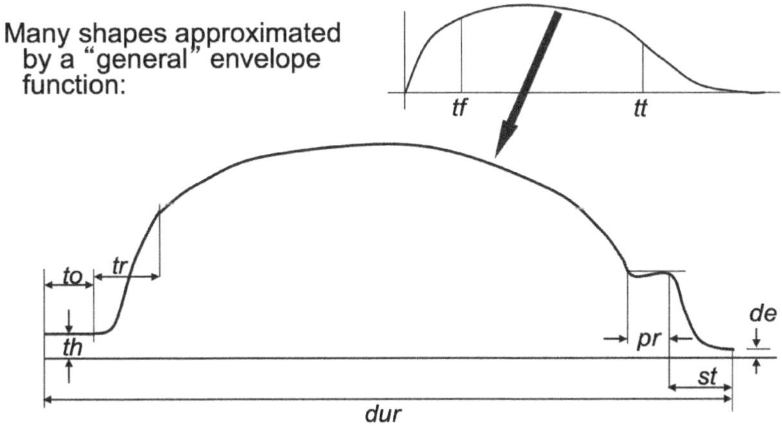

Figure 12.10: An amplitude envelope specification. In order to produce a wide variety of shapes based on the "tongue and breath" envelope model, we describe continuous envelopes with 9 parameters, as shown here.

The rules were developed by fitting generated envelopes to actual measured envelopes and generalizing from observed trends. Here is one example, illustrating the computation of the parameter *tf*. As shown in Figure 12.11, there are three cases. If coming from a slur and the direction is up, $tf = 0.1$. If the direction is not up, $tf = 0.4$. If *not* coming from a slur, $tf = 0.03 - 0.01 \times \log_2(dur)$.

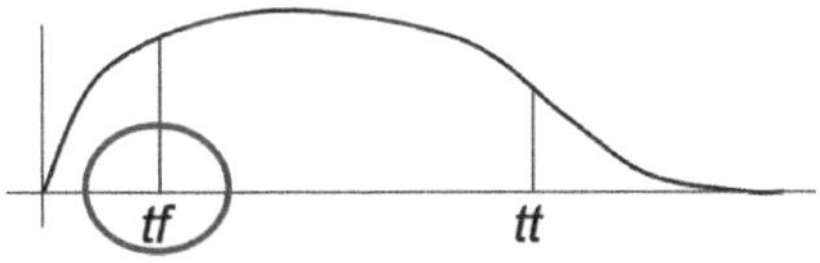


```
(cond (from-slur
        (setf takefrom (if direction-up 0.1 0.04)))
       (t
        (setf takefrom (+ 0.03 (* 0.01 (- log-dur))))))
```

from-slur \ direction-up	t	f
t	0.1	0.04
f	$0.03 - 0.01 \times \log_2(dur)$	

Figure 12.11: Computing envelope parameters. This example shows how the parameter *tf* is derived from score features *from-slur*, *direction-up*, and *dur*.

Similar rules are used to compute all 9 parameters of every envelope. The score-to-envelope mapping is hand-crafted and far from complete and perfect, but the result, at least for simple scores, is quite good and sounds very natural. Constructing mappings between multi-dimensional spaces (in this case, from multiple features of scores to multiple envelope parameters) is a natural problem for machine learning. In fact, my student Ning Hu created an automated system to analyze audio recordings of acoustic instruments and create both a spectral interpolation synthesis model, and a performance model that includes amplitude envelopes and vibrato. No manual rule construction or design was required (38).

12.2.6 Summary and Discussion of Spectral Interpolation

Spectral Interpolation Synthesis is based on modeling "real" performances, using measurements of spectra and other audio features to model what the listener hears without any modeling of the physical instrument. The performance model results in phrase-long control functions rather than individual notes. Since control functions are based on note-to-note transitions and context, the method requires some look-ahead. (The shape of the envelope depends on the pitch and articulation of the following note.)

12.2.7 Conclusions

What have we learned? First, envelopes and control are critical to music synthesis. It is amazing that so much research was done on synthesis algorithms without much regard for control! Research on the spectral centroid showed statistically valid relationships between score parameters and envelope shape, which should immediately raise concerns about sampling synthesis: If samples have envelopes "baked in", how can sampling *ever* create natural-sounding musical phrases? Certainly not without a variety of alternative samples with different envelopes and possibly some careful additional control through amplitude envelopes, but for brass, that also implies spectral control. Large sample libraries have moved in this direction.

The idea that envelopes have an overall "breath" shape and some fine details in the beginning and ending of every note seems to fit real data better than ADSR and other commonly used models. Even though spectral interpolation or even phrase-based analysis/synthesis have not become commonplace or standard in the world of synthesis, it seems that the study of musical phrases and notes in context is critical to future synthesis research and systems.

12.3 Algorithmic Control of Signal Processing

In the previous section, we looked carefully at some ideas on the synthesis of acoustic instrument sounds. In this section, we consider something that has no basis in the acoustical world: the direct generation and control of audio through algorithms.

There are relatively few works that push decision making, selection, wave shape, and parametric control down below the note level and into the audio signal itself. Ianis Xenakis developed a system called GENDYN that creates waveforms from line segments using algorithmic processes (99). Herbert Brün's SAWDUST is another example, described as a program for composing waveforms (see Section 7.1.2). Curtis Roads wrote the book *Microsound* (76), which concerns granular synthesis and more generally the realm between samples and notes. We have explored granular synthesis with Nyquist in some detail. In this section, we will look at signals controlled by (Nyquist) patterns and patterns controlled by signals.

12.3.1 Sounds Controlled by Patterns

In Figure 12.12, we see some code and a generated control function (a Nyquist signal). The signal is created by the SAL function `pat-ctrl`, which takes two patterns as parameters. The first pattern (`durpat`) returns durations and the second (`valpat`) returns amplitude values. As seen in the generated signal, `durpat` alternates between 0.1 and 0.2, while `valpat` cycles through the stair-step values of 0, 1, 2.

12.3.1.1 Pat-ctrl

The implementation of `pat-ctrl` is shown below. This is a recursive sequence that produces one segment of output followed by a recursive call to produce the rest. The duration is infinite:

```
pat-ctrl(make-cycle({0.1 0.2}), ;duration
         make-cycle({0 1 2}))   ;amplitude
```

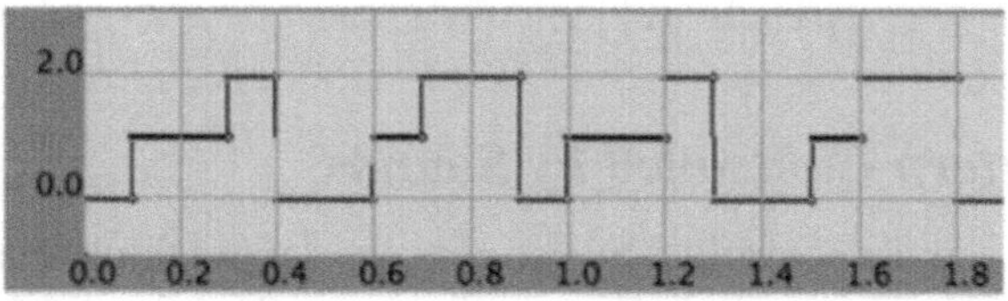

Figure 12.12: The `pat-ctrl` function creates a piecewise-constant function where each step has a duration and amplitude determined by the two pattern generator object parameters. Each pair of numbers retrieved from the two patterns produces one step in the stair-step-like function.

```
define function pat-ctrl(durpat, valpat)
     return seq(const(next(valpat), next(durpat)),
                pat-ctrl(durpat, valpat))
```

We can use `pat-ctrl` to construct a frequency control function and synthesize that frequency contour. The function `pat-fm`, shown below, adds the result of `pat-ctrl` to a `pitch` parameter, converts the pitch from steps to Hz, and then synthesizes a sinusoid. If `durpat` returns very small values, the resulting sound will not have discernible pitch sequences, at least not at the level of segment durations returned by `durpat`. However, higher-level structures in `durpat` and `valpat` will create structured timbral variations that catch our attention. In other words, the intent here is to modulate the sine tone at audio rates using complex patterns and resulting in novel sounds.

```
define function pat-fm(durpat, valpat, pitch, dur)
  begin
    with hz =
      step-to-hz(pitch + pat-ctrl(durpat, valpat))
    return pwl(0.01, 1, dur - 0.1, 1, dur) *
             hzosc(hz + 4.0 * hz * hzosc(hz))
  end
```

12.3.1.2 Using Scores

One long sine tone may not be so interesting, even if it is modulated rapidly by patterns. The following example shows how we can write a score that "launches" a number of `pat-fm` sounds (here, the durations are 30, 20, 18, and 13 seconds) with different parameters. The point here is that scores are not limited to conventional note-based music. Here we have a score organizing long, overlapping, and very abstract sounds:

```
exec score-play(
 {{ 0 30 {pat-fm-note :grain-dur 8 :spread 1
             :pitch c3 :fixed-dur t :vel 50}}
  {10 20 {pat-fm-note :grain-dur 3 :spread 10
             :pitch c4 :vel 75}}
  {15 18 {pat-fm-note :grain-dur 1 :spread 20
             :pitch c5}}
  {20 13 {pat-fm-note :grain-dur 1 :spread 10
             :pitch c1}}})
```

12.3.2 Pattern Controlled by Sounds

If we consider sounds controlled by patterns, we should think about the opposite. Here, we will look at control envelopes (which are also of type `SOUND` in Nyquist) and how they can be used in patterns. (Maybe you can also think of interesting ways for *audio* sounds to control patterns.)

When constructing sequences of events, scores, and `score-gen` may be all you need. But if you want to influence the evolution of fine-grain decisions, such as pattern output over time, then perhaps envelopes and other controls can be useful. This relates to a concept we saw before: *tendency masks*, which specify long-term trends. A standard example is: randomly choose the next pitch between an upper and lower bound, where the bounds are given by functions that change over time.

To implement something like tendency masks in patterns, we will use Nyquist `SOUND`s to specify the global continuous evolution of parameter values. To access the sound at a particular time, we use `sref(`*sound*`,` *time*`)`. Note that *sound* can be any `SOUND`, but it might be most convenient to use a piecewise linear envelope.

In `sref`, *time* is relative to the environment, so *time* = 0 means "now". And remember that while behaviors start at "now", existing sounds have a definite start time. So when we write `sref(`*sound*`, 0)`, it means access *sound* at the current time, not access the beginning (time 0) of *sound*.

12.3.2.1 A Template for Global Control Using Sounds

Here is an example you can build on for controlling patterns with sounds. There are three definitions:

- `pitch-contour` defines a time-varying contour that we want to use with some pattern computation;
- `get-pitch` is a function that simply accesses the pitch contour at the current time (indicated by time 0);
- `pwl-pat-fm` is a function that will create and use a pattern. Within the pattern, we see `make-eval({get-pitch})`. The `make-eval` pattern constructor takes an *expression*, which is expressed in Lisp syntax. Each time the pattern is called to return a value, the expression is evaluated. Recall that in Lisp, the function call syntax is `(`*function-name arg1 arg2* `...)`, so with no arguments, we get `(`*function-name*`)`, and in SAL, we can write a quoted list as `{`*function-name*`}`. Thus, `make-eval( {get-pitch})` is the pattern that calls `get-pitch` to produce each value:

```
variable pitch-contour =
           pwl(10, 25, 15, 10, 20, 10, 22, 25, 22)

function get-pitch()
  return sref(pitch-contour, 0)

function pwl-pat-fm()
  begin
    ...
    make-eval(get-pitch),
```

```
    ...
  end

play pwl-pat-fm()
```

We can do something similar with `score-gen`, using a `SOUND` to provide a time-varying value that guides the progress of some parameter. In the following example, the variable `pitch-contour` is accessed as part of the `pitch:` calculation.

```
begin
  with pitch-contour =
           pwl(10, 25, 15, 10, 20, 10, 22, 25, 22),
       ioi-pattern = make-heap(0.2 0.3 0.4)
  exec score-gen(
      save: quote(pwl-score),
      score-dur: 22,
      pitch: truncate(
          c4 + sref(pitch-contour, sg:start) +
          #if(oddp(sg:count), 0, -5)),
      ioi: next(ioi-pattern),
      dur: sg:ioi - 0.1,
      vel: 100)
end
```

You can even use the envelope editor in the NyquistIDE to graphically edit `pitch-contour`. To evaluate `pitch-contour` at a specific time, `sref` is used as before, but the *time* parameter to `sref` is `sg:start`, not 0. We need to use `sg:start` here because the entire `score-gen` computation is performed at time 0. We are not in a behavior, and there is no environment that changes the current time with each new note. Since everything is (normally) relative to time 0, we use `score-gen`'s special `sg:start` variable to refer to the "current" time, that is, the start time of each note.

12.4 3D Sound

We now turn to the topic of sound as originating in 3D space. We know from previous discussions of perception that there are various cues that give the impression of the origin of sounds we hear. In computer music work, composers are interested in simulating these cues to simulate a 3D sonic environment. Earlier, we introduced the idea of head-related transfer functions and the simulation of spatial cues over headphones. In this section, we expand on this discussion and also consider the use of multiple speakers in rooms and particularly in concert halls.

12.4.1 Introduction

To review from our discussion of sound localization, we use a number of cues to sense direction and distance. Interaural time difference (ITD) and interaural amplitude difference (ILD) give us information about direction in the horizontal plane, but suffers from symmetry between sounds in front and sounds behind us. Spectral cues help to disambiguate front-to-back directions and also give us a sense of height or elevation. Reverberation, and especially the direct-sound-to-reverberant-sound ratio gives us the impression of distance, as do spectral cues.

12.4.2 Duplex Theory

In the *duplex theory* of Lord Rayleigh, sound localization is achieved through a combination of ITD and ILD (36). ITD is caused by the difference in distance between our ears and the sound source when the source is to the left or right. The time difference is related to the speed of sound, and remembering that sound travels about 1 foot per millisecond, we can estimate that ITD is a fraction of a millisecond. (No wonder our ears can perceive time so precisely—at least precise relative timing between left and right ears is useful for localization.)

The ILD is caused by the masking effect of our heads when sound comes from one side or the other. Since different frequencies refract around our heads differently, the ILD is frequency dependent and more pronounced at higher frequencies where the wavelengths are short and our head does a better job of shielding one ear from the sound.

In duplex theory, there is ambiguity caused by symmetry. Any direction from the head falls on a cone-shaped surface, where the apex of the cone is at the head and center line of the cone runs through the two ears. This set of ambiguous directions is called the *cone of confusion* (Figure 12.13) because every point on the cone produces the same ITD and ILD.

In fact, the duplex theory ignores the pinnae, our outer ears, which are not symmetric from front-to-back or top-to-bottom. Reflections in the pinnae create interference that is frequency-dependent and can be used by our auditory system to disambiguate sound directions. The cues from our pinnae are not as strong as ITD and ILD, so it is not unusual to be confused about sound source locations, especially along the cone of confusion.

12.4.3 HRTF: Head-Related Transfer Functions

When sound reaches our ears from a particular direction, there is a combination of ITD, ILD, and spectral changes due to the pinnae. Taken together, these cues can be expressed as a filter called the head-related transfer function, or HRTF (54). We can measure the HRTF, for example, by placing tiny microphones in the

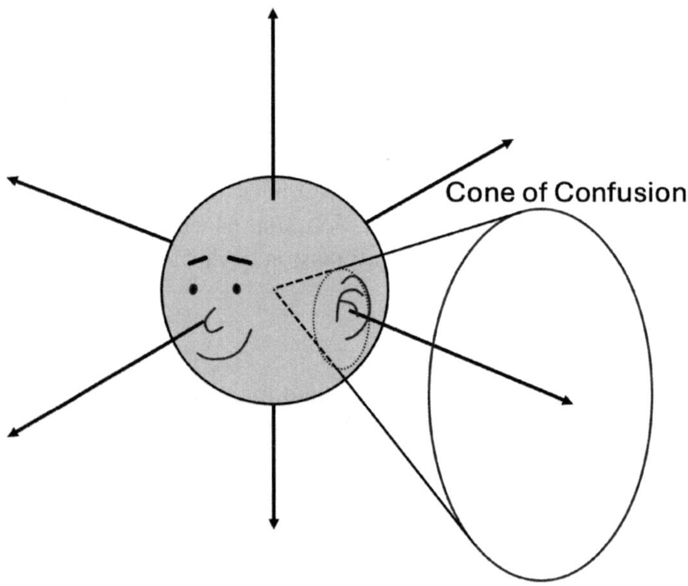

Figure 12.13: The "cone of confusion", where different sound directions give the same ITD and ILD.

ears of a subject in an anechoic chamber, holding their head steady, and recording sound from a speaker placed at a carefully controlled angle and elevation. There are some clever ways to estimate the HRTF, but we will skip the signal processing details. To fully characterize the HRTF, the loudspeaker and/or listener must be moved to many different angles and elevations. The number of different angles and elevations measured can range from one hundred to thousands.

To simulate a sound source at some angle and elevation, we retrieve the nearest HRTF measurement to that direction and apply the left and right HRTFs as filters to the sound before playing the sound to the left and right ears through headphones. (See Figure 12.14.)

One way to implement the HRTF filters is to compute the HRIR, or head-related impulse response, which is the response of the HRTF to an impulse input. To filter a sound by the HRTF, we can convolve the sound with the HRIR. If the sound is moving, it is common to interpolate between the nearest HRTFs or HRIRs so that there is no sudden switch from one filter to another, which might cause pops or clicks in the filtered sound.

12.4.4 HRTF, Headphones, and Head Tracking

When HRTFs are used, the listener normally wears headphones, which isolate sounds to the left and right ears and eliminate most of the effects of actual room

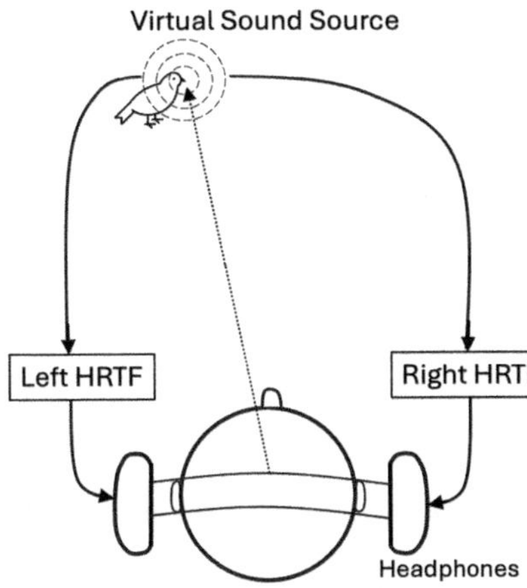

Figure 12.14: Sound is localized with HRTFs by filtering a sound to simulate the effect of delays, head, and ears on the sound. A different filter is used for left and right channels, and the filters are different for different directions.

acoustics in the listening space. Headphones have the problem that if the listener moves their head, the simulated space will rotate with the head and the headphones. To solve this problem, headphones are often tracked. Then, if the head turns 20° to the left, the virtual sound source is rotated to the right to compensate. Headphones with head tracking are sometimes combined with virtual reality (VR) goggles that do a similar thing with computer graphics: when the listener turns 20° to the left, the virtual world is rotated to the right, giving the impression that the world is real and we are moving the head within that world to see different views.

12.4.5 *Room Models*

An alternative to HRTFs and headphones is to use speakers in a room to create the effect of localized sounds. One approach is to use ray-tracing ideas from computer graphics to estimate a sound field in an imaginary space. One difficulty is that sound is slow and has long wavelengths relative to objects and rooms, which means that refraction is significant—sound does not always travel in straight lines! The refraction is frequency dependent. Nevertheless, ray tracing can be used to develop early reflection models for artificial reverberation that convey the geometry of rooms, even if the simulation is not perfect (63).

12.4.6 *Doppler Shift*

Another interesting process that works well with loudspeakers is the simulation of motion using Doppler shift. Sound at a distance is delayed. When sound sources move, the distance changes, so does the delay, and the change creates Doppler shift, or a change in frequency. Doppler shift can be modeled with actual delay consisting of buffers of samples, perhaps with some interpolation to "tap" into the delay at fractional positions. Sometimes, we can just use frequency modulation to give the effect of Doppler shift without any real simulation of delay. If there are multiple reflections, each reflection can have a different Doppler shift. This could add additional realism, but I have never seen a system that models reflections with individual Doppler shifts.

12.4.7 Reverberation

Doppler shift is enhanced through the use of reverberation. If a sound is receding rapidly, we should hear several effects: the pitch drops, the sound decreases in amplitude and the ratio of reverberation to direct sound increases. Especially with synthesized sounds, we do not have any pre-conceptions about the absolute loudness of the (virtual) sound source. Simply making the source quieter does not necessarily give the impression of distance, but through the careful use of reverberation, we can give the listener clues about distance *and* loudness.

12.4.8 Panning

Stereo loudspeaker systems are common. A standard technique to simulate the location of a sound source between two speakers is to "pan" the source, sending some of the source to each speaker. Panning techniques and the "hole-in-the-middle" problem were presented in detail in Section 10.3.6. Panning between two speakers can create ILD, but not ITD or spectral effects consistent with the desired sound placement, so our ears are rarely fooled by stereo into believing there is a real 3D or even 1D space of sound source locations.[2] Finally, room reflections defeat some of the stereo effect or at least lead to unpredictable listening conditions.

12.4.9 Multi-Speaker Playback

If two speakers are better than one, why not many speakers? This is not so practical in the home or apartment, but common in movie theaters and concert halls, especially for concerts of computer music. "Surround Sound" systems are available as consumer audio systems as well. In general, the simulation of direction is

[2]Thus, the whole idea of stereo is highly suspect. Could it be that stereo was promoted by manufacturers who wanted to sell more gear? There were multi-speaker systems in use before consumer stereo, and experiments have shown that three-channel systems (adding a center channel) are significantly better than stereo. My guess is that stereo is ubiquitous today because it was both interesting enough to sell to consumers yet simple enough to implement in consumer media including the phonograph record and FM radio. Even though we have only two ears, stereo with two channels falls far short of delivering a full two-dimensional sound experience, much less three dimensions.

achieved by choosing the nearest speaker in the desired direction. Often, sound is panned between the nearest 2 speakers when speakers are in a plane around the audience, or between the nearest 3 speakers when speakers are arranged in a dome (72). Chowning combined panning, reverberation, and loudness to simulate moving sound sources (10).

At the risk of over generalization, there are two general schools of thought on sound reproduction with loudspeakers. One school views loudspeakers as an approximation to some ideal. In this view, loudspeakers should have high fidelity to recreate any desired source sound with minimal alteration. When many speakers are used, they are almost invariably identical and uniformly distributed to allow panning to any angle. The focus is on sound content, and any speaker limitations are just a necessary evil.

The other school views electro-acoustic music more holistically. Loudspeakers are a part of the process. Rather than bemoan speaker imperfections, we can create an "orchestra" of loudspeakers of different types and placement. Composers can utilize directionality and frequency responses of different loudspeakers with musical intent. We embrace the fact that sound comes from loudspeakers rather than trying to hide it.

Recently, a new approach to sound localization with loudspeakers has come under investigation. The technique, called *wavefield synthesis*, uses a large array of speakers to reproduce the wave front of an imaginary 3D or 2D scene. Imagine a cubical room with one wall open and sound sources outside the room. Imagine an array of microphones on a grid stretched across the open wall, capturing the incoming sound wave at 100 or more locations. Now, imagine closing the wall, replacing each microphone with a small loudspeaker, and playing back the recorded sound wave through 100 or more loudspeakers. In principle, this should reproduce the entire incoming sound wave at the wall, creating a strong 3D effect. Of course there are questions of directionality, how many speakers are needed, whether to use a 2D or 1D array, room reflections, etc. An example of wavefield synthesis and playback is an auditorium at the Technical University of Berlin, which has 832 audio channels. Small speakers are placed in a continuous line on the left, front, and right walls. The speakers are separated by only 10 cm, but because of the small size, there are larger speakers just below them, every 40 cm. A small cluster of computers is used to compute each channel based on the precise delay from virtual sound sources. The results are quite impressive and unlike any typical speaker array, giving the impression that sounds are emerging from beyond or even within the line of speakers.

12.4.10 Summary

In this section, we have reviewed multiple perceptual cues for sound location and distance. HRTFs offer a powerful model for simulating and reproducing these cues, but HRTFs require headphones to be most effective, and since headphones move with the head, head tracking is needed for the best effect. For audiences, it is more practical to use loudspeakers. Multiple loudspeakers provide multiple point sources, but usually are restricted to a plane. Panning is often used as a crude approximation of ideal perceptual cues. Panning can be scaled up to multiple loudspeaker systems. Rather than treat speakers as a means of reproducing a virtual soundscape, loudspeaker "orchestras" can be embraced as a part of the electroacoustic music presentation and exploited for musical purposes. Finally, wavefield synthesis offers the possibility of reproducing actual 3D sound waves as if coming from virtual sound sources, but many speakers are required, so this is an expensive and still mostly experimental approach.

Chapter 13

Audio Compression

Topics Discussed: Coding Redundancy, Intersample Redundancy, Psycho-Perceptual Redundancy, Huffman Coding

13.1 Introduction to General Compression Techniques

High-quality audio takes a lot of space—about 10 M bytes/minute for CD-quality stereo. Now that disk capacity is measured in terabytes, storing uncompressed audio is feasible even for personal libraries, but compression is still useful for smaller devices, downloading audio over the Internet, or sometimes just for convenience. What can we do to reduce the data explosion?

Data compression is simply storing the same information in a shorter string of symbols (bits). The goal is to store the most information in the smallest amount of space, without compromising the quality of the signal (or at least, compromising it as little as possible). Compression techniques and research are not limited to digital sound-data compression plays an essential part in the storage and transmission of all types of digital information, from word-processing documents to digital photographs to full-screen, full-motion videos. As the amount of information in a medium increases, so does the importance of data compression.

What is compression exactly, and how does it work? There is no one thing that is "data compression". Instead, there are many different approaches, each addressing a different aspect of the problem. We'll take a look at a few ways to compress digital audio information. What's important about these different ways of compressing data is that they tend to illustrate some basic ideas in the representation of information, particularly sound, in the digital world. For a more complete coverage of compression, see *Introduction to Data Compression* (81).

DOI: 10.1201/9781003782711-13

There are three main principles or approaches to data compression you should know:

- *Coding Redundancy* eliminates extra bits used to represent symbols. For example, computer code generally uses 8-bit characters, but there are less than 100 different characters, at least for written English. We could use 7 bits per character for an immediate savings of 12.5%, and a variable-length encoding would be even more efficient.
- *Intersample Redundancy* looks at how sequences of symbols can be represented more compactly. For example, a fax machine could send a black-and-white image as a sequence of bits for black and white, e.g., 1111111000011111100110100000..., but since there are typically large black and white regions, we can encode this as the number of 1's followed by the number of 0's followed by the number of 1's, etc. The same bits could be represented as 7 4 6 2 2 1 1 5 ..., which is typically much more compact.
- *Psycho-Perceptual Redundancy* considers the waste of transmitting information that will never be perceived. A 16-bit audio recording contains a lot of information and detail we cannot hear. Yes, in the worst case, you really need 16 bits, and yes, in the worst case you really need a frequency response up to 20 kHz, but a lot of the audio information represented in the samples is inaudible, and that fact can be used to send less data.

13.2 Coding Redundancy

Let's look at how these principles are used in audio data compression. Starting with *coding redundancy*, we can think of each sample as a "symbol" that must be represented in bits. In "uncompressed" audio, each sample is encoded as a number on a linear scale. This is the so-called *PCM*, or *pulse-code modulation* representation.[1]

Another representation of samples uses a more-or-less logarithmic encoding called μ-law. This representation is not truly logarithmic and instead uses a floating-point representation with 1 sign bit, 3 exponent bits, and 4 mantissa bits. The encoding spans a 13-bit dynamic range where the quantization levels are smaller at low amplitudes. A less common but similar encoding is A-law, which has a 12-bit dynamic range.

[1] I've always thought PCM was odd terminology. It literally refers to the *transmission* of binary codes through pulses—see Patent US2801281A—which misses the point that this is about *representation*, not *transmission*, but since this work came out of a phone company, maybe it is not so surprising that PCM was viewed as a form of transmission.

Figure 13.1 shows a schematic comparison of (linear) PCM to μ-law encoding. The tick-marks on the left (PCM) and right (μ-law) scales show actual values to which the signal will be quantized. You can see that at small signal amplitudes, μ-law has smaller quantization error because the tick marks are closer together. At higher amplitudes, μ-law has larger quantization error. At least in perceptual terms, what matters most is the signal-to-noise *ratio*. In μ-law, quantization error is approximately proportional to the signal amplitude, so the signal-to-noise ratio is roughly the same for soft and loud signals. At low amplitudes, where absolute quantization errors are smaller than PCM, the signal-to-noise ratio of μ-law is better than PCM. This comes at the cost of lower signal-to-noise ratios at higher amplitudes. All around, μ-law is generally better than PCM, at least when you do not have lots of bits to spare, but we will discuss this further in Section 13.2.2.

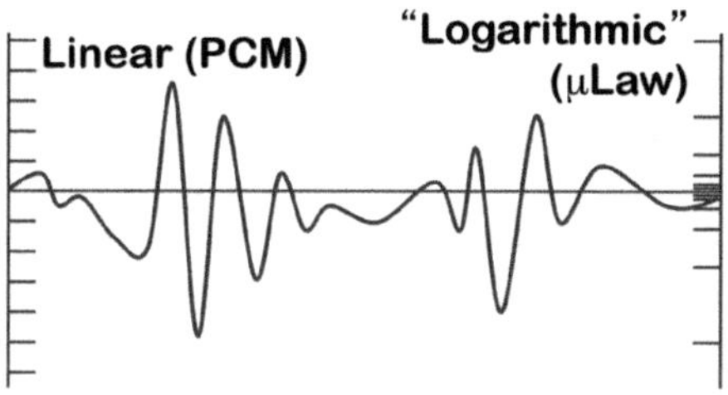

Figure 13.1: μ-law vs. PCM. Quantization levels are shown at the left and right vertical scales. μ-law has a better signal-to-quantization-error ratio at lower amplitudes but a higher ratio than PCM at higher amplitudes.

13.2.1 μ-law Implementation

To convert from 8-bit μ-law to PCM, we can treat the μ-law code as an unsigned integer, from 0 to 255, and store the corresponding PCM value in a table. Then, translation from μ-law to PCM is a simple table lookup: `ulaw_to_pcm[ulaw_code]`.

To convert from PCM to μ-law, we could also use a table to map from each of 2^{16} 16-bit PCM values to the corresponding μ-law value. It turns out the low-order 2 bits of the 16-bit code do not matter, so we can reduce the table size to 2^{14}, and we can use symmetry around zero to reduce the table size to 2^{13} or 8 kB.[2]

13.2.2 Discussion on μ-law

μ-law is used mainly for telephony where the sound quality is enough for speech intelligibility, but not good for music. For music, we might consider using more

[2]Of course, you could also do binary search to find the nearest μ-law code using the much smaller `ulaw_to_pcm` table, but it is much faster to use direct lookup.

bits to get lower noise. Studies show that with 16-bit samples, linear is better than logarithmic encodings, perhaps because quantization noise at 16-bits is so quiet that you simply cannot hear it. Finally, if you cannot afford 16-bits, you are much better off looking to other techniques.

μ-law was chosen as an example of coding redundancy. You might say that μ-law does not actually represent PCM samples, so this is not a true example of coding redundancy. It all depends on what it is you think you are encoding, and you could certainly argue that μ-law is based on perceptual principles so it is really an example of psycho-perceptual redundancy, which we will take up later.

A good example of "pure" coding redundancy is Huffman Coding, where each symbol is assigned a unique string of bits. Symbols that are very common receive shorter bit strings, and rare symbols use more bits. In most music audio, low amplitude samples are more common than high amplitude samples, which are used only for peaks in the signal. Analyzing one of my live recordings, I estimated that the 16-bit samples could be encoded with an average of 12 bits using a variable-length Huffman Code, which would eliminate much of the coding redundancy in the linear encoding. We will discuss Huffman Codes later as well.

13.3 Intersample Redundancy

Audio signals also exhibit *intersample redundancy*, which means that samples can be predicted from previous samples, so we do not really need all those bits in every sample. The simplest predictor is to guess that the next sample is the same as the current one. While this is rarely exactly true, the error is likely to be a small number.

13.3.1 DPCM – delta PCM

We can encode the error or *delta* from one sample to the next rather than the full value of each sample. This encoding, called DPCM, or *delta PCM* saves about 1 bit per sample in speech, giving a 6 dB improvement in signal-to-noise ratio for a given bit rate.

Figure 13.2 shows a DPCM-encoded signal using single bit samples. With a single bit, you can only indicate "go up" or "go down", so if the signal is constant (e.g., zero), the samples alternate 1's and 0's. Note that when the signal to be encoded (the solid line) changes rapidly, the 1-bit DPCM encoding is not able to keep up with it.

A DPCM encoder is shown in Figure 13.3. This is a common configuration where the output (on the right) is fed into a *decoder* (labeled "Integrate" in the figure). The decoded signal is subtracted from the incoming signal, providing a differ-

Figure 13.2: DPCM. The solid line is encoded into 1's and 0's shown below. The reconstructed signal is shown as small boxes. Each box is at the value of the previous one plus or minus the step size.

ence that is encoded as bits by the box labeled "Quantize". In this way, the overall encoding process drives the error toward zero.

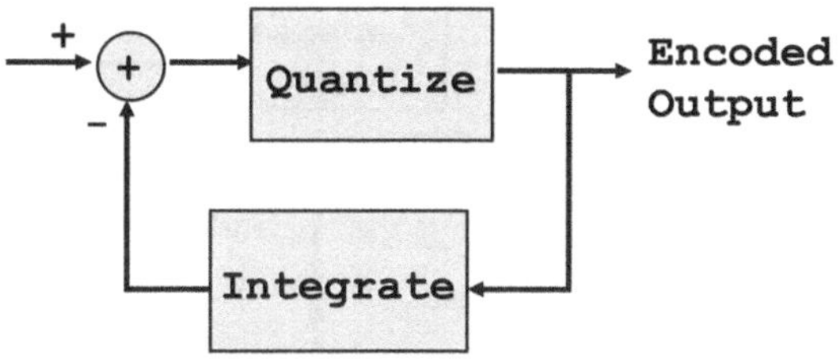

Figure 13.3: DPCM Coder. A reconstructed signal is subtracted from the signal to be encoded (at left) to decide whether the next output should be up (1) or down (0).

13.3.2 ADPCM – Adaptive Delta PCM

You can see that the DPCM coder suffers when the input changes rapidly (the limited step size means that the encoded signal cannot change fast enough) and when the input does not change at all (the minimum step size introduces error and noise). In *Adaptive Delta PCM* (ADPCM), the step size is variable. In the one-bit case, repeating bits mean the encoded signal is moving too fast in one direction, so the step size is increased to keep up. Alternating bits mean the encoded signal is overshooting the target, so the step size is decreased. ADPCM achieves an improvement of 10–11 dB, or about 2 bits per sample, over PCM for speech.

Figure 13.4 illustrates the action of ADPCM. Notice how the steps in the encoded signal (shown in small squares) change. In this example, the step size changes by a factor of two, and there is a minimum step size so that reasonably large step sizes can be reached without too many doublings.

Figure 13.5 shows a schematic of an ADPCM coder. It is similar to the DPCM coder except repetitions or alternations in the output bits are used to modify the

Figure 13.4: ADPCM. The step size is increased when bits repeat, and the step size is decreased (down to a minimum allowed step size) when bits alternate.

step size. The step size is also incorporated into the decoder labeled "Integrate", which decodes the signal.

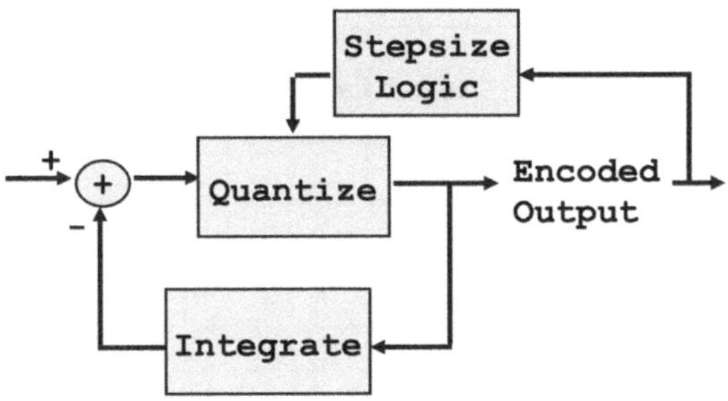

Figure 13.5: ADPCM Coder. This is similar to DPCM, but the step size is variable and controlled by additional logic that looks for same bits or alternating bits in the encoded output.

13.3.3 Adaptive Prediction

If the previous sample is a good predictor and helps us to encode signals, why not use more samples to get even better prediction? A simple N_{th}-order predictor forms a weighted sum of previous samples to predict the next sample. If the weights are adapted, this is called *adaptive prediction*. The gain is about 3 or 4 dB, or a fraction of a bit per sample, and there is little to be gained beyond 4th- or 5th-order prediction.

13.3.4 DPCM for High-Quality Audio

It might seem that we could replace 16-bit PCM with DPCM. Maybe 12 bits would be enough to store deltas, or maybe we could get better-than 16-bit quality with only 16 bits. Unfortunately, to encode *any* PCM signal with N-bit samples, you need $(N+1)$-bit deltas because the delta must span the entire range of an N-bit number, plus it needs a sign bit for the direction of change. Thus, DPCM at the same bit rate cannot be a lossless encoding. In careful listening experiments, PCM is slightly better than DPCM.

13.3.5 Review

The term PCM refers to uncompressed audio where amplitude is converted to binary numbers using a linear scale. By coding differently with μ-law and A-law, we can achieve better quality, at least for low-fidelity speech audio. Using *intersample redundancy* schemes such as DPCM and ADPCM, we can achieve further gains, but when we consider very high quality audio (16-bit PCM), these coding schemes lose their advantage.

As we will see in the next section, *psycho-perceptual redundancy* offers a better path to high-quality audio compression.

13.4 Psycho-Perceptual Redundancy and MP3

We have seen how *coding redundancy* and *intersample redundancy* are used in compression, especially for speech signals. For high-quality music audio, the FLAC lossless encoder can compress audio by about 50%, which gives an idea of the redundancy in PCM. To get well beyond a 2:1 compression ratio, we must turn to lossy schemes, where the original audio is not preserved, but where the differences are not perceptible and therefore acceptable in most applications.

13.4.1 Masking and Perceptual Coding

Our auditory system is complex and has some surprising behaviors. First, our ears act as filter banks, separating frequencies into different channels. There is some interaction between frequencies so that a loud sound in a channel *masks* or covers up soft sounds in adjacent channels. Masking also applies within a channel so that if you mix soft noise with a loud sound, the noise will be inaudible. This means that it is not always necessary to encode audio with very low noise. We can get away with a lot of quantization as long as there is sound to mask the quantization noise.

Another form of masking occurs over time. A loud sound masks soft sounds that follow for a brief period of time. Most of the masking dissipates within 100 ms. Amazingly, masking also works *backwards* in time: a loud sound can mask sounds that happened a few milliseconds earlier!

Another important idea for compression is that when we are digitizing a narrow frequency channel, we do not have to sample at the Nyquist rate. This matters because if we model human hearing and split a sound into, say, 32 channels, we might expect that we need 32 times as many samples. But suppose we have a channel with frequencies from 1,000 to 1,100 Hz. Rather than sample at 2,200 Hz or higher, we can frequency shift the signal down to the range of 0 to 100 Hz. Now, we can sample at only 200 Hz and capture all of the signal. To recover the original sound, we have to frequency shift back to the 1,000 to 1,100 Hz range. In theory, you can encode a signal as N bands, each at $1/N$ of the sample rate, so the total information is the same.

13.4.2 Some Insight on Frequency Domain and Coding

All perceptual coding is done in the frequency domain even though PCM works in the time domain. Redundancy is hard to find in the time domain because sound is vibration, implying constant change. Spectral data tends to be more static. The spectrum at time t is a good predictor for spectrum at time $t+1$. In tonal music, the spectrum also tends to be relatively sparse. It is non-zero only where there are sinusoidal partials. Sparse data is easier to encode efficiently.

13.4.3 MP3 – MPEG Audio Layer 3

MPEG is a video compression standard. Within MPEG is the "MPEG Audio Layer 3" standard for audio compression, commonly known as "MP3". This standard specifies how to decode audio so that MP3 files are treated consistently. Interestingly, the standard does *not* specify how to *encode* audio, so there are slight variations among encoders, resulting in different levels of quality and efficiency. In tests, a 6-to-1 compression of 48 kHz audio gives no perceptual difference from the original. The Fraunhofer Institute, who created the MP3 standard, claims 12-to-1 compression with no perceptual differences.

Let's take a high-level view of how MP3 works. The first step is to apply a filter bank that separates the signal into 32 bands of equal width. As described earlier, each band is sub-sampled by a factor of 32 to avoid increasing the overall sample rate. In practice, bands have some overlap and this sub-sampling causes some aliasing. Also, the filters and their inverses are slightly lossy in terms of recovering the original signal.

Next, a psychoacoustic model is applied to estimate the amount of masking that is present in each channel. This determines how much each band can be quantized. The model uses a 1024-point FFT and identifies sinusoids because the masking effect of sinusoids differs from that of noise. The model produces a signal-to-mask ratio for each of the 32 subbands.

Each subband is then transformed with a modified discrete cosine transform (MDCT) of length 18 or 6 subband samples. Essentially, this is a short-term frequency representation of the subbands, which allows for more efficient coding. For example, if there is only one sinusoid in the subband, only one MDCT coefficient should be high and others should be low. Next, the MDCT coefficients are quantized according to the signal-to-masking ratio. This results in 576 coefficients per frame (18 MDCT coefficients $\times$ 32 subbands).

The coefficients are ordered by increasing frequency because the highest frequencies tend to be zeros—these can be encoded without expending any bits. Next, there will be a run of coefficients that are –1, 0, or 1. These are encoded 4 at a time into an alphabet of 81 symbols. The remaining values are coded in pairs.

13.4.4 Details of Huffman Coding

To encode the MDCT coefficients, Huffman Coding is used. Huffman Coding is the most popular technique for removing coding redundancy. A Huffman Code is a variable length encoding of symbols into bit strings, and assuming that each symbol is encoded separately into a string of bits, Huffman Coding is optimal in producing the smallest *expected* bit length of any string of symbols.[3]

Figure 13.6 illustrates the Huffman coding process. To begin with, each symbol is given a probability. E.g., in English, we know that the letter E occurs about 12% of the time, while Z occurs only 0.07%. Thus, we should use fewer bits for E than Z. For this example, we encode only symbols A, B, C, D, E, and F, which we assume occur with the probabilities shown in Figure 13.6.

The algorithm produces a binary tree (Figure 13.6) using a simple process: Starting with the symbols as leaves of the tree, create a node whose branches have the 2 smallest probabilities. (This would combine D and F in Figure 13.6.) Then, give this node the probability of the sum of the two branches and repeat the process. For example, we now have C with probability 0.1 and the DF node with probability 0.1. Combining them, we get a new internal node of probability 0.2. Continue until there is just one top-level node. Now, each symbol is represented by the path from the root to the leaf, encoding a left branch as 0 and a right branch as 1. The final codes are shown at the right of Figure 13.6.

13.4.5 MP3 Coefficient Coding

Returning to MP3, the terminology of "codes" and "symbols" may be confusing. In Figure 13.6, the symbols were A, B, C, etc., but in general, these symbols can stand for numbers or even vectors. Any finite set of values can be considered a set of symbols that we can encode. In MP3, one of the things we want to encode

[3] Another technique, *arithmetic coding*, and some variations, offer even shorter encodings, essentially by representing symbols by fractional rather than whole bits.

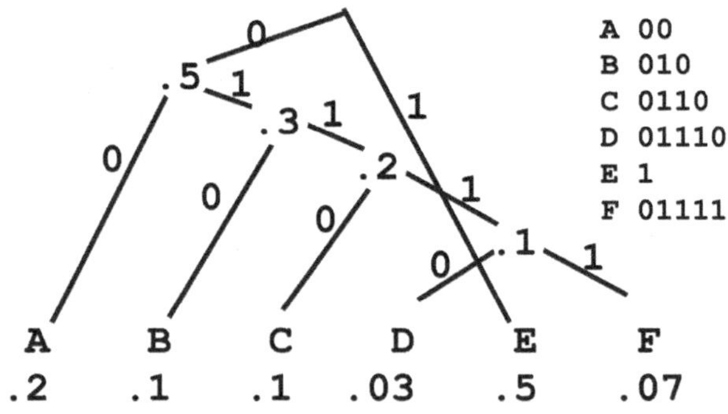

Figure 13.6: Huffman Coding Tree example.

are runs of coefficients -1, 0, or 1. These are grouped into 4, so the "symbols" are 4-tuples such as [-1, 0, 1, -1]. To make a Huffman Code, we can let:

A = [-1, -1, -1, -1]
B = [-1, -1, -1, 0]
C = [-1, -1, -1, 1]
D = [-1, -1, 0, -1]
E = [-1, -1, 0, 0]
F = [-1, -1, 0, 1]
etc.

Encoding in groups of 4 allows Huffman Coding to find a more compact overall representation.

13.4.6 Bit Reservoir and Bit Allocation

Even if audio encoding uses a fixed bit rate, some frames are going to be easier to encode than others. A trick used in MP3 is to take advantage of easy-to-compress frames. When bandwidth is left over, bits can be "donated" to a "bit reservoir" and used later to temporarily exceed the maximum data rate and improve the quality of more difficult frames.

Deciding how to use bits for encoding is a difficult problem. Encoders allocate bits to bands where the masking threshold is exceeded by quantization noise. The band is re-encoded and quantization noise is recalculated. This makes encoding slow.

13.4.7 Summary

Masking reduces our ability to hear "everything" in a signal, and in particular quantization noise. MP3 uses a highly quantized frequency-domain representation. Because of different quantization levels and coefficient sizes, Huffman coding is used to encode the coefficients.

13.5 LPC: Linear Predictive Coding

Another way to achieve compression is to use better, more predictive models of the source sound. This is especially important for voice, where a lot is known about the voice and where there is a big demand for voice data compression. For voice, source/filter models are used because the voice pitch and filter coefficients change slowly. Data rates for speech can be as low as 1 to 2 kbps (kilobits per second) and in cell phone communication are generally in the 5-10 kbps range.

LPC, discussed in Section 9.2, is an example of using intersample redundancy. Analysis estimates a vocal tract filter model that allows for good predictions of the output. By inverse filtering the desired signal, we get a source signal that is relatively easy to encode. Figure 13.7 illustrates the LPC model. This is also an example of an "object model" for data compression. The idea is to extract simple control parameters for an "object" that generates sound. The control parameters and object parameters can be quite small compared to the audio signal that is generated.

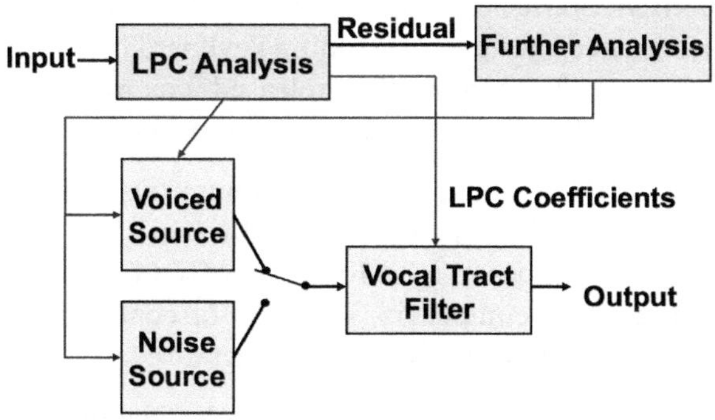

Figure 13.7: Linear Predictive Coding in Practice.

13.6 Physical Models – Speech Analysis/Synthesis

It seems feasible that object models and physical models can offer interesting compression techniques in the future. Our speech is controlled by muscles, and we know that muscles have low bandwidth compared to audio signals. Also, speech sounds are highly constrained. If we could transmit a model for speech production and muscle control parameters, perhaps the data rate for speech could be much lower and the quality could be higher.

13.7 Music Notation

The physical and object models approach to compression leads us to consider music notation. In some sense, music notation is high-level, low-bandwidth "control" information for performers who actually produce audio. Of course, in normal situations, no two music performances are alike, so we cannot really say that music notation is a compressed form of audio, but it is still interesting to consider notation, what it encodes, and what it does not.

Music notation is compact and symbolic as opposed to digital audio. Music notation is missing a lot of detail of how music is performed, for example details of instruments or muscle movement of performers. Furthermore, getting *any* musical rendition of music notation, complete with expressive interpretation and natural sounding voices and instruments is a big challenge that has not been automated.

Another representation that is similar to music notation is the performance information found in MIDI, or Musical Instrument Digital Interface. The idea of MIDI is to encode performance "gestures" including keyboard performances (when do keys go down?, how fast?, when are they released?) as well as continuous controls such as volume pedals and other knobs and sensors.

The bandwidth of MIDI is small, with a maximum over MIDI hardware of 3 KB/s. Typically, the bandwidth is closer to 3 KB/minute. For example, the complete works of ragtime composer Scott Joplin, in MIDI form, takes about 1 MB. The complete output of 50 composers (400 days of continuous music) fits into 500 MB of MIDI—less data than a single compact disc.

MIDI has many uses, but one big limitation is the inability in most cases to synthesize MIDI to create, say, the sound of an orchestra or even a rock band. An exception is that we can send MIDI to a player piano to at least produce a real acoustic piano performance that sounds just like the original. Another limitation, in terms of data compression, is that there is no "encoder" that converts music audio into a MIDI representation.

13.8 Deep Networks

An exciting development in audio compression is the use of deep neural networks (DNNs). Conceptually, audio compression introduces an *encoder*, that converts input audio into a compact representation, and a *decoder*, that converts the compact representation back into an approximation of the original audio. In machine learning terms, we can think of the encoder and decoder simply as functions from vectors (a slice of audio) to vectors (the encoding) and from the encoding back to audio. Often, DNNs require input/output pairs to serve as training data, but if we set up the encoder and decoder as a single deep network, the desired output is identical to the input, so we do not need labeled training data. This is sometimes called *unsupervised learning* and specifically an *autoencoder*. Both encoder and decoder are trained simultaneously on a wide assortment of audio to minimize a *loss function* which ideally estimates the perceptual difference between input and output. Since *human* perception and rating is not practical in training, various estimates are substituted. For example, loss can include such things as differences in the spectra, time-domain waveform, and some model of perceptual difference. An example is EnCodec (32).

By taking advantage of both intersample redundancy (encoder and decoder might utilize audio context) and perceptual redundancy, DNN approaches to audio compression can deliver high compression and high quality. This approach to audio compression will certainly evolve and improve with learning technologies.

13.9 Summary

We have discussed three kinds of redundancy: *coding redundancy*, *intersample redundancy*, and *psycho-perceptual redundancy*. μ-law, ADPCM, etc. offer simple, fast, but not high-quality or high-compression representations of audio. MP3 and related schemes are more general, of higher quality, and offer higher compression ratios, but the computation is fairly high. Neural networks achieve even higher compression ratios, being extremely powerful in learning and using intersample redundancy. We also considered model-based analysis and synthesis, which offer even greater compression when the source can be accurately modeled and control parameters can be estimated. Music notation and MIDI are examples of very abstract and compact digital encodings of music, but currently, we do not have good automatic methods for encoding and decoding.

Chapter 14

Computer Music Futures

Topics Discussed: Computer Accompaniment, Style Classification, Music Alignment, Human-Computer Music Performance

14.1 Introduction

Let's take a step back from details and technical issues to think about where computer music is heading, and maybe where music is heading. This chapter is a personal view, and I should state at the beginning that the ideas here are highly biased by my research, which is in turn guided by my own knowledge, interests, abilities, and talents.

I believe that if we divide computer music into a "past" and "future", the "past" is largely characterized by the pursuit of sound and the concept of the instrument. Much of the early work on synthesis tried to create interesting sounds, model acoustic instruments or reproduce their sounds, and build interfaces and real-time systems that could be used in live performance in the same way that traditional musicians master and perform with acoustic instruments. The "future", I believe, will be characterized by the model of the musician rather than the instrument. The focus will be on models of music performance, musical interaction among players, music described in terms of style, genre, "feel", and emotion rather than notes, pitch, amplitude, and spectrum. A key technology will be the use of AI and machine learning to "understand" music at these high levels of abstraction and to incorporate music understanding into the composition, performance, and production of music.

Much of my research has been in the area of music understanding, and in some sense, the "future" is already here. Everything I envision as part of the future has

DOI: 10.1201/9781003782711-14

some active beginnings well underway. It's hard to foresee the future as anything but an extension of what we already know in the present! However, I *have* witnessed the visions of others as they developed into reality: high-level languages enabling sophisticated music creation, real-time control of sound with gestural control, and all-digital music production. These visions took a long time to develop, and even if they were merely the logical progression of what was understood about computer music in the 1970s or 1980s, the results are truly marvelous and revolutionary. I think in another 20 or 30 years, we will have models of musicians and levels of automatic music understanding that make current systems pale by comparison.

The following sections describe a selection of topics in music understanding. Each section will describe a music understanding problem and outline a solution or at least some research systems that address the problem and show some possibilities for the future.

14.2 Computer Accompaniment

A basic skill for the musically literate is to read music notation while listening to a performance. Humans can follow quite complex scores in real time without having previously heard the music or seen the score. The task of Computer Accompaniment is to follow a live performance in a score and to synchronize a computer performance (16, 25). Note that the computer performs a pre-composed part, so there is no real time composition involved but rather a responsive synchronization. There are now many accompaniment systems, at least in the literature, as well as a few commercial systems. A partial list includes (6, 96, 1, 35, 73, 66, 52, 8).

Accompaniment systems have two basic parts. First, a score-follower matches an incoming live performance signal (usually either audio or data taken directly from a piano-like keyboard using the MIDI protocol) to a machine-readable note-list or score. Second, an accompaniment algorithm uses score location to estimate tempo, position, and decide how to schedule upcoming notes or sound events in the accompaniment score.

The score-following component of Computer Accompaniment can be dissected further into two sub-tasks as shown in Figure 14.1.

14.2.1 Input Processing

The first task, the Input Processor, translates the human performance (which may be detected by a microphone or by sensors attached to keys) into a sequence of symbols, which typically correspond to pitches. (In some systems, match-

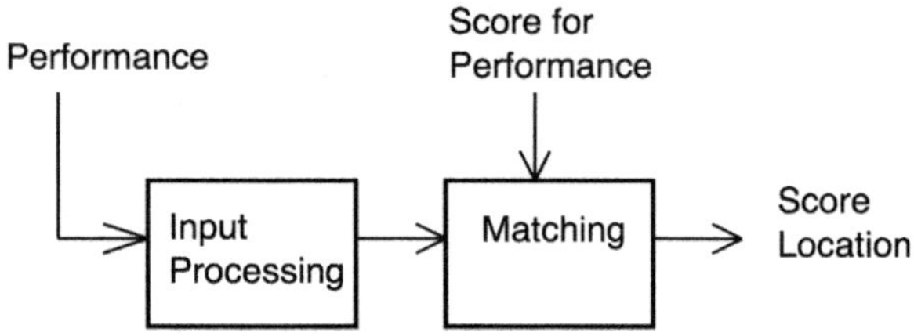

Figure 14.1: Score following block diagram.

ing is done according to spectra or even some latent vector constructed through machine learning without any discrete or symbolic intermediate representation.) When converting microphone input to symbols, the pitch must be estimated and quantized to the nearest semitone, and additional processing is useful to reduce the number of false outputs that typically arise.

14.2.2 Matching

The Matcher receives input from the Input Processor and attempts to find a correspondence between the real-time performance and the score. The Matcher has access to the entire score before the performance begins. As each note is reported by the Input Processor, the Matcher looks for a corresponding note in the score. Whenever a match is found, it is output. The information needed for Computer Accompaniment is just the real-time occurrence of the note performed by the human and the designated time of the note according to the score. Here, we are ignoring the other approach that aligns sampled features (spectra, pitch, amplitude, etc.) rather than a discrete sequence of note onset events.

Since the Matcher must be tolerant of timing variations, matching might be performed on sequences of pitches only. This decision throws away potentially useful timing information, but it makes the Matcher completely time-independent. One problem raised by this pitch-only approach is that each pitch is likely to occur many times in a composition. In a typical melody, the same pitches occur in many places, so there may be many candidates to match a given performed note.

The Matcher described here overcomes this problem and works well in practice. Many different matching algorithms have been explored, often introducing more sophisticated probabilistic approaches (66), but my goal here is to illustrate *one* simple approach. The Matcher is derived from the dynamic programming algorithm for finding the longest common subsequence (LCS) of two strings. Imagine starting with two strings and eliminating arbitrary characters from each string until the remaining characters (subsequences) match exactly. If these strings represent the performance and score, respectively, then a common subsequence represents a potential correspondence between performed notes and the score (see

Figure 14.2). If we assume that most of the score will be performed correctly, then the longest possible common subsequence should be close to the "true" correspondence between performance and score.

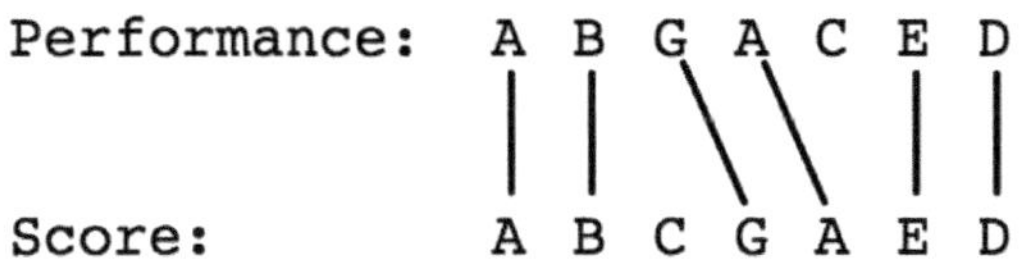

Figure 14.2: Illustration of the longest common subsequence between a performed sequence and a score sequence.

In practice, it is necessary to match the performance against the score as the performance unfolds, so only an initial prefix of the entire performance is available. This causes an interesting anomaly: if a wrong note is played, the LCS algorithm will search arbitrarily far ahead into the score to find a match. This will more than likely turn out not to be the best match once more notes are played, so the algorithm will recover. Nevertheless, being unreasonably wrong, even momentarily, causes problems in the accompaniment task. To avoid skipping ahead in the score, the algorithm is modified to maximize the number of corresponding notes minus the number of notes skipped in the score. Other functions are possible, but this one works well: the matcher will only skip notes when their number is offset by a larger number of matching notes.

The Matcher is an interesting combination of algorithm design, use of heuristics, and outright ad-hoc decisions. Much of the challenge in designing the Matcher was to model the matching problem in such a way that good results could be obtained efficiently. In contrast to the other accompaniment systems emerging at the same time, this Matcher designed by the author could easily match sequences of 20 or more pitches in real time, even on very slow microprocessors of the day, making it very tolerant of errors. (Consider a naive algorithm that tests all different ways to align performed notes to score notes. The number of possible alignments grows exponentially with the number of notes, so sequences of length 20 performed notes plus 20 score notes have about 10^{12} possible alignments, and even modern computers cannot do this in real time.)

Polyphonic matchers have also been explored. One approach is to group individual notes that occur approximately simultaneously into structures called *compound events*. A single isolated note is considered to be a degenerate form of compound event. By modifying the definition of "matches", the monophonic Matcher can be used to find a correspondence between two sequences of compound events. Another approach processes each incoming performance event as it occurs with no regard to its timing relationship to other performed notes. It is important in this case to allow notes within a chord (compound event) in the score to arrive in any order. (Note that the "pure" LCS algorithm disallows reordering.) The resulting algorithm is time-independent (6).

The Matcher performs a fairly low-level recognition task where efficiency is important and relatively little knowledge is required. When matches are found, they are output for use by an Accompaniment Performance subtask, which uses knowledge about musical performance to control a synthesizer. Several systems have been implemented based on these techniques, and the results are quite good. (You can find a video demonstration at `https://www.cs.cmu.edu/~rbd/videos.html`.)

The Matcher has also been extended to handle trills, glissandi, and grace notes as special cases that would otherwise cause problems, and this version has been used successfully for several concerts. A commercial Computer Accompaniment system, SmartMusic, was derived directly from the author's work and has been used mainly for music education since the 1990s. Other accompaniment systems include Tonara, Antescofo (11), Music Plus One (74), ACCompanion (8), and the author's Accomplice.

14.3 Style Classification

Many computer music applications can benefit from higher-level music understanding. For example, interactive performance systems are sometimes designed to react to higher-level intentions of the performer. Unfortunately, there is often a discrepancy between the ideal realization of an interactive system, in which the musician and machine carry on a high-level musical discourse, and the realization, in which the musician does little more than trigger stored sound events. This discrepancy is caused in part by the difficulty of recognizing high-level characteristics or style of a performance with any reliability.

Our experience has suggested that even relatively simple stylistic features, such as playing energetically, playing lyrically, or playing with syncopation, are difficult to detect reliably. Although it may appear obvious how one might detect these styles, good musical performance is always filled with contrast. For example, energetic performances contain silence, slow lyrical passages may have rapid runs of grace notes, and syncopated passages may have a variety of confusing patterns. In general, higher-level musical intent appears chaotic and unstructured when presented in low-level terms such as MIDI performance data.

Machine learning has been shown to improve the performance of many perception and classification systems (including speech recognizers and vision systems). This section describes a machine-learning-based style classifier for music (26). Our initial problem was to classify an improvisation as one of four styles: lyrical, frantic, syncopated, or pointillistic (the latter consisting of short, well-separated sound events). We later added the additional styles: blues, quote (play a familiar tune), high, and low. The exact meaning of these terms is not important. What really matters is the ability of the performer to consistently produce intentional and different styles of playing at will.

The ultimate test is the following: Suppose, as an improviser, you want to communicate with a machine through improvisation. You can communicate four different tokens of information: lyrical, frantic, syncopated, and pointillistic. The question is, if you play a style that you identify as frantic, what is the probability that the machine will perceive the same token? By describing music as a kind of communication channel and music understanding as a kind of decoder, we can evaluate style recognition systems in an objective scientific way.

It is crucial that this classification be responsive in real time. We arbitrarily constrained the classifier to operate within five seconds.

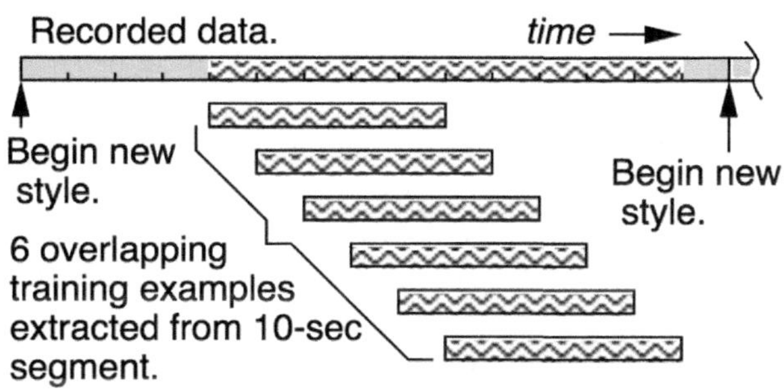

Figure 14.3: Training data for a style recognition system is obtained by asking a human performer to play in different styles. Each style is played for about 15 seconds, and 6 overlapping 5-second segments or windows of the performance are extracted for training. A randomly selected style is requested every 15 seconds for many minutes to produce hundreds of labeled style examples for training.

Figure 14.3 illustrates the process of collecting data for training and evaluating a classifier. Since notions of style are personal, all of the data is provided by one performer, but it takes less than one hour to produce enough training data to create a customized classifier for a new performer or a new set of style labels. The data collection provided a number of 5-second "windows" of music performance data, each with a label reflecting the intended style.

The data was analyzed by sending music audio from an instrument (a trumpet) through an IVL Pitchrider, a hardware device that detects pitch, note-onsets, amplitude, and other features and encodes them into MIDI. This approach was used because, at the time (1997), audio signal processing in software was very limited on personal computers, and using the MIDI data stream was a simple way to pre-process the audio into a useful form. We extracted a number of features from each 5-second segment of the MIDI data. Features included average pitch, standard deviation of pitch, number of note onsets, mean and standard deviation of note durations, and the fraction of time filled with notes (vs. silence).

Various style classifiers were constructed using rather simple and standard techniques such as linear classifiers and neural networks.

While attempts to build classifiers by hand were not very successful, this data-driven machine-learning approach worked very well, and it seems that our particular formulation of the style-classification problem was not even very difficult. All of the machine-learning algorithms performed well, achieving nearly perfect classification in the 4-class case, and around 90% accuracy in the 8-class case. This was quite surprising since there seems to be no simple connection between the low-level features such as pitch and duration and the high-level concepts of style. For example the "syncopation" style is recognizable from lots of notes on the upbeat, but the low-level features do not include any beat or tempo information, so evidently, "syncopation" as performed happens to be strongly correlated with some other features that the machine learning systems were able to discover and take advantage of. Similarly, "quote", which means "play something familiar" is recognizable to humans because we might recognize the familiar tune being quoted by the performer, but the machine has no database of familiar tunes. Again, it must be that playing melodies from memory differs from free improvisation in terms of low-level pitch and timing features, and the machine learning systems were able to discover this.

You can see a demonstration of this system by finding "Automatic style recognition demonstration" on `https://www.cs.cmu.edu/~rbd/videos.html`. Since this work was published, machine learning and classifiers have been applied to many music understanding problems including genre recognition from music audio, detection of commercials, speech, and music in broadcasts, and the detection of emotion in music (65).

14.4 Audio-to-Score Alignment

The off-line version of score following is called *audio-to-score alignment*. *Off-line* means that we do not need to output alignment or location data in real time. Instead, we get to observe the entire audio stream and the entire score before computation begins. This means that we can look ahead into the data for both audio and score. As a result, ambiguous information can be resolved by finding clearer matches happening both earlier and later.

This turns out to be a very big advantage. Earlier we said that computer accompaniment systems work in real time and perform quite well, which is true, but that is partly because accompaniment systems tend to be built for monophonic instruments (those that produce one note at a time). Dealing with polyphony (multiple notes) or something as complex as an orchestra or even a popular music recording poses a very challenging problem to detect notes accurately, so algorithms based on discrete note sequences are not likely to work well. Our ability to do real-time score following is greatly diminished when the input consists of *polyphonic music audio*.

These problems are compensated for by the additional power of using look-ahead in a non-real-time audio-to-score alignment system. This section outlines the basic principles that were originally described in a paper from my research group (40), and then presents some applications and opportunities for this technology.

14.4.1 Chroma Vectors and Similarity

In a monophonic score follower or polyphonic MIDI score follower, we normally use note pitch as the "feature" that we match between performance and score. With polyphonic audio, extracting pitches is difficult and unreliable, but another feature, called the *chroma vector* (97), has been shown to be quite useful and robust. The *chroma vector* is related to the spectrum. You might think the spectrum would be a good feature itself since it requires very little interpretation and certainly contains all the necessary information about the performance. The problem with the spectrum is that just by playing a little louder (brighter) or changing the microphone location, we can get fairly large shifts in the spectrum. Also, to align audio recordings to symbolic representations, we would need a way to determine the spectrum from symbolic representations, i.e., we need to synthesize a band or orchestra in a way that accurately reproduces the spectrum of the recorded version. Our symbolic descriptions do not contain enough information and our synthesis methods are not good enough to reproduce spectra.

The chroma vector divides the spectrum into semitones, i.e., we look at frequency bands for C1, C#1, D1, ... B1, C2, C#2, D2, ... B2, and all the way to the top octave. Then, we take all the magnitudes in the spectrum for pitch class C, namely the frequency bands for all the octaves of C: C1, C2, C3, etc., and add the magnitudes together to get one number we will call C. Then we do the same for C-sharp: C#1, C#2, C#3, etc., and then D1, D2, D3, etc., and all the other pitch classes. The result is a vector of 12 elements: C, C#, D, D#, E, F, F#, G, G#, A, A#, B. To finish processing, the chroma vector is often normalized to have a sum-of-squares magnitude of one so that scaling the amplitude of the source signal has no effect on the chroma vector.

You can think of chroma vectors as a summary or projection of the detailed spectrum into a simpler representation. A sequence of chroma vectors over time is analogous to a spectrogram, and we call it a chromagram.

Because this projection averages a lot of information and totally collapses octave information, it tends to be a robust indicator of melody and harmony, but at the same time, chroma vectors tend to have little to no information about timbre, so you get roughly the same chroma vector whether you play a chord on a piano or with an orchestra or synthesize the sound.

14.4.2 The Similarity Matrix and Dynamic Time Warping

Now that we have a robust representation of polyphonic music performances, we can compare a performance to a score. To get a chromagram from a score, we can either synthesize the score and compute the chromagram from audio, or we can make a direct "chroma-like" representation by simply representing any note with pitch class C as the vector 100000000000, C# as 010000000000, and so on. We could scale these vectors according to loudness indicated in the score. For chords, we just add the vectors from the notes of the chord. After normalizing the sums, we get something compatible with and similar to chromagrams.

To compare a performance chromagram to a score chromagram, we typically construct a full "similarity matrix" that compares every chroma vector in the performance to every chroma vector in the score. (Actually, we only have to compute 1/2 of this matrix since we use a commutative similarity function.) One way to compare vectors x and y is to use their Euclidean distance (distance is the opposite of similarity, so when we say "maximize similarity", it is equivalent to saying "minimize distance").

$$distance(x,y) = \sqrt{\sum_{i=1}^{n}(x_i - y_i)^2}$$

Figure 14.4 illustrates the similarity matrix comparing a MIDI-based chromagram (horizontal) to a chromagram of the recording of the same song by the Beatles (vertical). Notice that there is a dark narrow path near the diagonal from lower left (0, 0) to the upper right. Since dark represents high similarity (smaller distance), this is the path where the MIDI-based chromagram best aligns with the score-based chromagram.

To find the alignment path automatically, we look for a path from lower left corner to upper right corner in the similarity matrix that minimizes the sum of distances along the path. This is a standard problem called dynamic time warping and uses the same general dynamic programming approach used in the longest common subsequence (LCS) problem. Once the best path is computed, we have a mapping from each score position to the corresponding score location.[1] Audio-to-score alignment has been pursued and developed by many researchers (64).

[1] Technically, the MIDI file used in this example is essentially a note list and not a score in the sense of common practice music notation. It might be better to say this is *signal-to-symbol* alignment, but symbol

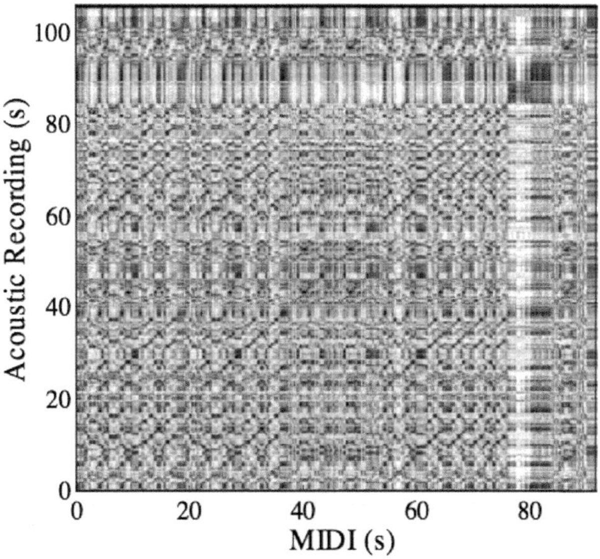

Figure 14.4: A similarity matrix illustrating data used for audio-to-score alignment. Darker means more similar.

14.4.3 Applications of Audio-to-Score Alignment

One application of audio-to-score alignment is to make navigation of audio easier. Figure 14.5 shows an experimental version of Audacity that was extended by the author to "warp" the tempo of a MIDI file to align to an audio recording. This is *not* simply a synthesized version of the MIDI file. The MIDI file came from a MIDI library, and the audio is a commercial recording of a Haydn symphony. By aligning these two different representations, we can immediately see much more of the music structure. For example, if one were looking for the places where the whole orchestra plays a long note together, it is much easier to find those spots with the MIDI file as a reference.

In studio recordings of new music, scores are often prepared using music notation software, so it is often the case that machine-readable common practice notation is available. In principle, that information could be used to display music notation to aid navigation in a future audio editor.

Alignment has also been used in systems to identify "cover songs", (83) which are versions of popular songs performed by someone other than the original recording artists. Another interesting possibility is to use alignment to provide meta-data or labels for audio. This data can then be used to train machine learn-

is a vague term, so it is common to use *score* to refer to any representation of notes or sound events with some indication of timing and properties such as pitch.

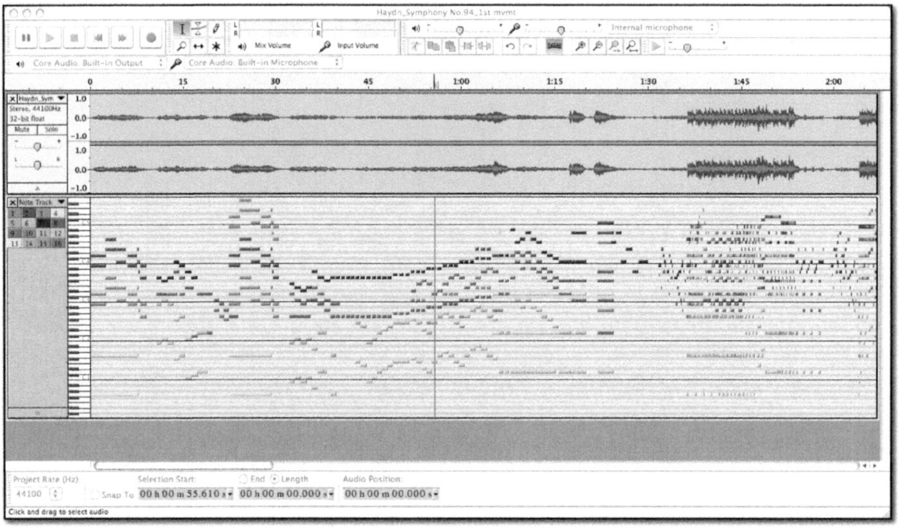

Figure 14.5: Alignment of MIDI in a piano-roll display to audio in an experimental version of the Audacity audio editor.

ing systems to identify chords, pitches, tempo, downbeats, and other music information (39).

14.5 Human-Computer Music Performance

Another interesting application for computers in music is live performance of popular music such as rock, jazz, and folk music. By and large, "popular" music has a definite form and steady tempo, but players often have the possibility to interpret the score rather freely. A consequence is that players synchronize more by beat than by note-by-note score following. In fact, many times there is no note-level score for guitars or drums, and even vocalists sing expressively without strictly following notated rhythms.

Computers are often used in such music, but computers play sequences at a strict tempo, and human musicians are forced to play along and synchronize to the computer (or even a digital audio recording, sometimes referred to as a *backing track*). This type of performance is restrictive to musicians, who often end up focused more on keeping with the computer than playing musically, and it is usually not enjoyable to have a completely inflexible tempo.

As an alternative, imagine a system where computers could follow humans, much like in computer accompaniment systems, only now with popular beat-based music. One could imagine a computer using beat-tracking algorithms to find the beat and then synchronize to that. Some experimental systems have been built with this model, but even state-of-the-art beat tracking (another interesting research problem) is not very reliable. An alternative is simple foot tapping using a sensor that reports the beat to the computer.

In addition to beats, the computer needs to know when to start, so we can add sensors for giving cues to start a performance sequence. Just as human conductors give directions to humans—play something now, stop playing, play louder or softer, go back and repeat the chorus, etc.,—we can use multiple sensors or different gestures to give similar commands to computer performers.

We call this scenario Human-Computer Music Performance (HCMP) (23), with terminology that is deliberately derived from Human-Computer Interaction (HCI) since many of the problems of HCMP are HCI problems: How can computers and humans communicate and work cooperatively in a music performance? The vision of HCMP is a variety of compatible systems for creating, conducting, cueing, performing, and displaying music. Just as rock musicians can now set up instruments, effects pedals, mixers, amplifiers, and speakers, musicians in the future should be able to interconnect modular HCMP systems, combining sensors, virtual performers, conducting systems, and digital music displays as needed to create configurations for live performance.

Some of the interesting challenges for HCMP are:

- Preparing music for virtual players: Perhaps you need a bass player to join your band, but you only have chord progressions for your tunes. Can software write bass parts in a style that complements your musical tastes?
- Sharing music: Can composers, arrangers, and performers share HCMP software and content? How can a band assemble the software components necessary to perform music based on HCMP?
- Music display systems: Can digital music displays replace printed music? If so, can we make the displays interactive and useful for cueing and conducting? Can a band leader lead both human and virtual performers through a natural music-notation-based interface?

Clearly, music understanding is important for HCMP systems to interact with musicians in high-level musical terms. What if a band leader tells a virtual musician to make the music sound more sad? Or make the bass part more lively? HCMP is an example of how future music systems can move from a focus on instruments and sounds to a focus on music performance and musical interaction.

14.6 AI and Machine Learning

Nearly every facet of computing and society is affected by recent advances in artificial intelligence (AI) and especially machine learning. Computer Music is certainly feeling this impact. Some important capabilities achieved with deep neural networks include:

- *source separation*, where input music audio is split into multiple tracks with (relatively) isolated vocals, drums, bass and other components, opening up many possibilities for analysis, audio processing, and production, replacing tracks, etc. (37, 28),
- *audio restoration*, where an estimate of the original source is recovered from audio with artifacts such as background noise, reverberation, distortion and even dropouts (90),
- *audio mastering*, where final touches are applied automatically to music recordings to achieve overall spectral balance, clarity, dynamics compression and artificial reverberation. Once an expensive process performed by experts, automated systems now master millions of songs (89).
- *chord recognition* from audio input has become highly accurate (61).
- *singing voice modification and synthesis*, a rapidly evolving area, has introduced systems that can replace a singer's voice with that of another (also known as *singing voice transfer*, a subclass of "deep fakes"). Other systems create singing voices directly from music notation.
- *popular song composition and audio production*, often referred to using the ambiguous term *music generation*, allows users to obtain entire songs in audio form based on text descriptions and/or lyrics. Although control, creativity and audio quality are all quite limited as of 2026, the results are listenable and show great promise, for example, as audio tracks for videos on social media. The state of the art is improving rapidly. Suno (`suno.com`) is a good example.

New capabilities are certain to appear at a rapid pace. These developments are changing the practice of computer music creation. However, just as synthesizers and sequencing introduced in the 20th century did not replace live musicians but were integrated into many aspects of composition, performance, and music production, we can expect that AI and machine learning will follow a similar path.

A major shortcoming of neural networks is that they learn from existing data, whether it be text, images, or music. This approach seems unlikely to create innovative music that breaks with tradition (consider Igor Stravinsky, John Cage, Charlie Parker, and a host of others). Perhaps breakthroughs in machine learning will lead to more creative systems. Meanwhile, there are many opportunities to explore how performing artists and composers can guide AI systems to achieve human artistic goals. It seems that incorporating neural networks into real-time music performance systems is wide-open for exploration, less demanding of corporate-level computing resources, and tailored to the skills and sensibilities of musicians.

14.7 Summary

Music understanding encompasses a wide range of research and practice with the goal of working with music at higher levels of abstraction that include emotion, expressive performance, musical form and structure, and music recognition. We have examined just a limited selection of music understanding capabilities based on work by the author. These include:

- computer accompaniment—the computer as virtual interactive and responsive musical accompanist,
- automatic style recognition—the detection of different performance styles using machine classifiers,
- audio-to-score alignment—the ability to match sounds to symbolic representations of music event sequences, and
- Human-Computer Music Performance—an evolving practice of bringing virtual performers into collaboration with humans in live performance.

All of these tasks rely on new techniques for processing musical information that we call *music understanding*. In addition, we took a brief look at the rapidly evolving capabilities of AI and machine learning technologies for creating music.

Chapter 15

Where Next?

This book has introduced fundamental technologies of digital audio, sound synthesis, and music creation by computer. We have touched on some related fields including musical acoustics, music perception, music theory, music information retrieval, and music understanding.

Our goal has been to focus on music synthesis and composition, particularly through the programming language Nyquist, as this offers tremendous flexibility and a chance to build a wide range of computational models and abstractions around music. While Nyquist is quite general for signal processing and automation, extending even to music composition, this is not to say Nyquist is the best approach to every task. Clearly, there are *less general* systems that are *more powerful* in the sense that they make it easier to do the limited set of things they are intended to do. If you want to edit recorded audio, by all means use an editor like Audacity or your favorite digital audio workstation. If you want to synthesize a rock drum track, by all means use a commercial drum machine. Hopefully, this book has enabled you to better understand and apply these more specialized systems and to go far beyond them when the need arises.

In addition, this book is just an introduction to a rapidly growing field. Our goal has been to remain compact and only cover essential and important information, providing a readable basis for exploring further. To learn more, it is good to have some idea of what is out there and where to look for it. This final chapter is by no means comprehensive, but it offers some directions for study and some references to consider.

DOI: 10.1201/9781003782711-15

15.1 NIME and Physical Computing

In 2001, a workshop called "New Interfaces for Musical Expression" or NIME was organized to discuss physical controls and interfaces that sit between performers and computer music systems. The annual NIME conference continues to draw researchers who study sensors, control strategies, haptics, robots, and many other topics, often with an emphasis on user studies, adopting methodologies from psychology and human factors. NIME proceedings are all online and free (`https://www.nime.org`).

In the early days, it was an accomplishment simply to combine a sensor, a microcontroller, and perhaps a MIDI interface to send controls to a synthesizer, and many projects explored variations of this configuration. Today, parts are available "off-the-shelf" to quickly put together the electronics needed for a computer music instrument controller. See offerings from `https://www.adafruit.com` and `https://www.sparkfun.com` for example. If you have no electronics skills, it could be quite liberating to master some basic skills. Many universities offer courses in "physical computing" or "Internet of Things" where you can learn to assemble small self-contained computing devices with sensors and outputs of various kinds. If not, look for Electrical Engineering courses in digital electronics or microcomputers/microcontrollers with lab sections where you actually build things.

15.2 Music Information Retrieval, AI, and Machine Learning

Almost coincident with the beginnings of NIME, a new field emerged combining library science, data retrieval, computer music, and machine learning called Music Information Retrieval (MIR). Like NIME, the International Society for Music Information Retrieval (ISMIR) conference draws hundreds of researchers every year who present work which has steadily drifted from retrieval problems and library science to more general research on music understanding and music composition by computer. This field is strongly weighted toward popular music and commercial music. Proceedings tend to be very technical and are available online at `https://ismir.net`.

ISMIR has become a favorite venue for applications of machine learning to music. Although research on machine learning in music is increasingly published in major machine learning conferences, ISMIR has by far the greatest variety and concentration of this work.

Some textbooks, mainly for graduate students, have appeared, including *Fundamentals of Music Processing* (65), which has a large collection of online support material. George Tzanetakis created an online course on MIR for Kadenze.

(https://www.kadenze.com/courses/machine-learning-for-music-information-retrieval/info)

15.3 Signal Processing

Our introduction to music signal processing is an attempt to convey "what every computer scientist should know" about signal processing. A more rigorous approach is certainly possible, and to design new algorithms or really master the application of signal processing to music, there is much more to learn. Julius Smith has a wonderful resource consisting of multiple online books (https://ccrma.stanford.edu/~jos). A formal Electrical Engineering course in Signals and Systems or Advanced Digital Signal Processing is a good way to learn more. The book *Audio Content Analysis* introduces many signal processing techniques for music analysis (53) with more formal and complete descriptions. There are online materials for this book as well. Another conference series, DAFX, has many papers on various synthesis and analysis techniques for music (https://www.dafx.de) and there is a book: *DAFX - Digital Audio Effects* (100).

15.4 Real-Time Systems

It is surprising given the importance of time in music that there is not more literature on building real-time systems for music. There are some important techniques, but few good sources to learn from. One recommendation is Ross Bencina's blog (http://www.rossbencina.com/code/real-time-audio-programming-101-time-waits-for-nothing). Ross Bencina and I gave a workshop and wrote a short document with some good references. This might be a good starting point for further reading (https://www.cs.cmu.edu/~rbd/doc/icmc2005workshop/real-time-systems-concepts-design-patterns.pdf).

15.5 General Computer Music

Beyond these more specialized areas, there are many musicians, scientists, and engineers who simply create and explore music with computers. There are too many ideas to classify or label them. Literally thousands of papers on computer music are reported in *Proceedings of the International Computer Music Conference* (ICMC), available free online from the International Computer Music Association (https://computermusic.org). Two main publications on Computer Music are the *Computer Music Journal* (https://www.computermusicjournal.org) and *Journal of New Music Research*. Unfortunately, neither of these journals is open, but your library may have access to online content. *Computer Music Journal* has a wide readership and tends to be less technical and less academic, while *Journal of New Music Research* has more in-depth articles and work related to contemporary art music. There is a good deal of overlap in topics, and both are important resources.

There are many more conferences we have not mentioned. Most of these conferences publish proceedings online. Searching the Internet for scholarly articles in journals and conferences is a good way to learn, and you will get to know which journal and conferences are most relevant to your personal interests.

Finally, AI systems are quite good at producing tutorials, surveys, and literature reviews. While they sometimes make false claims (be careful!), they are trained on millions of technical papers, and they can usually answer basic questions correctly and quickly. Unlike the early days, papers on computer music and related fields are now spread across hundreds of journals and conferences, and the search and digest capabilities of AI systems are now a critical resource for students and researchers.

References

[1] Bridget Baird, Don Blevins, and Noel Zahler. Artificial intelligence and music: Implementing an interactive computer performer. *Computer Music Journal*, 17(2): 73–79, 1993.

[2] Huda Barakat, Oytun Turk, and Cenk Demiroglu. Deep learning-based expressive speech synthesis: A systematic review of approaches, challenges, and resources. *EURASIP Journal on Audio, Speech, and Music Processing*, 2024(11), 2024.

[3] Arthur H. Benade. *Fundamentals of Musical Acoustics*. Dover Publications, Garden City, NY, 2nd revised edition, 1990.

[4] Stefan Bilbao, Charlotte Desvages, Michele Ducceschi, Brian Hamilton, Reginald Harrison-Harsley, Alberto Torin, and Craig Webb. Physical modeling, algorithms, and sound synthesis: The ness project. *Computer Music Journal*, 43(2-3): 15–30, 2019.

[5] H. S. Black and J. O. Edson. Pulse code modulation. *AIEE Transactions (American Institute of Electrical Engineers)*, 66: 895–899, 1947.

[6] Josh Bloch and Roger B. Dannenberg. Real-time accompaniment of polyphonic keyboard performance. In *Proceedings of the 1985 International Computer Music Conference*, pages 279–290, San Francisco, August 1985. Computer Music Association.

[7] Claude Cadoz, Annie Luciani, and Jean-Loup Florens. Cordis-anima: A modeling and simulation system for sound and image synthesis: The general formalism. *Computer Music Journal*, 17(1): 19–29, 1993.

[8] Carlos Eduardo Cancino-Chacón, Silvan Peter, Patricia Hu, Emmanouil Karystinaios, Florian Henkel, Francesco Foscarin, Nimrod Varga, and Gerhard Widmer. The accompanion: Combining reactivity, robustness, and musical expressivity in an automatic piano accompanist. In *Proceedings of the Thirty-Second International Joint Conference on Artificial Intelligence (IJCAI-23)*, pages 5779–5787, 2023.

[9] John M. Chowning. The synthesis of complex audio spectra by means of frequency modula- tion. *Journal of the Audio Engineering Society*, 21(7), 1973.

[10] John M. Chowning. The simulation of moving sound sources. *Computer Music Journal*, 1(3): 48–52, 1977.

[11] Arshia Cont. Antescofo: Anticipatory synchronization and control of interactive parameters in computer music. In *Proceedings of the 2008 International Computer Music Conference*, pages 33–40, 2008.

[12] Perry R. Cook. A meta-wind-instrument physical model, and a meta-controller for real time performance control. In *Proceedings of the International Computer Music Conference (ICMC)*, 1992.

[13] Perry R. Cook. Singing voice synthesis: History, current work, and future directions. *Computer Music Journal*, 20(3): 38–46, 1996.

[14] Perry R. Cook and Gary P. Scavone. The synthesis toolkit (stk). In *Proceedings of the International Computer Music Conference (ICMC)*, pages 164–166, San Francisco, CA, 1999. International Computer Music Association.

[15] Margaret Cychosz, Matthew B. Winn, and Matthew J. Goupell. How to vocode: Using channel vocoders for cochlear-implant research. *The Journal of the Acoustical Society of America*, 155: 2407–2437, 2024.

[16] Roger B. Dannenberg. An on-line algorithm for real-time accompaniment. In *Proceedings of the 1984 International Computer Music Conference*, pages 193–198, San Francisco, June 1985. Computer Music Association.

[17] Roger B. Dannenberg. Abstract time warping of compound events and signals. *Computer Music Journal*, 21(3): 61–70, Fall 1997.

[18] Roger B. Dannenberg. The implementation of nyquist, a sound synthesis language. *Computer Music Journal*, 21(3): 71–82, 1997.

[19] Roger B. Dannenberg. Machine tongues xix: Nyquist, a language for composition and sound synthesis. *Computer Music Journal*, 21(3): 50–60, Fall 1997.

[20] Roger B. Dannenberg. Languages for computer music. *Frontiers in Digital Humanities*, 5: 26, 2018.

[21] Roger B. Dannenberg. *The Nyquist Reference Manual*. Roger B. Dannenberg, 2025. Available as doc/nyquistman.pdf in the Nyquist download at sourceforge.net.

[22] Roger B. Dannenberg and Istvan Derenyi. Combining instrument and performance models for high-quality music synthesis. *Journal of New Music Research*, 27(3): 211– 238, September 1998.

[23] Roger B. Dannenberg, Nicolas E. Gold, Dawen Liang, and Guangyu Xia. Bootstrap learning for accurate onset detection. *Computer Music Journal*, 38(2): 36–50, summer 2014.

[24] Roger B. Dannenberg, Hank Pellerin, and Istvan Derenyi. A study of trumpet envelopes. In *Proceedings of the International Computer Music Conference*, pages 57– 61, San Francisco, 1998. International Computer Music Association.

[25] Roger B. Dannenberg and Christopher Raphael. Music score alignment and computer accompaniment. *Communications of the ACM*, 49: 38–43, August 2006.

[26] Roger B. Dannenberg, Belinda Thom, and David Watson. A machine learning approach to musical style recognition. In *Proceedings of the 16th International Society for*

Music Information Retrieval Conference (ISMIR), pages 344–347, San Francisco, 1997. Computer Music Association.

[27] Hugo Tremonte de Carvalho. An introduction to markov chains in music composition and analysis. *MusMat Brazilian Journal of Music and Mathematics*, III(2): 18–43, December 2019.

[28] Alexandre Défossez. Hybrid spectrogram and waveform source separation. In *Proceedings of the ISMIR 2021 Music Demixing Workshop (MDX)*, 2021.

[29] Charles Dodge and Thomas A Jerse. *Computer Music: Synthesis, Composition, and Performance*. Schirmer Books, New York, 2nd edition, 1997.

[30] Mark Dolson. The phase vocoder: A tutorial. *Computer Music Journal*, 10(4): 14–27, 1986.

[31] Scott A. Van Duyne and Julius O. Smith III. Physical modeling with the 2-d digital waveguide mesh. In *Proceedings of the International Computer Music Conference (ICMC)*, pages 40–47, San Francisco, CA, 1993. International Computer Music Association.

[32] Alexandre Défossez, Jade Copet, Gabriel Synnaeve, and Yossi Adi. High fidelity neural audio compression, 2022.

[33] John M. Eargle. *Handbook of Recording Engineering*. Springer, New York, 4th edition, 2005.

[34] Neville H. Fletcher and Thomas D. Rossing. *The Physics of Musical Instruments*. Springer-Verlag, New York, 2nd edition, 1998.

[35] Loren Grubb and Roger B. Dannenberg. A stochastic method of tracking a vocal performer. In *Proceedings of the 1997 International Computer Music Conference*, pages 301–308, 1997.

[36] William M. Hartmann, Brad Rakerd, Zane D. Crawford, and Peter Xinya Zhang. Transaural experiments and a revised duplex theory for the localization of low-frequency tones. *Journal of the Acoustical Society of America*, 139(2): 968–985, 2016.

[37] Romain Hennequin, Anis Khlif, Felix Voituret, and Manuel Moussallam. Spleeter: A fast and efficient music source separation tool with pre-trained models. *Journal of Open Source Software*, 5(50): 2154, 2020.

[38] Ning Hu. *Automatic Construction of Synthetic Musical Instruments and Performers*. PhD thesis, Carnegie Mellon University Computer Science Department, 2013.

[39] Ning Hu and Roger B. Dannenberg. Bootstrap learning for accurate onset detection. *Machine Learning*, 65(2–3): 457–471, 2006.

[40] Ning Hu, George Tzanetakis, and Roger B. Dannenberg. Polyphonic audio matching and alignment for music retrieval. In *2003 IEEE Workshop on Applications of Signal Processing to Audio and Acoustics*, pages 185–188. IEEE, 2003.

[41] Jennifer Iverson. Technosynthesis: From vocoder speech to electronic music. In *Electronic Inspirations: Technologies of the Cold War Musical Avant-Garde*, pages 167–194. Oxford University Press, 2019.

[42] Julius O. Smith III. Efficient simulation of the reed-bore and bow-string mechanisms. In *Proceedings of the International Computer Music Conference (ICMC)*, pages 275–280. International Computer Music Association, 1986.

[43] Julius O. Smith III. Physical modeling using digital waveguides. *Computer Music Journal*, 16(4): 74–91, 1992.

[44] Julius O. Smith III. Commuted synthesis of the bowed string. In *Proceedings of the International Computer Music Conference (ICMC)*, pages 64–71, San Francisco, CA, 1993. International Computer Music Association.

[45] Julius O. Smith III. *Spectral Audio Signal Processing*. W3K Publishing, Stanford, CA, 2011.

[46] W. Kaegi and S. Tempelaars. Vosim—a new sound synthesis system. *Journal of the Audio Engineering Society*, 26(6): 418–425, June 1978.

[47] M. Karjalainen, V. Valimäki, and Z. Janosy. Towards high quality sound synthesis of the guitar and string instruments. In *Proceedings of the 1993 International Computer Music Conference*, pages 56–63. University of Michigan Publishing, 1993.

[48] K. Karplus and A. Strong. Digital synthesis of plucked-string and drum timbres. *Computer Music Journal*, 7(2): 43–55, Summer 1983.

[49] Kevin Karplus and Alex Strong. Digital synthesis of plucked-string and drum timbres. *Computer Music Journal*, 7(2): 43–55, 1983.

[50] Jean Laroche and Mark Dolson. Improved phase vocoder time-scale modification of audio. In *Proceedings of the IEEE Workshop on Applications of Signal Processing to Audio and Acoustics (WASPAA)*, pages 91–94, New Paltz, NY, 1999. IEEE.

[51] Victor Lazzarini. *Spectral Music Design: A Computational Approach*. Oxford University Press, Oxford, UK, 2021.

[52] Lin Hao Lee. Musical score following and audio alignment. Meng final year project report, Imperial College London, UK, 2022.

[53] Alexander Lerch. *An Introduction to Audio Content Analysis: Applications in Signal Processing and Music Informatics*. Wiley, 2012.

[54] Song Li and Jürgen Peissig. Measurement of head-related transfer functions: A review. *Applied Sciences*, 10(14): 5014, 2020.

[55] Gareth Loy. *Musicmathics, Volume 1: The Mathematical Foundations of Music*. MIT Press, Cambridge MA, USA, 2011.

[56] Max V. Mathews. The digital computer as a musical instrument. *Science*, 142(3592): 553–557, November 1963.

[57] Max V. Mathews. *The Technology of Computer Music*. MIT Press, Cambridge, MA, 1969.

[58] R. J. McAulay and T. Quatieri. Speech analysis/synthesis based on a sinusoidal representation. *IEEE Transactions on Acoustics, Speech, and Signal Processing*, 34: 744– 754, 1986.

[59] Michael E. McIntyre, Robert T. Schumacher, and Jim Woodhouse. On the oscillations of musical instruments. *The Journal of the Acoustical Society of America*, 74(5): 1325– 1345, 1983.

[60] Michael E. McIntyre and Jim Woodhouse. On the fundamentals of bowed-string dynamics. *Acustica*, 43(2): 93–108, 1979.

[61] Matt McVicar, Raúl Santos-Rodríguez, Yizhao Ni, and Tijl De Bie. Automatic chord estimation from audio: A review of the state of the art. *IEEE/ACM Transactions on Audio, Speech, and Language Processing*, 22(6): 1049–1065, 2014.

[62] F. Richard Moore. *Elements of Computer Music*. Prentice Hall, NJ, USA, 1990.

[63] F. Richard Moore. A general model for spatial processing of sounds. *Computer Music Journal*, 7(3): 6–15, Autumn 1983.

[64] Alia Morsi and Xavier Serra. Bottlenecks and solutions for audio to score alignment research. In *Proceedings of the 23rd International Society for Music Information Retrieval Conference (ISMIR)*, 2022.

[65] Meinard Müller. *Fundamentals of Music Processing: Audio, Analysis, Algorithms, Applications*. Springer, New York, 2015.

[66] Eita Nakamura, Yasuyuki Saito, Nobutaka Ono, and Shigeki Sagayama. Merged-output hidden markov model for score following of midi performance with ornaments, desynchronized voices, repeats, and skips. In *Proceedings of the 11th Sound & Music Computing joint with the 40th International Computer Music Conference*, pages 1185–1192. Computer Music Association, 2014.

[67] H. Nyquist. Certain topics in telegraph transmission theory. *Trans. AIEE*, 47: 617–644, April 1928.

[68] Alan V. Oppenheim, Ronald W. Schafer, and John R. Buck. *Discrete-Time Signal Processing*. Pearson, Upper Saddle River, NJ, 3rd edition, 2009.

[69] Ken C. Pohlmann. *Principles of Digital Audio*. McGraw-Hill Education, New York, 6th edition, 2010.

[70] Giovanni De Poli. A tutorial on digital sound synthesis techniques. *Computer Music Journal*, 7(4): 8–26, 1983.

[71] Zdeněk Průša and Nick Holighaus. Phase vocoder done right. In *Proceedings of the 25th European Signal Processing Conference (EUSIPCO 2017)*, pages 1006–1010, Kos, Greece, August 2017.

[72] Ville Pulkki. Virtual sound source positioning using vector base amplitude panning. *Journal of the Audio Engineering Society*, 45(6): 456–466, 1997.

[73] Christopher Raphael. Automatic segmentation of acoustic musical signals using hidden markov models. *IEEE Transactions on Pattern Analysis and Machine Intelligence*, 21(4): 360–370, 1999.

[74] Christopher Raphael. Music plus one and machine learning. In *ICML'10: Proceedings of the 27th International Conference on International Conference on Machine Learning*, pages 21–28, Madison, WI, 2010. Omnipress.

[75] Bernard E. Richardson. The acoustical development of the guitar. *Catgut Acoustical Society Journal*, 2(5): 1–10, May 1994.

[76] Curtis Roads. *Microsound*. MIT Press, 2004.

[77] Curtis Roads. *The Computer Music Tutorial*. The MIT Press, Cambridge, MA, 2nd edition, 2023.

[78] Curtis Roads and Paul Wieneke. Grammars as representations for music. *Computer Music Journal*, 3(1): 48–55, March 1979.

[79] Xavier Rodet. Time-domain formant-wave-function synthesis. *Computer Music Journal*, 8(3): 9–14, Autumn 1984.

[80] Thomas D. Rossing, F. Richard Moore, and Paul A. Wheeler. *The Science of Sound*. Addison-Wesley, Reading, MA, 3rd edition, 2002.

[81] Khalid Sayood. *Introduction to Data Compression*. Morgan Kaufmann, Waltham, MA, 4th edition, 2012.

[82] Manfred R. Schroeder. Natural sounding artificial reverberation. *Journal of the Audio Engineering Society*, 10(3): 219–223, 1962.

[83] Joan Serrà and Emilia Gómez. Audio cover song identification based on tonal sequence alignment. In *Proceedings of the IEEE International Conference on Acoustics, Speech and Signal Processing (ICASSP)*, pages 61–64, 2008.

[84] Marie-Helene Serra, Dean Rubine, and Roger Dannenberg. Analysis and synthesis of tones by spectral interpolation. *Audio Engineering Society Journal*, 38(3): 111–128, March 1990.

[85] Xavier Serra and Julius O. Smith III. Spectral modeling synthesis: A sound analysis/synthesis system based on a deterministic plus stochastic decomposition. *Computer Music Journal*, 14(4): 12–24, 1990.

[86] C. Shannon. A mathematical theory of communication. *Bell System Technical Journal*, 27: 379–423, July and October 1948.

[87] Mary Simoni and Roger B. Dannenberg. *Algorithmic Composition: A Guide to Composing Music with Nyquist*. The University of Michigan Press, Ann Arbor, 2013.

[88] J. H. Smith and J. Woodhouse. The tribology of rosin. *Journal of the Mechanics and Physics of Solids*, 48: 1633–1681, 2000.

[89] Jonathan Sterne and Elena Razlogova. Machine learning in context, or learning from landr: Artificial intelligence and the platformization of music mastering. *Social Media + Society*, 5(2), 2019.

[90] Jiaqi Su, Zeyu Jin, and Adam Finkelstein. Hifi-gan: High-fidelity denoising and dereverberation based on speech deep features in adversarial networks. In *Proceedings of the Annual Conference of the International Speech Communication Association (INTERSPEECH)*, pages 4506–4510, 2020.

[91] C. Sullivan. Extending the karplusstrong algorithm to synthesize electric guitar timbres with distortion and feedback. *Computer Music Journal*, 14(3), Fall 1990.

[92] Siu-Lan Tan, Peter Pfordresher, and Rom Harré. *Psychology of Music: From Sound to Significance*. Routledge, New York, 2010.

[93] Heinrich Taube. Sal: A simple algorithmic language in common music. In *Proceedings of the 2007 International Computer Music Conference*, pages 121–124, San Francisco, 2007. International Computer Music Association.

[94] Barry Truax. Organizational techniques for c:m ratios in frequency modulation. *Computer Music Journal*, 1(4): 39–45, Winter 1978. reprinted in Foundations of Computer Music, C. Roads and J. Strawn (eds.). MIT Press, 1985.

[95] Barry Truax. Real-time granular synthesis with a digital signal processor. *Computer Music Journal*, 12(2): 14–26, 1988.

[96] Barry Vercoe. The synthetic performer in the context of live performance. In *Proceedings of the 1984 International Computer Music Conference*, pages 199–200, San Francisco, June 1985. Computer Music Association.

[97] Gregory H. Wakefield. Audio thumbnailing of popular music using chroma-based representations. *IEEE Transactions on Multimedia*, 7(1): 123–132, 2004.

[98] Arnold Whittall. *The Cambridge Introduction to Serialism*. Cambridge University Press, New York, 2008.

[99] I. Xenakis. *Formalized Music: Thought and Mathematics in Music*. Pendragon Press, Stuyvesant NY, 1992.

[100] Udo Zölzer, editor. *DAFX: Digital Audio Effects*. John Wiley & Sons, Chichester, UK, 2nd edition, 2011.

Index

For Product Safety Concerns and Information please contact our EU representative GPSR@taylorandfrancis.com Taylor & Francis Verlag GmbH, Kaufingerstraße 24, 80331 München, Germany

Batch number: 10725802

Printed by Printforce, the Netherlands